Minnesota Injustice

Harlot of Injustice

Plus

How We Can Improve Our Legal System

Dale Nathan

ALETHOS PRESS LLC
PO Box 600160
St. Paul, MN 55106

Minnesota Injustice: True Court Horror Stories – With Names

ISBN 0-9702509-8-3

Printed by Bethany Press International
Bloomington, MN

Artwork by Dane Dinger, of St. Paul, MN

10 9 8 7 6 5 4 3 2 1

Dedicated To

Chris-Ann R. Wilkoske

My book is dedicated to my daughter Chris-Ann Wilkoske who came to me as a foster child. During the first 15 years of her life, she was raised by a loving but afflicted mother in a dysfunctional home that lacked a father or father image. Despite her troubled beginning, and despite many trials and ordeals after she left my care, she matured into a good and beautiful young woman whom I love very much.

And

Beverly J. and Russell D. Oberg

From 1978 until they retired in the fall of 2003, Beverly J. Oberg and her husband, Russell D. Oberg, my dearest friends, cared for over 400 homeless or troubled teenage and preteenage boys and girls. Many were homeless or troubled; some just needed a temporary home. Their loving but stern care in their home and in their Independent Living Skills program based in the other unit of their duplex taught these children the character and discipline needed for a happy and successful adult life. Russ and Bev are among Minnesota's elite in service to community, commitment to justice, and devotion to Christ.

Here, take your gratuity.

(A rule issued by judges for themselves only lets them accept as many $150 gratuities – gifts – as they want, without reporting them to anyone. Minnesota Supreme Court Order, dated November 1, 1995.)

Contents

Acknowledgements

Several associates and friends contributed immeasurably to this book. I am profoundly grateful to each.

Dane Dinger, who created the cover and each of the illustrations, was brilliant in presenting complex legal system problems and proposed reforms in poignant visual images that portray core concepts with great clarity and impact.

Dave Racer patiently guided me in composition and enhanced the text with insights gained from years of experience as an author, newspaper editor and radio broadcaster, candidate for political office, and campaign manager.

My very good and learned lawyer friend whom I have not named for the reasons stated in the prologue spent countless hours reviewing what I wrote. He suggested numerous changes that added considerable clarity and scholarship to the manuscript.

Carrie Jensen, an incredibly hard working scopist, thoroughly cleansed my book of grammar, syntax, typographical, spelling and other errors, which make reading it so much easier. After I found Carrie, I learned that a scopist is a professional proofreader. I highly recommend Carrie to any writer who aspires to an error-free work.

My sincere thanks to Minnesota's appellate court administrative office and Tax and Compensation Court Chief Judges for the information on case filings, dispositions and judge salaries that they so kindly provided.

My daughter Chris-Ann and dear friends Bev and Russ blessed and inspired me with their unflagging support without which I could not have completed my book. Words are not adequate enough to express my heartfelt gratitude.

Although not directly involved in creating this book, Kyle Tyacke, the superb webmaster who greatly enhanced the website I provided to him, contributed mightily to the success of my work by portraying it on the internet so effectively.

Bethany Press International was magnificent in providing me perfect, yet very reasonably priced, printing services.

Thanks are due the American Bar Association, the office of United States Supreme Court Justice Sandra Day O'Connor, and the library staffs at the William Mitchell College of Law, Minnesota Supreme Court Law Library and Ramsey County Law Library, for their generous assistance in locating and providing materials I read in preparing for composition.

The views expressed in this book are exclusively mine and do not necessarily express the opinions of any of the people who helped me in my work.

Foreword
By Dale Nathan

Many Minnesotans believe our court and legal system needs a major overhaul. This is the first of a planned series of books based on that premise. Sequels to this edition will supplement the rationale for reform and include more detail on specific proposals.

Our next book, scheduled for release in the last quarter of 2004 or first quarter of 2005, will be hardback. In addition to supplementing this book, it will have special features we believe you will find to be entertaining and useful.

Many chapters of our next book will begin with a "legal gem." Each gem captures and encapsulates a modicum of legal wisdom that will enable you to better understand and cope with our court and legal system. Here is an example:

"What do you call a lawyer who has an IQ of 80?"

"Your Honor."

Part I of our next book will consist of a new group of true Minnesota court horror cases. We ask our readers who have or know of such a case to inform us about it by sending a description of the case to us at:

by e-mail: dalenathan@usfamily.net
by fax: 651-454-0507
by mail:

Dale Nathan
P.O. Box 211284
Eagan, MN 55121-1284

With your permission, we will include the cases we select in our next book. We plan to continue publishing summaries of such cases until we cannot find any more.

Part II of our next book will contain something this book does not - expositions on selected legal topics. Each exposition will educate the reader in a few pages on a topic of law such as real estate transactions, wills and probate, insurance and health benefits, child custody, maintenance and child support, and other topics up to an approximate total of 10. Our objective is to familiarize readers with the basics incidental to each topic so each can more competently cope with legal matters that involve that topic.

Proposed reforms such as a plan to select judges solely on merit, report cards on judges who seek re-election, public financing of judge elections, outsourcing prisoner care and rehabilitation, using ignition interlocks to reduce repeat DWI offenses, installing camcorders in courtrooms, and others will be laid out in far greater detail than in this book for possible consideration by the next Minnesota legislature.

Finally, we note that legal system reform may be needed in many states in addition to Minnesota. It is possible that the Minnesota Injustice series will stimulate the writing of comparable series in many other states.

Definition of a good judge

A good judge does not need to have a great legal mind or be a genius; it is sufficient if he or she uses common sense and basic values, as well as the law, in making judgments that are fair and sensible, and appropriately penalizes persons who, after a fair trial, are found to be guilty of a crime or other illegal behavior.

– By the author

What is your definition of a good judge? In the sequel to this book, which will be published in the near future, we will include definitions of a good judge provided to us by our readers. If you have such a definition, we may, with your consent, include it in our next book. Send your definition:

By e-mail to: dalenathan@usfamily.net

By mail to: Dale Nathan
PO Box 211284
Eagan, MN 55121-1284

This is for the judge's re-election campaign. Don't tell him.

(A judge's campaign committee can accept
an unlimited amount of money.)

Prologue

This book was written for three reasons. The first is to inform you of what you probably know: our court and legal system is badly broken. It needs to be fixed. The second is to identify the major problems that make justice unavailable and unaffordable for most Minnesotans. The best reason for the book is the third one. It is to educate you on common sense reforms that will dramatically increase the availability of affordable justice.

The primary focus of the book is on Minnesota's judges. They are the state's custodians of justice. As you will see, they routinely fail to provide it.

Our legal system is not just badly broken. It frequently malfunctions or does not function at all, resulting in harsh injustice instead of justice.

Horror Cases With Names

Part I of the book consists of horror cases of injustice in Minnesota courts. These are but an ice crystal atop a massive iceberg of horror cases. The cases in Part I were chosen because they are true, incredible, shocking and heartbreaking. They exemplify what is wrong with our court system.

The cases show in stark detail that judges can, if they choose, separate parents and children without good reason, ruin businesses, cheat providers of labor and materials out of payments due them, help big businesses rob the government, condone racism and racial profiling, disregard police brutality, destroy the lives of people, and do so without fear of personal consequences. No one holds judges accountable for their court actions. The system protects even the worst among them. Judges have nearly absolute power in their courtrooms.

Many judges practice favoritism. While claiming to cover their eyes, judges look the other way as their re-election committees accept campaign contributions of tens of thousands of dollars from lawyers and law firms who practice in their courtrooms. Any lawyer or law firm and others can give an unlimited amount to a judge's campaign committee. A judge's re-election committee can spend without limit on his or her re-election campaign.

Judges belong to a closed fraternity. They know which judges are abusive and dishonest, incompetent, pompous and insensitive. Yet, they refuse to speak out against these bad judges. They follow the golden rule of judicial politics: never speak evil against your brethren on the bench.

Bad judges must be exposed. The people of Minnesota need to awaken from their apathy and learn how the system is malfunctioning. The horror cases in this book are intended to shock your complacency about the legal system and persuade you to join in the effort to make positive reform happen.

THE PROBLEMS

The horror cases in Part I illustrate major problems with our legal system. Part II describes these problems. First, except for a very few people, justice is unaffordable. Only a tiny fraction of citizens can pay tens of thousands of dollars for lawyer fees and court costs. Hundreds of Minnesotans, probably thousands, sit in jail or prison at a huge cost to Minnesota taxpayers because public defenders are stretched too thin and are without the resources they need to provide adequate defenses. Many news stories have reported incidents of convictions that wrongfully imprisoned people for years and in some cases resulted in execution for crimes they did not commit.

At the same time, influential criminal lawyers win unjust concessions from judges they befriend with generous campaign contributions and numerous gratuities. As a reward, judges set low bail, accept incomprehensible plea bargains and impose light sentences that free felons to return to the streets and endanger the public. Money buys influence from those who are supposed to be above being bought.

At variance with our state constitution, judges are rarely selected by the people; they are appointed by the state's top politician, the governor. Uninformed voters do not really re-elect incumbent judges. They usually know nothing about them. Seldom does a judge even face opposition for re-election.

Along with judges throughout America, Minnesota judges usurped power to wrongfully hurt people who come before them. They can intentionally hurt anyone they want - a family, children, someone they just do not like. If they choose to do so, they can ruin a business just for political reasons, throw an innocent person in jail, unjustifiably destroy a career, and get away with it scot-free. Judges have "judicial immunity" - the power to abuse without penalty.

Because they lack adequate financial resources, indigent low-income parents unjustifiably lose their children to foster care at an enormous cost to taxpayers. Worse yet is the damage done to families split apart, to children who suffer lifetime scars, and to their children who are often re-cycled into the same bad system. Judges who should know better refuse to stand up to social workers and other government agents, unwilling to risk the retribution of public employee unions.

Unlimited campaign contributions and gifts called gratuities have corrupted Minnesota's judges. Under a rule they made up on their own, that applies only to themselves, a judge can take gratuities of up to $150 each as many times per day as he or she wants. Like some lawyers, politicians and big business executives, some judges are corrupt.

Studies published by the Supreme Court of Minnesota and civic organizations report rampant racism and racial profiling in our legal system. But neither the Supreme Court of Minnesota nor any other Minnesota court has taken any effective action to end the abominations of judges who dispense justice based on the color of a person's skin.

Minnesota's courts are choked with lawsuits. In 2003, more than 2 million files were opened in Minnesota's court system. They make clearing the calendar the primary objective of daily court hearings, not providing justice. Many of these cases enriched lawyers while families were destroyed, children damaged, lives and careers ruined, and those with bodily injuries under-compensated for their loss.

Oversized damages awards enrich a few while costing the economy tens of millions of dollars. Contingent fee and class action lawsuits make litigation a sport of the rich rather than the pursuit of justice.

Class action lawsuits drain tens of millions of dollars from society into the pockets of rich lawyers. Typically, little is left for the victims of corporate fraud and wrongdoing.

Legal doctrines like joint and several liability and vicarious liability burden defendants with high-dollar judgments even if there was only partial fault on their part or, in a vicarious liability case, no fault at all.

Countless cases demonstrate how these court failings fly in the face of justice, punish good people and give breaks to crooks.

Judges and Lawyers

Lawyers fear judges. There is good reason for that. Judges have enormous unchecked power over lawyers.

In one case, a district court judge ordered a lawyer to tell him what he had been told by his client. When the lawyer refused on the basis of attorney-client privilege, the judge put him in jail for over six weeks. The Minnesota Court of Appeals approved what the district court judge did. It did not matter that the district court judge's order was illegal and unethical.

A judge can ruin a lawyer. He or she can fine a lawyer thousands of dollars and put him or her in jail on the spot for any reason the judge chooses. A judge can rule against a lawyer out of spite. It is very easy for a judge to ruin a lawyer's reputation.

Lawyers know a judge can severely damage them. They cower before judges. Like subjects before their king, lawyers ply judges with adulation. Gaining a judge's good will is very important to a lawyer's career. Most judges expect or even require a humble demeanor from lawyers. When a lawyer is faced with a choice of fighting for the rights of his client or offending the judge, almost all will abandon the client.

In truth, judges are dictators. We live in a land of petty dictatorships ruled by judges. Once a judge gets jurisdiction over a lawyer, or any person for that matter, the judge can ruin him or her.

In a purported democracy, lawyers are afraid to criticize judges.

In a land of freedom, lawyers are oppressed.

Because they fear judges, and for another reason, few lawyers are working for or want significant change in our court and legal system. The additional reason is that the existing system treats lawyers very well.

Most lawyers earn a very good income from their practice or their corporate job. They live in expensive homes in prosperous suburbs. Often, they and their spouses and children drive prestigious suburban utility vehicles or sports cars. Their income enables them to spend weekends at their lake cabins, or on their boats, or both. It also pays for their children's college educations.

Successful lawyers get along with judges. It is bothersome sometimes when justice is difficult or impossible to get, but lawyers seldom blame themselves when that happens. It is the system that they did not create and cannot control. Their consciences are clear. They do not see any compelling need to change the system that treats them so well and do not want to be a troublemaker.

Few, if any, judges want significant change in the current court and legal system. Why should they? They earn well over $100,000 per year, have excellent health care plans mostly paid for by the taxpayers, and can look forward to generous pensions when they retire. Gratuities (gifts) of up to $150 each supplement their income. They are free to accept as many such gratuities per day as they wish.

Their office commands honor and respect. People look up to them. Their job is risk-free. They can make any decision they wish to make without fear of any consequence. Re-election is virtually guaranteed.

It is not likely that lawyers and judges will instigate significant change in our court and legal system. For that to happen, it must be forced - by the people.

Reforms That Will Bring Justice

Citizens can demand changes to the legal system that will make real justice available and affordable for all. Legislators can be lobbied and convinced to reform our court and legal system; those legislators who refuse to do so can themselves be replaced. The many good judges who serve with distinction can work from the inside to bring needed reform, once they feel public wrath over the current system.

Part III of the book proposes doable reforms, among which is making judges accountable for their decisions. A special court to try judges that can award damages to victims of clearly wrongful decisions would sharply curtail judge wrongdoing. Loss of pay, fines, suspensions and possible removal from office also will provide strong incentives for judges to do the job right. Another important reform is public disclosure of misdeeds and injustices. Judges and bureaucrats are human (really) and fear being embarrassed. Forcing them by law to disclose the details of their activities is a powerful deterrent to improper actions and behavior.

An extremely important reform is to get politics out of the judge selection and re-election processes. We can accomplish this with a merit plan like that referred to as the "Missouri Plan" because Missouri was the first of 15 states to adopt such a plan. Supreme Court Justice Sandra Day O'Connor wrote positively about this plan in the case of Republican Party of Minnesota v. White. This case concerned a candidate for the Minnesota Supreme Court, Gregory Wersal, who won the right to be able to state his positions on issues as part of an election campaign. Prior to this decision, incredibly, candidates for judge could not tell the voters their positions on the issues!

Chapter 16 in Part III tells how we can greatly reduce the cost of justice for nearly everyone by simplifying and expediting court procedures. Some of the proposed methods are to provide public services to facilitate fact-finding, improve the use of mediation and arbitration at less expense, authorize resolution of child custody and visitation and marital property distribution by nonpartisan experts, and, similarly, rely on neutral experts to determine damages awards in personal injury cases. Health care and insurance costs will be reduced if we limit awards for damages to what is reasonable. Simplifying and expediting court procedures as proposed above will substantially reduce out-of-sight amounts for lawyer's fees.

We can and we should greatly expand the number of public defenders and increase their resources to assure that every person accused of a crime, no matter how poor, will be adequately defended. We must do the same in juvenile court proceedings to assure that every litigant in such a proceeding is effectively represented, especially in cases that involve the custody of a child. It is critical that public defenders be fully independent of and free from pressure by county authorities.

We can and should abolish campaign contributions for judges. We can replace such financing with public financing as in North Carolina and other states. As an alternative, we can discourage the obvious ploy for judge favoritism by barring lawyers and law firms from appearing before judges they supported financially. The Minnesota Supreme Court by itself could abolish the obnoxious rule that allows judges to accept unlimited $150 gratuities.

Report cards at judge re-election time will give the voting public a basis for deciding on whether or not to re-elect a judge to office. Judge mistreatment of people who appear before them will largely disappear if we videotape court proceedings and use the video as the basis for disciplining the offending judge.

There is one sure way we can get the justice we want: boot judges out of office. What is most important to a judge, even more than providing justice, is staying in office. Judges cherish the power and prestige of their office. They bask in the reverence and deferential treatment they expect and often demand. They prefer the current easy re-election process. Judges do not want voters to challenge their performance. Regrettably, it is not currently practical to inform the average voter on which judges are good and which are bad. The only option is to vote against all incumbent judges until we have a new system.

Chapter 18 tells how we can boot judges out of office. It is surprisingly simple, but it will not be easy. According to the Minnesota Secretary of State, votes for a fictitious person such as Mickey Mouse are counted and have the same validity as votes for anyone else. If Mickey Mouse gets the most votes in a judge election or re-election, he wins the office. Since Mickey Mouse does not exist, a vacancy is declared and the governor appoints a new judge.

Every two years, approximately one-third of all judges stand for re-election. In every election the ballot you receive has a line under the name of each incumbent judge for a write-in vote. If most of the votes are for the same fictitious person, the incumbent judge is defeated. We propose that you join other voters in casting write-in votes for Mickey Mouse. Driving judges from office is a sure way to get their attention and convince them of the public's insistence on reform.

It is not the means we lack to free society from injustice; it is the lack of knowledge and lack of determination to force change. In America, the people truly have power - the power to make our court and legal system what we want it to be. Minnesota can make its legal system what it ought to be – the world's and history's finest. If together we assert our power we can reach the goal of this book - affordable justice for all.

Let the journey begin.

Part I

True Horror Cases – With Names

All of the cases summarized in Part I of this book are actual Minnesota court cases. All information is truthful. The court file number of each case is contained in our website:

http://www.mncourtreform.org

Send us your horror story.

A sequel to this book is planned for release before or in the first quarter of 2005. If you would like us to consider your story, please e-mail it to dalenathan@usfamily.net or mail it to: Dale Nathan, P.O. Box 211284, Eagan, MN 55121.

The Young Sex Perverts (Ages 4 and 6)

James H. Clark, Jr., Ramsey County Judge
John F. Connelly, Ramsey County Judge
Joanne M. Smith, Ramsey County Judge
Teresa R. Warner, Ramsey County Judge
Paul Magnuson, Former Chief Judge, U.S. District Court for Minnesota
Anthony McWell, Ramsey County Child Protection Worker
Ann O. Ploetz, Assistant Ramsey County Attorney
Karen J. Garvin, Assistant Public Defender, Ramsey County
Julie Russomanno, Guardian Ad Litem
Minnesota Supreme Court
Minnesota Appeals Court Judges Bruce Willis, Gordon W. Schumaker, Edward J. Parker

Case Summary

A child protection worker, with the judge's help, and the help of Ramsey County officials, permanently separated a mother (Mother) from her four children and ended all contact among them because the mother, a white woman, dated a black man for a while, and because she would not "cooperate" with the child protection worker. The child protection worker insisted that she had to reconcile with her former companion, the father of two of her children, who repeatedly beat and raped her for more than five years, sometimes in front of her children.

While her 12-year-old daughter was in foster care, the child protection worker, despite Mother's frantic objections, allowed the girl to be in the apartment of Mother's former companion. He assaulted and probably raped the girl, which the child protection worker blamed on Mother and used as the basis for denying her any visitation with her children for months.

Shortly before a trial on Mother's right to have custody of her two youngest children, girls then four and six years old, Mother was scheduled to have unsupervised visitation with them on weekends. Two days before this visitation was to begin, an incident happened between the child protection worker and Mother at her home. He brought Mother's two youngest girls to her home for visitation supervised by him. Mother's oldest daughter happened to be there at the time. In front of her children, the child protection worker accused Mother of using drugs and lying. This provoked a heated denial.

The next day, the child protection worker wrote a letter to Mother with a copy to her lawyer in which he called off the promised unsupervised visitation because of the incident the day before. He said she could have only supervised visitation at an office in a county building on weekdays during regular business hours, which were the hours Mother had to be at her job. These two events happened only two weeks before the trial on her parental rights to her two youngest children.

Four weeks before the argument at Mother's home, the child protection worker had arranged for a psychologist who gets over 90 percent of her business from Ramsey County to write a letter in which she recommended that Mother, whom she had never evaluated or even met, not have unsupervised visitation with her two youngest girls. She said in her letter that the girls had "acted-out sexually toward adult males," and blamed Mother, even though the girls had been in foster care for more than one-and-one-half years.

In testimony at the trial, the child protection worker admitted that he acted unprofessionally in stirring up an argument with Mother just before she was to have weekend visits with her two young daughters.

Mother lost custody of her four children. She is not even allowed contact with them or they with her.

Additional Information and Comment

The parent-child relationship is one of the most protected rights a person has in the United States, perhaps the most important right. Federal courts have said this about that right:

> Parents have a "fundamental liberty interest in the care, custody, and management of their children." Bohn v. County of Dakota, 772 F. 2d 1433 (8th Cir. 1985); Fitzgerald v. Williamson, 787 F. 2d 403 (8th Cir. 1986); Ruffalo by Ruffalo v. Civiletti, 702 F. 2d 710 (8th Cir. 1983); Santosky v. Kramer, 455 U.S. 745, 102 S.Ct. 1388, 71 L.Ed 2d 599 (1982); Stanley v. Illinois, 405 U.S. 645, 92 S.Ct. 1208, 31 L.Ed. 551 (1972). Respondent's interest in preserving and maintaining her family is among the strongest recognized in law. A "parent's interest in the custody of his or her child is among the most basic and fundamental of the liberties protected by the Constitution." Davis v. Page, 618 F. 2d 374 (5th Cir. 1980). The constitutional interest "in the development of parental and filial bonds free from government interference has many avatars .... [A]bove all, it is manifested in the reciprocal rights of parent and child to one another's companionship." Franz v. United States, 707 F. 2d 582, addendum at 712 F. 2d 1428 (D.C. Cir. 1983).

As stated by the 8th Circuit in Bohn, supra,

> "The privacy and autonomy of familial relationships ... are unarguably among the protectible interests which due process protects. We can conceive of no more important relationship, no more basic bond in American society, than the tie between parent and child." Bohn, 772 F. 2d at 1435

Put simply, a child should never be separated from his or her parents unless that is absolutely unavoidable to protect the child.

The case of "The Young Sex Perverts" and others like it show that Minnesota social workers, court officials and judges often do not regard the parent-child relationship as highly as the law requires. The court record in "The Young Sex Perverts," which is a public record, not only shows failure to help keep families together, it shows a deliberate effort to break up a family.

1. After Mother separated from the man who savagely abused her, the court denied her custody of her children because she could not find suitable housing. The child protection worker did nothing to help her. He sent her to another county agency. That agency told her it would help her financially if she found the housing she needed.

2. Although Mother worked full time at about $10 per hour, she still could not find housing for herself and her children. The reasons are understandable: she had a prior eviction (unlawful detainer judgment) and bankruptcy attributable to the severe drug and alcohol abuse of her companion who did not work and stole her money to pay for his drugs and alcohol. In addition, there was a history of her former companion damaging rental property and, despite her attempts to get away from him, he followed her and harassed her. The authorities did nothing to protect Mother from this abuse.

3. A short time after Mother separated from the man who abused her, the child protection worker demanded that she participate in joint counseling with the objective of re-uniting with him. Her former companion had physically beaten her regularly for several years and raped her two or more times per week sometimes in front of her children. But the child protection worker did not understand that the last person in the world a battered woman wants to see is the person who battered her. The child protection worker never asked the batterer to reform himself or apologize to Mother. He faulted Mother for not "cooperating" by not participating in joint counseling.

4. For months, Mother faithfully visited her children while they were in foster care and had them for unsupervised visitation on weekends, all without significant incident. She properly cared for her children while they were with her. The foster mother who cared for Mother's two youngest children during this time was highly complimentary of Mother.

5. During this period, Mother, who is white, dated a black man for a while. The child protection worker found out about this and told Mother to "stick to your own kind." Mother took and passed a lie detector test to verify that the child protection worker said this. Shortly after the child protection worker learned that Mother was dating a black man, he began the process to terminate Mother's parental rights to her two youngest children and put her two oldest children in permanent foster care.

6. Next, the child protection worker attempted to place the two youngest children with their father - the man who had beaten and raped Mother. The child protection worker approved arrangements for all four children to be together at this man's apartment. While she was at his apartment, the man sexually assaulted Mother's then 12-year-old daughter. The police filed a report, but the county never prosecuted him.

7. After this incident, the child protection worker denied Mother any access to her children for months while the sexual attack was being "investigated." Later, he alleged that Mother had not visited her children and was not interested in them even though she demanded many times that she be allowed to be with them.

8. After he made up his mind to terminate Mother's parental rights to two of her children, he demanded that Mother see a psychologist he had selected and who would be paid by Ramsey County. Mother did not want to see this psychologist. The child protection worker told her she could not get her children back unless she did as he commanded her.

9. Before Mother went to this psychologist, the child protection worker visited him and told him all about Mother.

10. The psychologist tested Mother, interviewed her, and performed a brief parenting evaluation. He concluded that Mother would never be able to parent her children.

11. It turns out this psychologist was not even licensed when he evaluated Mother. In Minnesota, it is illegal for a person to practice psychology without a license.

12. The court-appointed a Guardian Ad Litem to recommend what was in the best interests of the children. She filed her report, in which she recommended that Mother's parental rights be terminated – before she even met Mother.

13. Until the pre-trial conference, which usually occurs just before trial, a public defender represented Mother. She did nothing for Mother. She did not have the time or resources to do anything for her.

14. At about this time, Ramsey County prosecuted Mother's then 11-year-old son for sexually abusing his sisters when they were 3 and 5. The instance of the alleged sexual abuse occurred at the apartment of the man who had battered Mother when the four children were alone with him. The man taught the boy to sexually molest his sisters. This was not brought out at the boy's trial by the public defender who met and represented him at trial the same day. The boy was put into institutions for sexually troubled children for more than two years.

15. Several months prior to the trial on Mother's parental rights, she met a man who respected and treated her well. They began a relationship and she moved into his home. It was a spacious home and could house all of Mother's children. The child protection worker inspected and approved the home. By then it was shortly before the trial was to begin. That was when the child protection worker broke his promise to let Mother have unsupervised visitation with her two youngest daughters on weekends.

16. A new lawyer, not a public defender, began representing Mother at the pre-trial conference. He protested against the child protection worker's racism and refusal to help reunite Mother and her children, and said he would inform the public of the wrongdoing of the child protection worker and others who were helping him hurt Mother and her children. Judge James H. Clark, Jr., responded that juvenile court proceedings were confidential and fined Mother's lawyer $1,500 after he published information about the case.

17. A month before Mother's trial started, she found a Ph.D. psychologist she trusted and received counseling from her many times. That psychologist concluded that Mother had some emotional conditions, but that these conditions were treatable and found no reason to believe Mother was unable to parent her children. She testified for Mother at her trial and filed reports of her findings, which contradicted the findings of the unlicensed psychologist who had conducted the earlier evaluations of Mother.

18. Mother proved all of the above during eight days of trial

that, for unavoidable reasons, took place over a seven-month period. It did not matter. Judge Clark terminated Mother's parental rights to her two youngest children.

19. Mother's appeal to the Minnesota Court of Appeals was futile. Judge Bruce D. Willis, who wrote the unpublished decision denying Mother's appeal, lied and knew he was lying when he wrote in the decision that Mother refused to participate in individual therapy. He knew that Mother refused to participate in individual therapy with psychologists who were selected and paid by Ramsey County. It is undeniably clear that she participated in individual therapy.

Judge Willis lied when he wrote that Mother did not make progress in therapy. Two reports in the record written by the Ph.D. therapist who treated Mother, a woman of impeccable credentials and integrity, described substantial progress by Mother and a favorable prognosis. Judge Willis lied yet again when he wrote that Mother refused to participate in family therapy. She tried as hard as she could to participate in therapy with her children, as her case plan required. She was unable to do that because the child protection worker would not make her children available for such therapy.

20. Justice Alan Page wrote a one-sentence order refusing to consider Mother's appeal to the Minnesota Supreme Court.

21. In separate proceedings, Judges Joanne M. Smith and Teresa R. Warner gave Ramsey County the right to permanently separate Mother from her other two children. Mother is not allowed to have any contact with her children, nor they with her.

22. Mother brought an action in the United States District Court for the District of Minnesota in which she described the actions of Judge Clark and Ramsey County officials that were violating her parental rights. Chief Judge Paul Magnuson threw the case out of court and fined Mother's lawyer $2,500.

THE JUDGE WHO MADE HOUSE CALLS

Thomas H. Carey, Hennepin County Judge (retired in Florida)
Court of Appeals Judges Harvey Holtan, Edward Toussaint, Jr., Robert H. Schumacher

Case Summary

A small painting company (Painter) provided materials and labor to paint a luxury home to sell to a couple (Buyers), one of whom was a Hennepin County attorney, and the other a prominent Hennepin County businessman. Buyers agreed to pay the general contractor (Builder) his costs plus a percentage for profit. The final cost of the home far exceeded the budget and Buyers did not have enough money to pay the full price. Painter completed his work, which was inspected and accepted by Builder's construction superintendent (later fired by Builder).

After Builder refused to pay Painter the $20,000 balance that was due, Painter recorded a mechanic's lien on the home. Buyers used a falsified closing statement to close around the mechanic's lien. When the judge learned that Painter's claim was for "only" $20,000, he demanded that the case be settled. He did not want to waste his time on a small claim. He refused to allow a claim of fraud by Painter based on the falsified closing statement. Buyers refused to offer anything to Painter. He asked for a trial. During trial, the judge decided to personally inspect the home as part of the proceedings, in effect making himself a witness. This is illegal. Rule 605 of the Minnesota Rules of Evidence prohibits a judge presiding over a trial from being a witness in the trial. Further, it had been over a year since Painter had painted it.

At Buyers' home, Buyers took Judge Carey on a tour. They pointed out deficiencies they said were there when they moved in and began residing in their new home more than a year earlier. Builder testified at trial that these deficiencies had been corrected shortly after Buyers had moved in and even claimed money from Painter for making the corrections.

The judge found as a fact that Builder's employees had corrected alleged deficiencies in Painter's work and deducted the amount claimed by Builder for the correction work from the amount claimed by Painter. He also found that Painter's alleged deficiencies still existed even though Builder's employee had corrected them. On the basis of his findings of fact, the judge denied Painter recovery of any of his $20,000 claim and fined his attorney $20,000 because, despite five witnesses including the discharged construction superintendent, he said the case was completely without merit and never should have gone to trial.

The Minnesota Court of Appeals reversed the fine against Painter's lawyer, but refused to reverse the decision against Painter since the trial court is the sole judge of credibility of witnesses, despite the glaring discrepancies in Judge Carey's findings of fact. Painter never received anything for his materials and labor.

Additional Information and Comment

Painter had been paid part of the subcontract price, but was owed an additional $20,000. But the cost to build the home was almost $1 million, far over Buyers' budget, who were short of money. In discovery, the process in a lawsuit of getting information from opposing parties, Painter learned that the contract between the general contractor and Buyers was a cost reimbursement plus fee contract. The pertinent part of this contract for the construction of the home stated:

> "4) In consideration of the covenants and agreements hereof . . ., the Owner/Buyer agrees to pay to the Builder the sum of all costs plus 10% profit in the following manner: Down payment of $35,000.00 at

the execution of this contract, balance at completion."

Like almost every home buyer, Buyers planned to finance the purchase of their home by borrowing money from a lender and giving the lender a mortgage interest in their new home. But the amount in loan proceeds approved by the lender they chose was not nearly enough to pay the balance owed subcontractors including Painter. In order to complete the closing and get ownership of the home built for them, Buyers would have to cheat by not paying subcontractors all of what was owed them.

Buyers knew this would not be easy to do. The lenders required title insurance as is typical in almost all home purchases. This insurance guarantees that title is clear at the time of closing without any liens including mechanic's liens. A form that had to be signed by the Buyers at the closing included this provision, "A sworn Construction Statement must be provided which lists all material suppliers, contractors and sub-contractors." A document entitled "Lenders Settlement Instructions," contained the following statement "NAMC [the lender] REQUIRES FIRST LIEN RIGHTS. NO EXCEPTIONS WILL BE PERMITTED ON THE FINAL TITLE POLICY."

To get through the closing, Buyers would need to get around the above requirements. They would need a closer to help them do this.

Most closings are documented in a form approved by the U.S. government because it often guarantees the loan. It is considered very risky to include false information in such a form. A warning in the form states: "WARNING: It is a crime to knowingly make false statements to the United States on this or any other similar form. Penalties upon conviction can include a fine or imprisonment. For details see: Title 18 U.S. Code Section 1001 and Section 1010."

Despite the above warning and the risks, Buyers signed a closing statement that contained false information to complete the closing. When they arrived at the closing for their new home, a closing statement already had been prepared as usually is the case. This first closing statement, which never was signed, showed that subcontractors had been paid $286,669.36 from the loan proceeds and $14,800 had been put in escrow to pay Painter (even though his claim was for $20,000). The buyers could not sign this proposed closing statement because they did not have the money to do so. Because of this, a second closing statement was prepared. It did not refer to any mechanic's lien or any money in escrow to pay off any mechanic's lien. Painter's mechanic's lien was ignored. This second closing statement did not show any amounts owed subcontractors even though in reality they were due $286,669.66. None of the sub-contractors except for Painter had recorded mechanic's liens against the new home and because of that their claims could be hidden.

Painter showed Judge Carey the falsified documents and explained how Buyers had committed a major crime and fraud against Painter and other subcontractors. Judge Carey was not interested. He refused to let Painter amend his first complaint to include allegations of fraud. He also refused to let Painter introduce any evidence of Buyers' fraud at the trial. Because of Judge Carey, Buyers got away with their illegal behavior.

THE TERRIFIED LITTLE GIRL (4 YEARS OLD)

Timothy L. Blakely, visiting Scott County Judge
William E. Macklin, Scott County Judge
Michael A. Young, Scott County Judge
Thomas R. Howe, Scott County Judge
R. Kathleen Morris, Attorney, Scott County, Parenting Time Investigator
Linda Gerr, Guardian Ad Litem
Minnesota Court of Appeals Judges Roland C. Amundson (later convicted of felony crimes and now in prison), Gary L. Crippen, Robert H. Schumacher, Randolph A. Randall, G. Barry Anderson

Case Summary

Mother and Husband, married over 20 years with several grown children, had a falling-out and separated. During the few months they were apart, Mother had an affair with a co-worker at the place where she worked. She and Husband reunited. Later, she found she was pregnant.

A few months later, Daughter was born. The co-worker found out and demanded to know if Daughter was his child. A paternity test proved that she was. The co-worker (Father hereafter) urged Mother to leave Husband and live with him and Daughter. Mother refused.

Father went to court to force Mother to give him visitation with Daughter. The court-appointed Guardian Ad Litem investigated, found Father to be unstable, and recommended supervised visitation, which the court ordered to take place at a children's safety center. The court also ordered Father to pay child support, which he failed to do.

Visitation was very troubled. Father was determined to get custody of Daughter and get Mother to live with him. During his time with Daughter at the visitation center, he repeatedly told her she would be coming to live with him. After one visit when she was three years old, Daughter told Mother and grandmother that Father had taken her to the bathroom and touched her genital area, but she would not repeat this story to an investigator and no finding of child abuse was made.

Visitation became more troubled. Daughter felt frightened of Father. She refused to visit him. Once, she locked herself in her room. Father went to court. He complained that Mother was denying him visitation, and he asked for unsupervised visitation. Scott County Judge Michael Young put Mother in jail for a short while to underscore the court's order to give Father the visitation specified in the judgment and decree, but he did not order unsupervised visitation.

Mother retained a lawyer to advise her on how she could protect Daughter and herself. He recommended that she consult a reputable child psychologist to evaluate Daughter and make recommendations on what was in Daughter's best interests. Mother followed her lawyer's advice. After several meetings with Daughter, the psychologist wrote reports in which she stated Daughter felt terrified of Father and that forced visitation with him was very harmful. She also reported that Daughter had told her of sexual abuse of her by Father. She recommended that Father work with a psychologist to eliminate the problems visitation caused and work toward unsupervised visitation.

Judge Timothy Blakely took over the case. He announced his view that every child should get to know his or her biological parents and his intent to give Father unsupervised visitation with Daughter. To reach this objective, he appointed R. Kathleen Morris as the parenting investigator to make recommendations. (She is the former Scott County Attorney who was defeated for re-election after she accused scores of parents of sexually abusing their children and arranged for them to be placed in foster homes.) Ms. Morris recommended that Father have extensive unsupervised visitation with

Daughter alone at his home. Judge Blakely would not listen to the child psychologist who had evaluated Daughter. He would not even accept her reports into evidence. Eventually, he ordered that Daughter have unsupervised visitation almost every weekend and half of all holidays with Father to make up for the past.

Today, at age seven, Daughter is an emotional and psychological wreck. She does not play with her friends and her neighbors on most weekends. Instead, she is forced to travel to Father's cabin in northern Minnesota and stay with him over the weekend. Conditions in Father's cabin are not as comfortable as in Mother's home and this bothers her. The cabin lacks hot water and toilet facilities (she uses an outhouse) and bathing facilities. There she spends most of her time sitting on a couch until she returns to Mother and Husband's home in the Twin Cities area.

Judges Blakely and Macklin have determined that it is in Daughter's best interests to spend almost every weekend with Father whether she likes it or not and regardless of how that affects her and her relationship with Father. These judges did not and will not consider the evaluations and recommendations of Daughter's psychologists on what is in Daughter's best interests. They choose to rely on the recommendations of a former Scott County Attorney who practices before them.

Additional Information and Comment

Before Judge Blakely took over the case, Mother and Father had appeared before at least five other judges. All had limited Father to supervised visitation. They did so because Guardians Ad Litem assigned to the case reported that Father's attitude and conduct were detrimental to the child. In her affidavit, one Guardian Ad Litem said:

> "5. I considered [Father] less than emotionally stable when I was working with him in 1998 because of his tenacity concerning visitation and his wishes to go for full custody with total disregard for the effect it would have on [Daughter].

"6. [Daughter] was very young when I was on the case and did not really know [Father]. Despite this, he told me several times he wanted visits and was going for full custody. I suggested that he move more slowly and establish a good relationship with [Daughter] and supervised visitation for the present.

"7. After I had several conversations with [Father] concerning [Daughter's] welfare and my recommendations, he became increasingly agitated and angry with me. During this period I received a message from [Father] stating '[GAL's name] you better start doing your f------ job.' I have since deleted the message.

"8. While I was the Guardian Ad Litem on the case, [Father] went to the I'm O.K. Visitation Center for visitation with [Daughter]. There were times when he screamed at me that I was not helping him. I explained again how this was about [Daughter] and what was best for her. I attempted to explain that he was having visits and we were moving forward. [Father] continued to scream at me and once left me abruptly."

The former Guardian Ad Litem was discharged at Father's request.

Although she strongly disliked Father and preferred that he not be in Daughter's life, Mother accepted that Father was entitled to visitation and did all that she could to give him the court-ordered visitation. This was very difficult for her. Father lived in a small town in central Minnesota. Mother lived in the Lakeville, Minnesota area. She worked 40 hours per week.

Father demanded that visitation be at a children's safety center in Belle Plain, Minnesota - a trip that took Mother 45 minutes each way. Mother objected to visitation in Belle Plain, Minnesota, because it put an enormous strain on her and the child.

Mother was greatly concerned about Father's behavior with

Daughter because she knew he took illegal drugs. She saw him do that at the company where they had worked together. She did not want Daughter alone with Father.

Mother was concerned because Daughter acted troubled after visits with Father. She acted frightened and often was sad and moody for days. She would not say what Father had told her during her time with him and neither Mother or Husband asked.

Daughter fought going to visitation. There were times when she had to be dragged to the car crying because she did not want to go see a person that to her was a stranger. Mother's husband was who she thought was daddy.

Stress forced Mother to seek a different location for visitation. Finally, two judges in two separate hearings ordered that the location of visitation be changed. It was, and visitation improved.

At the first hearing before Judge Blakely, he suggested that visitation be moved again – to the home of Mother's mother (Grandmother). Mother's lawyer countered with what he thought would be a better place. Grandmother worked at a motel that had an indoor swimming pool. Why not have four hours of visitation every Saturday at the motel where Father and Daughter could visit extensively and where Daughter could go swimming with her friends if she wanted to. This arrangement was acceptable to all, and visitation took place thereafter at the motel every Saturday morning for an entire summer.

Daughter still was not comfortable with Father. It was clear that something was very wrong.

While visitation was occurring at the motel, Judge Blakely issued an order based on the evidentiary hearing held the same day that the new visitation arrangement had been agreed upon. He ordered that Father would begin having unsupervised visitation with Daughter beginning in seven weeks. He issued this order despite hearing about the many problems Daughter experienced because of visitation with Father.

Mother asked Judge Blakely to reconsider his order for unsupervised visitation. She asked the judge to order that she, Father and Daughter be evaluated by psychologists and that she and Father be tested for drug usage.

Shortly thereafter, Judge Blakely sent a letter to the parties' lawyers. In the letter he made clear that Father was going to get unsupervised visitation with Daughter. He wrote:

> "I would like to reiterate at this point the importance that I place on the physical and emotional well-being of this child. I strongly believe that it is in the best interests of the majority of children to have a loving, positive relationship with **both** parents. To this end, I expect that your clients would put aside past animosities toward each other and work to encourage normal, healthy, loving attitudes of the child toward both parents. Anything less may endanger the child's emotional health." (emphasis in original)

Several days after he sent this letter, Judge Blakely presided over a hearing on Mother's motion for reconsideration. He ordered the parties to get the evaluations Mother wanted. Then, four days later, he appointed R. Kathleen Morris to be the Parenting Time Evaluator to investigate and make recommendations on visitation.

One of Ms. Morris' first actions was to visit the psychologist who was going to evaluate Mother, Father and Daughter to determine why visitation was causing so many problems. After Ms. Morris visited this psychologist, she became hostile toward Mother for reasons never made known to her.

Before the court-ordered evaluations were performed and submitted to the court, Ms. Morris submitted a report to Judge Blakely in which she recommended that Father begin to have extensive unsupervised visitation with Daughter after a very short transition period.

In the meantime, Mother found a very reputable psychologist who agreed to evaluate Daughter. After several meetings with Daughter, she wrote three letters in which she reported that visitation by Daughter with Father was causing very serious problems that should be resolved before Daughter was forced to have unsupervised visitation with Father. In her first letter, she wrote:

> "At this point in time the source of [Daughter]'s anxiety or difficulty with visits is unclear. I would recommend that [Daughter] would have supervised vis-

> its for short periods of time (i.e., 1-2 hours) to increase the possibility of developing a positive relationship with her father, [Father]. Forcing a young child to have longer and longer visits before she is ready may exacerbate the situation, and actually accomplish the opposite goal. I recommend that, until the hearing, [Daughter] have short visits with [Father] at a visitation center for further observations. Even though it may not yet be clear where the disturbance is coming from, it seems apparent that these visits are stressful to [Daughter]. Increasing the length of the visits at this time, including having them be unsupervised, may only strengthen the negative emotion [Daughter] is experiencing. It seems to be in the best interests of [Daughter] and [Father] to set up visitation scenarios that are not stressful, and which could be positive and relationship building."

Judge Blakely refused to receive this letter into evidence or consider it, or to hear the testimony of the psychologist who wrote it. On the day it was given to him, he ordered the beginning of unsupervised visitation by Daughter with Father, and issued an order that Mother be arrested and taken to jail for not appearing before him. Later, he jailed Mother's lawyer because he refused to tell him what Mother had said to him. He demanded that Mother's lawyer violate the attorney-client privilege.

A few weeks later, the psychologist wrote her second letter. It states:

> "During a recent session . . ., [Daughter] made several comments that were noteworthy. On our way to the play therapy room, [Daughter] said '[Father] wants to put my mom in jail and kill her.' At that time, [Daughter]'s voice seemed to be high pitched and anxious. During the post session (with a parent/guardian and the child) [Daughter] offered another unsolicited comment. She looked directly at me

> and said '[Father] touched my butt, and I don't ever want to see him again.' She did not look down at the floor, nor did she look at [Mother] while she told me. If children are lying or not telling the truth, they often look at the floor or somewhere else rather than directly at the person. She did not seem to be interested or able to elaborate any further. I have since called Child Protective Services and filed a report with them about what [Daughter] said. This is the second time [Daughter] has made an unsolicited comment to me about [Father] while looking directly at me. The other comment, as mentioned in the previous letter, was 'I don't like to see [Father]. I hate him.'"
>
> "In summary, [Daughter] has made some statements that indicate strong emotion and distress surrounding [Father]. I continue to recommend that [Daughter] be allowed to work through those feelings and given time for us to understand more fully what she needs. Forced unsupervised visitation at this point could be harmful for [Daughter]. I reiterate again that short supervised visitations should occur at a visitation center until more information is available to determine what is in [Daughter]'s best interest."

This letter was sent to Judge Blakely. Nothing changed. Mother was in hiding with Daughter after emergency appeals had been made to the Minnesota Court of Appeals to stop Judge Blakely from hurting Daughter and Mother, and to get Mother's lawyer out of jail.

A month later, the psychologist said this in her third letter:

> "This letter is an update to my previous letters. As I stated before, [Daughter] has demonstrated anxiety and fear about visiting [Father]. At this time I cannot state with certainty all the reasons for [Daughter]'s anxiety about visiting with [Father].

> Regardless of the reasons for the anxiety, [Daughter]'s well-being needs to be considered in the process of helping her to get to know her biological father. It is clear she has anxiety and confusion right now, so any plan for her welfare should take into account her current emotional state.
>
> "The purpose of this letter is to more clearly delineate some recommendations I have for [Daughter]. I continue to recommend that she be given time to work through her anxiety, as well as be allowed time to grow into a relationship with [Father]. It would be helpful for [Daughter] to begin visits with him in a therapeutic setting, such as the [psychologist's clinic]. If she does demonstrate anxiety, she will have someone qualified to help her with these emotions. It is essential that these therapeutic visits occur before there would be any move to unsupervised visits. If the move to unsupervised visits goes too quickly, the development of a relationship between [Daughter] and [Father] could be threatened. As long as [Daughter]'s anxiety decreases, then a plan could be set to begin a few short unsupervised visits. If [Daughter]'s anxiety continues to decrease, the plan could include a gradual increase of time for the unsupervised visits as well."

Mother submitted the psychologist's three letters to the Minnesota Court of Appeals in connection with her emergency appeals. They did not change any of Judge Blakely's decisions or do anything about his actions, with one exception. After Mother's lawyer had been in jail for almost seven weeks and still would not reveal what Mother had told him, the appeals court let him out.

Mother made a regular appeal to the Minnesota Court of Appeals. After several months, it denied her appeal. The Minnesota Supreme Court refused to review the matter. Mother and Daughter came out of months of hiding. Mother spent a month in jail. Daughter was forced to begin and continue unsupervised visitation with Father almost every weekend and one-half of all holidays. That has continued. It is believed that Father has told Daughter that he will have Mother sent back to jail if she misses visitation with him.

THE UGLY LIQUOR STORE

Thomas O. Hayes, Anoka County Judge

Case Summary

Lindstrom, Minnesota, decided to build a new liquor store. The city council invited interested construction companies to submit bids. Under the law, the company that proposed the lowest price would win the contract if it agreed to meet all specifications and proved that it was a qualified builder.

The invitation for bids issued by the City of Lindstrom was for the design and construction of a liquor store. If it had chosen to do so, the city could have contracted initially for just the design of the store it wanted. Award of a contract for just design services is not subject to the rule that it must go to the low bidder. It can be made on a basis that takes judgmental factors into account, although it must be on a fair basis.

The solicitation for bids issued by the City of Lindstrom stated that:

> "The criteria used to select the Firm to design and construct the project will include, but are not necessarily limited to:
>
> 1. Cost
> 2. Design
> 3. References and experience."

One of the members of the city council wanted a certain construction company to win. The owners of that company were political supporters. Before bids were submitted, he met with the owners of that company. At the city council meeting after that, the council voted to award the contract to the second low bidder – the city council member's political supporters. The council said it liked the design of the second low bidder better than the design of the low bidder.

The low bidder brought suit to stop the award and to get an order that the contract must be awarded to the low bidder as required by law. Anoka District Court Judge Thomas O. Hayes, a former county attorney, ignored the law. He approved the award to the second low bidder.

Before the Minnesota Court of Appeals, the second low bidder argued that a contract for the design and construction of a government building was not the same as a contract for just the construction of a government building and, therefore, was not subject to the rule that award of such a contract must be to the low bidder.

Judge Hayes was wrong, the appeals court concluded. It said:

> "[The low bidder] argues that the district court erred in concluding that the mixed design services and building construction contract for the municipal liquor store is not a contract subject to Minnesota's competitive bidding statute. [The low bidder] asserts that the contract is for the construction of a public building, a contract of the sort the legislature expressly contemplated when it enacted Minnesota's competitive biding statutes. We agree.
>
> "Competitive bidding statutes are designed to ensure that taxpayers 'receive the best bargain for the least money.' [citation omitted] The 'fundamental purpose of competitive bidding is to deprive or limit the discretion of contract-making officials in the areas which are susceptible to such abuses as fraud, favoritism, improvidence and extravagance' [citation omitted]"

After reviewing Minnesota's competitive bidding statutes, it was crystal clear to the appeals court that the contract for a new liquor store was subject to those statutes and had to be awarded to the low bidder. The court reversed Judge Hayes following a long and expensive appeal by the low bidder. This victory, however, came after the new liquor store had been built. Judge Hayes then awarded the low bidder the costs it incurred in preparing and submitting its proposal. Lindstrom taxpayers paid these costs as well as the higher price for the new liquor store, which exceeded the original low bid.

Additional Information and Comment

Fraud, corruption and favoritism in state and local government purchasing in Minnesota waste hundreds of millions of dollars every year, and probably increase your state and local tax burden by at least 25 percent. This waste could be largely eliminated by the Model State Procurement Code, a national model state law that was adopted and is in effect in more than 16 states. It is not even being considered by Minnesota's executive or legislative branches of government. (Libraries that have the text of the Model State Procurement Code are listed in a website that can be found by entering and searching, "Model State Procurement Code library.")

Consolidation of county and local government service agencies would eliminate additional hundreds of millions of dollars of expenditures each year by Minnesota's governmental units and lower taxes without reducing the quantity and quality of governmental services. Minnesota's legal system, however, does not require state, county and local government officials to give high priority to cost-effectiveness in governmental operations.

THE VANISHING BUILDERS

Timothy J. McManus, Dakota County Judge
James M. Rosenbaum, Chief Judge, U.S. District Court for the District of Minnesota

Case Summary

A scheme perpetrated by a major Minnesota lumber company through an unregulated private bank it created deprived hundreds of subcontractors of payment for their labor and materials. The private bank was a wholly-owned subsidiary of the lumber company. A national bank loaned the lumber company bank scores of millions of dollars that it then loaned to builders to finance the construction of homes.

The lumber company bank made loans to financially weak builders that could not qualify for construction loans from commercial banks which are regulated by federal and state agencies. Interest rates charged by the lumber company bank were substantially higher than those of commercial banks and the lumber company bank charged thousands more in fees and carrying costs.

The lumber company bank retained and controlled the proceeds of each loan. It paid subcontractors and vendors directly as long as funds were available. Products purchased from the lumber company always were paid for in full. The general contractor always was paid for its work, sometimes an obviously excessive amount. Occasionally, proceeds of a loan were used to pay the lumber company amounts owed for materials used on other construction projects.

Many of the financially weak builders completed construction of one or more homes financed by the lumber company bank and then went out of business, or simply disappeared. The lumber company bank foreclosed on its construction loan mortgage which generally used up all the equity in the home. There was nothing left to pay subcontractors for their labor and materials. The percentage of loans made by the lumber company bank to financially weak builders that went into default was five times as high as the rate for regulated commercial banks.

One of the subcontractors sued the lumber company and its bank for racketeering under a federal law known as the Racketeer Influenced Corrupt Organizations Act, 18 U.S.C § 1961 et seq. Federal Judge James Rosenbaum, now Chief Judge of the United States District Court for the District of Minnesota, demanded that the complaint, the document that started the lawsuit, be re-written several times; it did not have enough detail for him to see the fraud. He finally threw the lawsuit out of court because he was never satisfied with the complaint.

The subcontractor then sued in a Minnesota state court under a state law that provides relief for fraud. Judge Timothy McManus threw this suit out of his court without letting it go before a jury. He said there were no facts in dispute. The lumber company bank was simply foreclosing on its mortgage. The Minnesota Court of Appeals affirmed Judge McManus' ruling. Chief Justice Kathleen Blatz and the rest of the Supreme Court of Minnesota refused to review the matter. As a result, the lumber company got away with its frauds. It continues to make high risk loans to financially weak builders and defraud subcontractors out of payment for their labor and materials. After the subcontractor's appeals were denied, Judge McManus awarded judgment against the subcontractor for thousands of dollars of costs, including more than $5,000 for the work of an expert who never even testified.

Additional Information and Comment

The document that starts a civil lawsuit is called a "complaint." It is a statement of the plaintiff's claim against the person or persons being sued.

According to the official court rules of procedure, a complaint is sufficient to start a lawsuit if the information in it: (1) shows the court named in the complaint has "jurisdiction" – legal authority over the people named in the complaint and the legal authority to decide the dispute; (2) states what the claim is such as what the defendant or defendants did that was illegal or wrongful; and (3) states the relief that the plaintiff is or plaintiffs are seeking. (Rule 8 of the Rules of Civil Procedure.)

Rule 8(e) states: "(1) Each averment of a pleading shall be simple, concise, and direct. No technical forms of pleading or motions are required." The basic concept is fair notice. A complaint conforms to the rules of pleading if it presents "a generalized summary of the claim . . . sufficient to afford fair notice to the defendant. . . . [citation omitted]" The Federal Rules of Civil Procedure do not require a claimant to set out in detail the facts upon which he bases his claim. To the contrary, all the Rules require is "a short and plain statement of the claim that will give the defendant fair notice of what the plaintiff's claim is and the grounds upon which it rests." (Moore's Federal Rules Pamphlet, 1998, Part I, page 68.)

If a complaint alleges fraud, as the complaint did in the case of "The Vanishing Builders," Rule 9(b) of the Rules of Civil Procedure applies. It states: "In all averments of fraud or mistake, the circumstances constituting fraud or mistake shall be stated with particularity. Malice, intent, knowledge, and other condition of mind of a person may be averred generally." The rule requires that the complaint state details of the alleged fraud such as who committed the fraud, how the fraud was committed, and the time and place of the fraud. What Rule 9 prohibits is mere conclusions such as, the defendant defrauded me, without giving the defendant a fair idea of what the alleged fraud is.

By any fair measure, the complaint in the case before Judge James M. Rosenbaum more than met the requirements of Rules 8 and 9 of the Rules of Civil Procedure. It ran 33 pages long. Although length by itself does not satisfy the particularity test, this complaint included substantial detail: the names of the financially weak general contractors financed by the lumber company bank and their principal officers, the specific homes that were involved including the legal description of each, the mortgage and mechanic's lien documents recorded against each home including document numbers and dates of recording, the names of the officials of the lumber company bank who conceived the fraudulent scheme and implemented the loans, the default percentages on projects, some of which were more than 25 percent, the names of numerous subcontractors who never were paid for their labor and materials, and many other details.

The facts alleged in the complaint before Judge Rosenbaum were parallel to the facts in another case, Atlas Pile Driving v. Dicon Financial Co., 697 F.Supp 1058 (D.Minn 1988), aff'd, 886 F.2d 986 (8th Cir. 1989), in which the same kind of scheme to defraud was successfully alleged and proven. Although the complaint before Judge Rosenbaum was modeled after the complaint in the Atlas case, it simply was not good enough. In truth, no reasonable person could have failed to understand the fraud alleged in this complaint. Judge Rosenbaum chose to play dumb.

After two amended complaints both failed to please him, Judge Rosenbaum granted the defendants' motion for summary judgment, thereby keeping the case from proceeding before a jury. The federal court of appeals for Minnesota affirmed Judge Rosenbaum's decision. It played as dumb as he did.

Long after Judge Rosenbaum dismissed the case, it was discovered that he had personal contacts with the family that owned the lumber company and its bank. This was the subject of a complaint to the judge's ethic's committee. The complaint was ignored.

The complaint that did not have enough detail for Judge Rosenbaum had enough for Dakota County Judge Timothy J. McManus. He found a different reason for dismissing the lawsuit. He said there were no facts in dispute and could not see any wrongdoing in the defendants' conduct.

Many of the allegations in the complaint before Judge McManus were undisputed: the lumber company bank made loans to general contractors who officials of the bank knew from their loan applications were financially weak, all of these general contractors were fully paid for their work and then some, all vanished leaving scores of subcontractors without payment for their labor and materials, all the new home projects listed in the complaint went into foreclosure, and the bank recovered the full amount of every loan plus substantial amounts for interest and fees. Judge McManus could not comprehend the major fact in dispute: the lumber company bank and its officials and associates had engaged in a scheme to defraud subcontractors.

THE TORTURED CHILDREN

Dennis A. Challeen, retired Winona County Judge
Donna Thethewey, Ramsey County Referee
Robert Fletcher, Ramsey County Sheriff
David May, former Ramsey County
Director of Child Protection
Judge Dane Morey, Buffalo County, Wisconsin
Judge of Circuit Court
Ann M. Yelle, Stuart I. Berg, Buffalo County
Child Protection Officials
James Duvall, Buffalo County Attorney
Mark Perron, Ramsey County Assistant County Attorney
Brian Magruder, Ramsey County Human Services Department
John C. Shabaz, Wisconsin Federal District Court Judge
David C. Rice, Wisconsin Assistant Attorney General

Case Summary

After years of beatings and other kinds of abuse by her husband, the mother of their three children divorced him. The court awarded custody of the couple's three children to their mother. Their father, who did not work and received social security disability income (SSI), refused to pay any child support. Their mother, who did work, could not make ends meet. She urgently needed additional income. This led her to make a serious mistake. She sold some marijuana to an undercover officer.

The court sent her to jail and transferred custody of the parties' children to their father. He tortured them. He beat them, forced the two girls to watch pornography, refused to provide them with adequate clothing and other necessities, and often left them alone. His home was filthy, lacked hot water, and frequently lacked food.

Conditions became so bad that a county child protection worker filed a CHIPS (Child In need of Protective Services) petition charging the children's father with child abuse. An exhibit attached to the petition reported that he showed his son movies of naked men and women having intercourse, repeatedly hit the girls, that there was little to eat in the home, that the children often were left without supervision, that the home often was cold in the winter time because the wood furnace had died out, and that four times, one of the children was found by her school to have head lice.

A criminal complaint filed by the sheriff charged the children's father with engaging in violent, abusive, indecent, profane, boisterous, unreasonably loud and otherwise disorderly behavior, and making threats of bodily harm to his children. He pleaded no contest to these charges. However, he was allowed to keep custody of the children even though their mother had completed her jail time and begged for the return of her children.

Later, the children's mother moved for an investigation. Judge Dennis A. Chaleen appointed a licensed social worker to be the children's guardian ad litem (a person who investigates and reports to the court on children involved in a legal proceeding). She reported to the judge that the children were struggling in school, that the oldest girl had made repeated reports of abuse by their father, that clearly there were problems in his home, and that the children's schools considered their father to be a problem parent. Despite all this, Judge Chaleen refused to change custody.

One night, after more serious abuse, the children called their mother, and ran from their father's home to a meeting place where their mother picked them up and fled to her home in St. Paul, Minnesota. The next day, Ramsey County Deputy Sheriffs, with the cooperation of Ramsey County Child Protection, picked up the children and returned them to their father's county where they were put into separate foster homes.

Several months later, despite their father's refusal to cooperate, and strong warnings by social workers that he was a danger to his children, the court returned the children to their father. Three months later, after more beatings and torture, the children ran again to their mother's home. A new child protection worker finally determined that the children should be with mother and left them in her home. The county that put the children in foster care then forced their mother to pay thousands of dollars for the cost of foster care.

Additional Information and Comment

When the court transferred custody to him, the children's father was living in Wisconsin, just across the Mississippi River near Winona, Minnesota. After they began living with him, the children often complained of physical and sexual abuse by their father. Authorities removed the children several times from their father's home and placed them in foster homes.

A petition by a social worker employed by the Buffalo County, Wisconsin Department of Human Services, filed a CHIPS petition, charging him with abusing the children as follows:

> "Count One: The minor has been a victim of sexual or physical abuse including injury which is inflicted by another other than by accidental means.
>
> "Count Two: The father refuses or is unable for reasons other than poverty to provide necessary care, food, clothing, medical or dental care or shelter so as to seriously endanger the physical health of the child."

The children's mother asked Judge Challeen to investigate charges that the children's father abused them. He granted the motion and appointed a licensed social worker and guardian ad litem to investigate.

In her report the guardian ad litem stated:

> "The children have struggled in school academically. [The youngest daughter] has had four cases of head lice; [the oldest daughter] has made repeated reports of abuse perpetrated by father. These have involved the police, the Department of Human Services and

the County Attorney's Office in Buffalo County. The long and short of it is that [the oldest daughter] has recanted her reports. However, the school told me as recently as last week about another report of father physically abusing [his oldest daughter] and [his son], and [the oldest daughter] is of the belief, according to the school, that it doesn't do any good to tell adults anyway because they don't do anything. Clearly there are problems in the [father's] household.

"[The oldest daughter] has done very poorly academically in school and appears to school personnel to be very unhappy and dissatisfied with her home life.

"[The youngest daughter] struggles in school academically. She has difficulty with peer group relationships; she constantly seeks negative attention. In fact, she has an insatiable need for attention from adults.

"Cochrane-Fountain City School has a negative view of [the children's father] in terms of his support of the children and follow-through in supporting the children in their school endeavors. [The oldest daughter] will be going to summer school and has been referred to as emotionally disturbed for the fall. [She] appears to have no friends; [the boy and youngest daughter] on the other hand are easily led into negative activities. Cochrane-Fountain City School staff clearly believe that these children need to be in foster care.

"[The youngest daughter – about 10 at the time] is swearing a lot and [the boy] is stealing his sister's clothing.

"[A child protection worker] is visiting the family

> weekly on a voluntary agreement with [the father]. He stated the school called him two weeks ago stating that [the oldest daughter] was crying continually.
>
> "It is clear to me that Cochrane-Fountain City School staff consider [the father] to be an inadequate and a problem parent. . . . The children have clear social, emotional and academic problems; they are at-risk children."

A licensed social worker/therapist reported that the children were presently in a situation where the potential for violence "appears to be probable," and recommended that the children be removed from their father's home and custody.

Unknown to their father, the children began writing descriptions of the abuse they were suffering. The following excerpts illustrate the abuse inflicted on the children:

> "[My brother] was in the bathtub and he accidentally splashed some water onto the floor. He was about to clean it up when I called him upstairs. So he came upstairs where I was. I can't remember what we were talking about, but we talked for a while. Then, our dad called [my brother] downstairs. When he got downstairs our dad slammed him on the stairs and was yelling and spitting in his face while he was yelling. And he was telling [my brother] how sick and tired he was of us messing up the house. Then he told [my brother] how sick and tired of us acting like niggers.
>
> "When [my brother] told our dad to leave him alone because our dad was calling him a nigger and swearing and calling him names, so [my brother] ran and locked himself in the bathroom while dad was behind chasing him and when he got to the door he screamed and said open the door and [my brother] refused to open the door so our dad slammed his fist

on the door while telling [my brother] to open the door but [my brother] still refused to open the door then made a loud crack and our dad got madder and he almost knocked a piece of the door out. [My brother] finally opened the bathroom door and when he did our dad grabbed ahold of his shirt and his arm and twisted it around his back and pushed [my brother] down to the floor and as he pushed him to the floor with his arm behind his back [my brother's head hit the bathroom sink and he started to cry louder than he was when his arm got twisted behind his back. And as he was doing all of this he said don't you ever run away from me and when he hit his head he said, 'Ooh poor baby.'

"[My brother] forgot to bring one of our mixing bowls in the house after he fed my dog. Our dad found out and told me to bring the mixing bowl back into the house. He did but the bowl was a little cracked on the top and it was chewed up a little. Our dad grabbed the bowl and threw it and it hit him in the face, then he kneeled on his chest and [my brother] thought he broke his rib when it popped but he didn't.

"[My brother] said 'I'm sick and tired of working my butt off around the house and you don't do nothing but watch TV.' Our dad said, 'sick and tired of what? Doing this?' He started acting like he was masturbating.

"Our dad just came in, he smells and there is mud all over his nose. 'Sick.' He smells like beer really bad and he sure looks and talks like he's drunk. . . . I can't understand him much right now. He just told us to get our stuff on and to go with him it's time to go. I didn't think at the time. I should have told him that I wasn't going to go with him until he sobered up. I

> guess I didn't want to get him mad so he hurts us.
>
> "He said to my brother and I that the reason me and our dad got in fights last year is because I was going through puberty. He was referring to the time he choked me and put a pillow over my face so that my brother and sister couldn't see my face, because my face was starting to change colors.
>
> "Dad grabbed ahold of my sister and slammed her up against my door and my sister said, 'Don't hit me,' and she put her arms up in front of her face and then he grabbed one of her arms and hit her with her own hand and he said, 'Now what are you going to tell the judge? They won't believe you if you say that I hit you with your own hand. So now what are you going to tell them?' Then my sister was supposed to take her pill and she said, 'let me get some spit in my mouth,' because he wouldn't let her get any water but he kept saying no and he then jammed the pill down her throat."

Judge Dane Morey found that the father's home and his treatment of the children were unacceptable and placed the children in foster homes.

Anne M. Yelle, the lead child protection worker, Stuart I. Berg, the director of the department, and Buffalo County District Attorney, James Duvall made the determination to return the children to their father even though the children expressed their strong desire to live with their mother.

Buffalo County social workers, including Anne M. Yelle, told the children that their mother was selling drugs and in other ways slandered her and attempted to turn the children against her.

These same social workers, including Anne M. Yelle, terrorized the children by telling them that they would be put in cuffs and placed in detention if they did not agree to return to their father's home.

The social workers and Anne Yelle were so determined to return the children to their father that they refused to coordinate with or follow the recommendations of the youngest girl's foster parents and professional service providers in La Crosse County, before urging Judge Morey to order the children back to their father.

The social workers and Anne Yelle made their decision to send the children back to their father even though he repeatedly used profane language in the presence of the children – even when in-home counselors were present.

The social workers and Anne Yelle recommended returning the children to their father's home even though it was filthy and unsafe and had not been repaired or brought up to the fire and safety code as required by a court order.

After the children were returned to their father, he moved out of Wisconsin to Winona, Minnesota. Severe abuse continued and was reported to the Winona County Human Services Department. This lead to an investigation. One day while the investigation was in progress, the children were severely mistreated and fled to a neighbor's home. Their father had left the home for more drinking. The children called their mother who drove from her home in St. Paul and brought them back with her.

The children went into hiding. The Winona County child protection worker came to St. Paul and the children were produced for a meeting with him. Based on what the children told him and what he had learned, he let the children stay with their mother.

Buffalo County billed the children's mother for thousands of dollars to pay for the foster care they had provided over her objection. They still are collecting from the children's mother through tax intercepts.

The Billion Dollar Heist

John R. Tunheim, Federal District Court Judge
Ann Montgomery, Federal District Court Judge
(former U.S. Magistrate)
Jonathan Lebedoff, U.S. Magistrate
Raymond L. Erickson, U.S. Magistrate
Federal Appeals Court Judges
James B. Loken (Chief Judge), Gerald W. Heaney,
Pasco M. Bowman II, (former Chief Judge)

Case Summary

A government contractor bilked taxpayers out of more than a billion dollars by giving false information to the United States Navy that led the Navy to buy 1980s era computers at a price of $1 million each even though modern era computers with superior capability were available for about $20,000 each.

Judge John Tunheim, with the Navy's cooperation, dismissed the suit brought by an employee who was fired because he would not participate in the contractor's scheme to cheat the government. Judge Tunheim and other court officials covered up the fraud. On the recommendation of U. S. Magistrate Jonathan Lebedoff, Judge Tunheim penalized the employee and his lawyer for trying to expose the fraud.

(Before he was appointed to the federal bench, Judge Tunheim was the chairman of the U.S. Assassination Records Board, which reviewed records concerning the assassination of President John F. Kennedy. President Bill Clinton nominated him to be a federal judge in 1995. The review board's final report was that a single, illiterate, emotionally-disturbed vagrant was solely responsible for killing President Kennedy.)

In the wrongful discharge lawsuit brought by the former employee against the contractor, Judge Tunheim declared the facts to be different from what the evidence showed. On the basis of this distortion of the facts, Judge Tunheim granted summary judgment in favor of the contractor. The federal appeals court for Minnesota affirmed his decision. One appeals court judge did not even read Judge Tunheim's decision before the oral argument in that case.

In a separate whistle blower case started by the employee, the then United States Attorney, David L. Lillehaug, refused to prosecute the contractor in return for a political favor.

The obsolete computer fraud cost the U.S. Navy and U.S. taxpayers more than $1 billion than what it would have cost for computers that had as much and even more capability than the obsolete computers. Several other frauds described below robbed U.S. government agencies of more unknown millions of dollars.

Additional Information and Comment

Procurement Fraud 1 – The Obsolete Computer Fraud
Amount of the fraud – more than $1 billion

The UYK-43 (actually pronounced "yuk-43") computer is a ruggedized computer developed for the U.S. Navy. It was designed in the early 1980s and selected by the U.S. Navy as its standard computer. The Navy required that it be ruggedized so it could withstand very rough conditions. These computers were installed on almost every Navy and Marine Corps combat ship. Many ships had several UYK-43 computers.

The UYK-43 also was designated by the Navy as its standard computer for all of its other operations. The contractor became the sole source for the Navy's principal computer because it owned the design and was the only company that had the legal right to manufacture it.

Initial quantities of the UYK-43 were very expensive per unit.

After some quantity buys, the price per computer eventually stabilized to about $1 million each by the early 1990s.

During the cold war era that extended into the 1990s, the U.S. Navy, Marine Corps and Coast Guard purchased hundreds of UYK-43 computers. They were needed for new and retrofitted warships, and for ground operations. The cost to these agencies was enormous. It soon became a major problem as the federal government deficit grew to historic levels.

Computer technology advanced incredibly during the 1980s. By 1992, much of the 1982 computer technology had long been obsolete. Computers that were much smaller than the UYK-43 had far greater storage capacity and operated many times faster than 1982 computers. They used chips instead of printed circuit boards and vacuum tubes, making them far easier and less expensive to manufacture. By 1992, it was possible to manufacture a ruggedized computer for $20,000 that would far outperform the UYK-43.

A computer system consists of hardware and software. A computer will not operate at all without compatible software. Like computer hardware, computer software technology advanced dramatically from 1982 to 1992. But the software for the 1982 UYK-43 continued to be the 1982 software. Software created in the late 1980s was too advanced for the UYK-43 and that system could not use it.

The Navy and other federal agencies were desperate to reduce the price of the UYK-43 computer system. They knew they could buy computers that had the same capability as the UYK-43 for about $20,000 each. But the 1982 UYK-43 software would not operate on these advanced computers. To use the new era computers the 1982 UYK-43 software would have to be converted.

Only the contractor that created the 1982 UYK-43 software knew how to convert it, and, because it owned the software, had the sole legal right to do so. So the Navy went to the contractor and asked how much it would cost to convert the 1982 UYK-43 software to work with much cheaper modern computers.

This request put the contractor's management on the spot. If they allowed their engineers to convert the 1982 UYK-43 software so it would work on much cheaper computers manufactured by other companies it would result in the loss of sales. The government would buy the cheaper computers instead of hundreds of UYK-43 computers at $1 million each. There would be no sales of UYK-43 computers. Their bosses would not like that.

Navy contracting officials asked some of the contractor's software engineers if the 1982 UYK-43 software could be converted for use in 1992 computers manufactured by companies other than their employer. These engineers said they would look into it. They did and learned it was easy to do. They prepared to report this to the Navy.

Before the software engineers submitted their report to the Navy, the contractor's vice-president of marketing learned of it. He contacted the vice-president and general manager. They concluded it would be disastrous if such a report was given to the Navy. They instructed their software engineers to lie – to tell the Navy that converting the 1982 UYK-43 software so it would run on modern computers was too expensive or not practical. When the software engineers refused, management instructed the hardware engineers tell that to the Navy. They did.

The Navy and other federal government agencies still are buying the UYK-43 computer system at about $1 million each. Navy officials learned about the lawsuit brought by the contractor's employee who was fired because he would not lie or commit fraud. These Navy officials, as well as the contractor, did not want the court action to be successful or to become public information.

Procurement Fraud 2 – VAX Idle Computer Overcharges
Amount of the fraud – unknown millions of dollars

The DEC VAX was a large and expensive computer. The contractor purchased and leased several of these computers and installed them in their factory. These computers were used in performing contracts and company research projects. The cost of renting or purchasing these computers was charged directly to government contracts at hourly rates that were in proportion to the time the VAX computer or computers were used on each contract.

As a result of contract completions and the failure to win new contracts, there was a decline in the number of contracts to which these charges could be billed. This caused a substantial decline in the company's profit and even in losses. To reverse this, the contractor changed its method of charging projects for the use of VAX computers and so informed the government. Beginning on a specified date, these costs were included in engineering overhead, an indirect cost pool. Engineering overhead was allocated to contracts based on direct labor dollars.

Regulations required official approval of changes in accounting practices to assure that the government was not being charged more than what was justified. To get such approval, a contractor was required to inform the government of each change in its accounting practices and the cost impact on each contract being performed.

After the contractor changed its method for charging VAX computer use, its billings for VAX computer time greatly increased. The effect of these changes was that the government was charged for the cost of idle VAX computers – computers that were not used at all in performing government contracts. The contractor did this by bundling its VAX equipment and charging projects for the costs of all equipment in the bundle.

Thus, prior to the change, each project was charged only for the cost of each VAX computer or computers actually used in performing the contract. After the change, projects were charged rates for the costs of VAX computers based on the costs of all VAX computers, including some that were not used in performing the project that was charged. In fact, the contractor even made retroactive charges for previous use of VAX computers.

After the contractor changed the method for charging VAX computer time, it ordered projects to continue using VAX computers unless management approved exceptions and allowed some projects to discontinue using VAX computers and substitute other computers if that resulted in savings for the contractor.

One of the contracts the contractor was performing when it changed the method of charging VAX computer time was called the

TEAMS III contract. This was a task order contract. When the Navy wanted certain work, it issued a Task Assignment Record (TAR) describing the work it wanted done. The contractor then submitted a quotation that listed the level of personnel who would perform the work and an estimated total cost.

After the Navy approved the estimate, the work began. The employees who managed projects were known as project engineers. Certain project engineers managed TARs that used VAX computers. Charges for using VAX computers were charged to TAR accounts. After the rates for VAX usage increased substantially, project engineers complained to management because the increased costs were causing overruns on their projects. These costs were passed on to Navy customers.

For example, in just one project, the initial estimate for use of a VAX computer was less than $100,000. The final charge exceeded $300,000. In this manner, the contractor fraudulently charged the Navy millions of dollars for the use of VAX computers that were never needed nor used in performing work on the TARs or contracts charged for these costs.

After the VAX rates were increased substantially, retroactive charges for VAX computer time were made to TARs. These retroactive charges were illegal. This resulted in many overruns. In many instances, the retroactive charges were assessed after all work had been completed and the TAR closed out.

The contractor was faced with hundreds of thousands, perhaps millions of dollars of overruns on TARs. The contractors decided to transfer the overrun amounts to other TARs, even though there was no legal basis for doing so.

To get the government to approve the changes it made, the contractor submitted a cost impact statement to government officials responsible for approving payments. Instead of the millions of dollars of increased costs described above, this document reported that there was no significant cost impact as a result of the changes made in charging for the use of VAX computers and other equipment. Specifically, the cost impact statement states, "[T]he net cost impact to the Government on CAS [Cost Accounting Standards]-covered contracts . . was a decrease in costs of $96,501 even though the flexibly-priced (cost reimbursable type and fixed price incentive programs) programs showed an increase of $3,378."

With respect to the TEAMS III contract, the cost impact reported in the cost impact statement was $7,221. The actual cost increase was more than $1 million.

Procurement Fraud 3 – The Disclosure
Amount of the fraud – about $1 million

To win new contracts, contractors normally budget an amount each year for marketing. Because a portion of these costs are charged to government contracts, federal procurement regulations require annual approval of the amount of marketing costs to be charged to government contracts.

One year, the contractor made a major effort to win a huge contract. Its major competitor was IBM and it won the contract. In trying to win this contract, the marketing department spent most of its bid and proposal funds for that year. In order to continue marketing efforts, the contractor's management wanted to charge marketing expenses to the TEAMS III contract as part of the price of performing TARS (Task Assignment Records). They instructed the engineer who was the TEAMS III program manager to charge the TEAMS III contract for the costs of marketing.

This engineer refused because charging marketing costs directly to a government contract is illegal. He also refused to permit others to charge the TEAMS III contract for marketing efforts. Eventually, the contractor laid him off because he refused to cheat.

The engineer filed a lawsuit against the contractor in United States District Court, District of Minnesota, Court File Civil No. 3-92-252. He alleged wrongful discharge. The contractor settled and paid the engineer for his loss.

In his lawsuit, the engineer alleged illegal practices by the contractor including illegal charges to the TEAMS-III contract. The Navy became aware of these allegations and the Navy Criminal Investigative Service began an investigation.

The contractor conducted an internal investigation of its own concerning the engineer's allegations. Its investigators gathered information of illegal practices and prepared a document that became known as The Disclosure. The contractor sent The Disclosure to the Navy under a Department of Defense policy that provides that the consequences may be less severe if the contractor voluntarily discloses information about wrongdoing. In The Disclosure, the contractor reported illegal charges of about $120,000. At the time the contractor made this disclosure, the contractor and its attorneys knew that the actual amount of illegal charges to the TEAMS III contract was many hundreds of thousands of dollars.

The Disclosure also falsely reported that travel costs of a small number of trips made primarily for marketing purposes were improperly charged to the TEAMS III contract, principally by an engineer who performed work on TARS. In fact, a substantial amount of travel costs incurred primarily for marketing purposes were charged to the TEAMS III contract. The contractor knew these expenses had been illegally charged to the TEAMS III contract and hid this information from the Navy.

Procurement Fraud 4 – Illegal Substitution of Personnel and Labor Cost Mischarging
Amount of the fraud – at least $50,000

Erik was a project manager employed by the contractor. As a project manager he managed performance of TARs authorized by the Navy. Erik considered it his duty to assure that the work was done as required by the contract and that all charges to the TAR were legal and proper.

Erik was responsible for managing work on a TAR known as the ACDS Block 1 Sim Close TAR. It was for a scientific report the Navy wanted. While he was managing performance of this TAR, he wrote to his supervisor, pointing out that employees assigned to this TAR were being removed and laid off. His supervisor assigned less experienced and less-qualified personnel to take their place, which severely impacted the ability of the contractor to perform its contractual obligations under the TEAMS III contract.

Erik informed his management that the personnel changes would result in a report that was incomplete, inaccurate and of poor quality. After Erik said qualified and experienced personnel were needed to perform the work, his supervisor told him to use substitute personnel. Another supervisor told Erik to charge the time of the substitute personnel, whose rates of compensation were higher than the laid-off personnel, to engineering overhead.

These instructions by his supervisors were to perform illegal acts. It was illegal to substitute personnel after a TAR price had been negotiated without getting the Navy's approval. The contract required that the contractor inform the Navy of the changes and agree to a price reduction if the changes would decrease the cost of performance. The contractor instructed Erik not to inform the Navy of the substitutions.

The instruction given Erik by his supervisor to charge labor costs to overhead also was an instruction to perform an illegal act. The cost of performing a TAR must be charged directly to the contract, not to overhead.

Because he protested against and refused to perform orders to substitute personnel and charge the new personnel to overhead, Erik was quickly re-evaluated and ranked at the top on the layoff list. Then, he was laid off.

Procurement Fraud 5 -Fake Labor Rates/Cost Mischarging
Amount of the fraud – at least $1 million

Erik, as part of his duties, was involved in preparing price estimates of performing proposed TARs under the TEAMS III contract for submission to the Navy. The contractor program management and overall management instructed Erik to quote unrealistically low manday rates for TARs (Task Assignment Records), specifically TAR 367. At the time, The contractor was competing for the TEAMS IV contract, the proposed follow-on contract to the TEAMS III contract. The contractor wanted to deceive the Navy into believing that it could perform TARs for the rates proposed in its proposal for the TEAMS

IV contract.

The result of quoting unrealistically low manday rates for performing TAR 367 was that not all the tasks on TAR 367 were completed. Those that were completed were of inferior quality. Other project managers were ordered to quote unrealistically low manday rates (the rate for one day's work) for performing TARs and did so. These price estimates were inaccurate because the manday rates were intentionally understated. Many TARs overran the initial estimates because higher-grade personnel had performed the work or because work that had been performed by lower-grade personnel had to be corrected.

The intentional submission of inaccurate cost or pricing data is a violation of the law (31 U.S.C. § 3729 and 10 U.S.C. § 230b). It is procurement fraud.

Procurement Fraud 6 – Hiding Evidence Of Fraud
Amount of the fraud – unknown millions

During an investigation of contractor fraud, the Inspector General of the Department of Defense issued a subpoena and served it on Erik's lawyer. The subpoena ordered the lawyer to give the investigator evidence of the contractor's fraud that Erik had given him. Erik had been employed by the contractor for more than 20 years. In the last years of his employment, he received thousands of pages of documents in the course of his work that he believed were evidence of crimes by the contractor against the United States Government. He took these documents to his home and stored them in three barrels.

After he was discharged, the contractor learned of the documents in Erik's possession. The contractor did not want the government to see these documents. It told Erik that the documents were company property, that they were stolen, and must be returned to the contractor and not be delivered to or read by government investigators.

Erik refused the contractor's demands. He told the contractor that the records were evidence of crimes against the government. Because of that, the law not only gave him the right, but the obligation to turn the records over to government officials. His lawyer then delivered the records to the government's investigator who was very happy to get them. They supported the government's conclusion that the contractor had committed major fraud.

The contractor went to court. In a motion heard by U.S. Magistrate Raymond L. Erickson, the contractor claimed that the records were company property and demanded that they be returned to the company. Magistrate Erickson agreed. He ordered the records returned. To this judge, the fact that they were evidence of crimes against the U.S. Government was irrelevant. The government's investigator returned the records to the contractor.

Procurement Fraud 7 – North Warning Program Fraud
Amount of the fraud – about $100,000

The contractor performed a contract known as the North Warning, PB-21 program. It assigned the work to two of its plants, one in Minnesota, and the other in Canada. The Minnesota plant kept dollars that should have been returned to the customer because of agreements made during contract negotiations.

This contract was part of negotiations involving the "Ill Wind" scandal. The agreement was that the plant in Canada would contract all the circuit fabrication through its Minnesota plant at zero percent gross margin with zero percent fee. The plant in Canada assigned much of the work to the Minnesota plant, even though this work could have been subcontracted to another company which would have performed it at a much lower cost.

Contrary to its agreement with the U.S. Government, the Minnesota plant charged a 7 percent fee. The value of the purchase orders was $2.6 million, resulting in a fraud of more than $182,000.

Procurement Fraud 8 – SEM D Electronic Modules
Amount of the fraud – about $100,000

The subcontract was for production of SEM D electronic modules. The contractor was to demonstrate producibility of four unique-type modules currently being supplied by the Raytheon Corporation. These modules were referred to as the UCG group and contained Raytheon proprietary logic gate arrays.

Parallel to this effort was another subcontract with another prime contractor to qualify the contractor as a second source of these UCG modules on a Navy program known as the BSY-1 program. Instead of duplicating any production efforts in the factory, Steve, the project manager for the project, provided funding to the BSY-1 program manager to build the modules needed for delivery.

The UCG modules that the contractor manufactured did not conform with subcontract specifications and did not demonstrate producibility of SEM D electronics modules because the units manufactured by the contractor were built with used parts obtained from a Navy depot. Government procurement regulations bar a contractor from delivering products containing used parts unless it is specifically approved by the buying agency. The contractor violated the specifications because the Raytheon Corporation refused to sell its proprietary units to the contractor. As a result, the contractor had to deliver modules built with used parts to its prime contractor. But the contractor did not inform its prime contractor of the used parts or obtain the government's permission to do so.

The contractor never demonstrated production capabilities because it could not manufacture parts equivalent to the Raytheon Corporation proprietary parts. Despite its failure to meet the contract's requirement to demonstrate producibility of the SEM D electronic modules, the contractor collected the full amount of the subcontract price, which eventually was paid to the prime contractor by the Navy.

Procurement Fraud 9 – Navy AN/UYK-44 EP (Enhanced Processor) Chip Set Contract
Amount of the fraud – $100,000

This was a joint effort funded by the Canadian and U.S. governments. The contractor's plants in Canada and Minnesota worked on the project.

The program overran its budget by $200,000. The contractor hid the overrun by switching the additional costs to another contract that, unlike the Enhanced Processor Chip Set contract, was not a fixed price. The program to which the overrun was transferred was a cost reimbursement contract. Such switching is illegal. It clearly is fraudulent.

Steve questioned the illegal transfer. The department director told him to leave the issue alone. Eventually, Steve was laid off.

Procurement Fraud 10 – UYK-43 Computer
Amount of the fraud – unknown millions of dollars

The contractor falsified test results and provided falsified reports to the U.S. Navy to get the Navy to accept delivery of and pay for UYK-43 computers. By relying on the falsified data, the Navy purchased hundreds of UYK-43 computers, many of which were installed on combat ships, that did not meet contract specifications.

Prior to delivering UYK-43 computers to the government, the contractor was obligated by its contract to successfully run a factory acceptance test. The purpose of this test was to demonstrate that the computer complied with all specifications. Failure to pass the factory acceptance meant that the Navy would not accept or pay for the computers. False data were presented to the Navy that the computers had passed all requirements of the factory acceptance test. The Navy was misled to accept and pay for computers that did not conform to all of the specifications. The contractor collected millions of dollars by fraud.

Procurement Fraud 11 – Time Card Fraud
Amount of the fraud – unknown thousands or tens of thousands of dollars.

Employees were directed to charge their time spent preparing a proposal to the U.S. Post Office directly to overhead or to a cost reimbursement contract. There was a separate account for proposal costs known as the bid and proposal (B&P) account. Time spent supporting the proposal effort should have been charged to the B&P account, not overhead or an account for a contract being performed.

Unannounced audits of time card reporting were supposed to be conducted by department directors and administrative aides. On several occasions time cards would be caught not being filled out on a daily basis or simply left blank. This was in direct violation of company policy and agreements with the government. There never was any discipline of those who failed the audits. The general atmosphere in the company was one of a joke. One employee never passed an audit.

Federal judge's tolerance of procurement fraud.

Procurement fraud is not new. It existed before and after the U.S. Civil War when congress passed the False Claims Act, 31 USC §§ 3729 et seq., to try to stem this kind of fraud. Allegations of overcharging and corruption by the Halliburton Company subsidiary Kellogg Brown & Root show that our country still is afflicted with this problem. What may be new is the willingness of federal judges to cover up these crimes and protect their perpetrators.

Corrupt decisions like those of Judge Tunheim in the case of "The $1 Billion Heist" raise a perplexing and frightening question: why are federal judges allowing these frauds that so deplete our resources for the enrichment of a few warmongers? Are federal judges being paid off? In Chapter 4, we quote former federal appeals court judge Abner Mikva's description of instances of federal judges accepting lavish gifts from industry leaders who are seeking decisions that will benefit their industry. Perhaps consideration should be given to a federal law that bars federal judges from accepting gratuities. A proposed reform that would bar Minnesota state court judges from accepting gratuities is described in Chapter 15.

Other reforms could improve the quality of federal judges and their decisions. Chapter 12 proposes a system like the Missouri Plan for selecting candidates for state court judges solely on merit. This method could be employed to select candidates for federal judge. The current process for selecting candidates for federal judge, a lifetime appointment, is badly flawed. It is dominated by politics. Democrats frequently refuse to even consider candidates proposed by a Republican president and visa versa.

The Common Sense Commission proposed in Chapter 11 can publicize the bad decisions of federal judges and embarrass them in the same way as proposed with respect to state court judges. There is no legal barrier to the creation of a federal Judges and Public Officials Court like the court proposed in Chapter 11 that has jurisdiction to hear claims of misbehavior by federal judges and the power to award judgments in favor of victims of wrongful actions by federal judges.

Under the U.S. Constitution, federal judges are appointed to their office for life during good behavior. That should not be a license to hurt our country and its citizens.

The Desperate Mother

Earl F. Beddow, Jr., Ramsey County Referee
Paulette K. Flynn, Ramsey County Judge
Mary E. McGinnis, Ramsey County Referee
M. Michael Monahan, Ramsey County Judge
Gregg E. Johnson, Ramsey County Judge
Edward Toussaint, Jr., Chief Judge, Minnesota Court of Appeals
William Moore, Family Court Officer

Case Summary

Mother, an immigrant who was in the United States on a student visa, was so physically abused by her alcoholic husband that she took their child and fled to a woman's shelter. Even though she was at the shelter for months, and the shelter confirmed the abuse, judges and referees did nothing because the mother was unable to produce a witness who actually saw her husband beat her. Because she was in the United States on a student visa, it was illegal for her to work to support herself and her child. Referees Earl F. Beddow, Jr., Mary E. McGinnis, and Judges Paulette K. Flynn and M. Michael Monahan refused to award her anything for temporary child support or maintenance (formerly alimony).

Because a trial in her case was months away, Mother made an emergency appeal to the Minnesota Court of Appeals. Chief Judge Edward Toussaint, Jr. turned down Mother's appeal for emergency relief because she had not sent an affidavit (sworn statement of the facts) with her appeal, even though such an affidavit was in the court file. Judge Toussaint did not bother to ask for an affidavit to support the appeal. He was insensitive to Mother's situation and the danger to the child of losing her mother.

A legal aid lawyer finally won permanent residency status for Mother to stay in the United States and be with her child. Financially broke and with no way to pay her lawyer, she agreed to give her husband the home they had purchased and all of their property, and settled for $100 per month child support – far less than she needed to provide for herself and her child. Judge Gregg E. Johnson approved the settlement.

Additional Information and Comment

Her husband and his lawyer did everything they could to rush the divorce action to a conclusion. They knew that once the divorce became final, Mother would be deported because, unlike him, she did not have a basis on her own for staying in the United States. Her daughter, having been born in the United States, was a U.S. citizen and could stay. Mother feared that she would be deported without her daughter.

Mother was desperate to stall the divorce proceeding until she could get permanent status. She was desperate for money to provide for herself and her daughter but legally could not work. Because she was a foreign national, she was not eligible for public assistance. She was desperate for legal services but had no money to pay a lawyer or to pay litigation costs.

Her husband had a good paying job with the State of Minnesota and no fear of deportation. He was a permanent resident. In an effort to drive Mother from the United States, he contacted the U.S. Immigration and Naturalization Service and urged them to deport her. He told the agency she had married him just to get a basis for staying in his country.

Both Mother and her husband were from Kenya. In that country, women have few rights in the marriage relationship. A wife was expected to be her husband's servant and do his bidding. Mother, her husband felt, had stepped out of line in defying and asserting independence of him. If he wanted to drink, that was none of her concern.

Mother proved that her husband had an alcohol abuse problem. She did so by taking the deposition of her husband's former stepdaughter. He had been married before. That marriage ended in divorce. In her deposition, the former stepdaughter stated what she had been told by her mother:

> "A. She was worried that he had a drinking problem, and she said that when he was drinking, he was never mean, he didn't take an abusive slant but that he was difficult to reach, to talk to, that he didn't realize he had a problem, but she was worried he may. He didn't think so. And that's sort of the gist of our conversations.
>
> "Q. This is a yes or no question. Did your mother ever discuss with you the reasons for the breakup of her marriage to [Mother's husband]?
>
> "A. Yes.
>
> "Q. Was drinking one of those reasons?
>
> "A. Yes."

Mother begged the family court officer and the court to order a chemical evaluation of her husband before deciding on custody and what was in the best interests of the child. The family court officer refused to recommend a court-ordered evaluation. In his evaluation and recommendations report in which he recommended that Father have the primary custody of the parties' daughter, the family court officer wrote:

> "It appears from the available information provided, there was the issue of [Mother's husband's] chemical use which [Mother] expressed as being of grave concern and not fully explored in the initial report. [Mother] appears to suggest, from the available information, that [her husband's] 'drinking interferes with proper care of the child and poses a danger.' The quote taken from a letter written to this Family Court Officer dated January 30, 1996 from

[Mother's] attorney went on to state, 'If there is evidence of a drinking problem, we believe it should be considered in determining what is best for the child. RCCCD did not investigate Mother's allegations concerning Father's drinking because of a ruling by a family court referee in another proceeding (a petition for an order for protection). The referee, however, did not know of the information we obtained recently and are providing to you.'

"There has never been a question about [Mother's husband] having a chemical abuse problem during the 1980s, since it was during that time he had two DWI's in a five-year period. [His] last DWI was in 1986 when he underwent an outpatient chemical dependency treatment program. The fact [Mother's husband] has not been involved in another alcohol-related incident since, to support Mother's allegations, it did not make sense to subject [her husband] to a chemical dependency evaluation. However, as part of this updated report both parties underwent a chemical dependency evaluation. The evaluations were conducted by [evaluator], a licensed psychologist in private practice, who concluded [Mother] has 'at present no signs or symptoms to substantiate a chemical dependency problem.' This conclusion was derived from self report and verification sources which included [her husband] the only one to respond. [Mother's husband] reported not having any concerns about [her] use of chemicals.

"[The evaluator's] evaluation of [Mother's husband] relied on the same sources and concludes 'there are at present signs and symptoms to substantiate a chemical dependency problem. [Mother's husband] attended chemical dependency treatment in the past and was diagnosed as chemically dependent. He continues to use alcohol even though he has been

> diagnosed as chemically dependent. It is believed that a relapse prevention program on an outpatient basis would be beneficial for [Mother's husband].' There were three verification sources including [Mother], a person who met (Mother's husband] while attending school with [Mother], and a neighbor of [Mother's husband]. Only [Mother] reported having concerns about [her husband's] alcohol use.
>
> "[Mother's husband] had a second chemical dependency evaluation conducted by [evaluator] at Chemical Health Institute, Ms. [evaluator] relied on self report and collateral contacts and concludes: '[Mother's husband] exhibits no symptoms of alcohol dependency or abuse. His alcohol consumption typically remains within medically defined safe guidelines and social/legal limits of acceptability. This pattern has remained consistent for the last nine years with no clinically significant changes in frequency of use or amount consumed. From our knowledge of the disease of alcoholism, this consistency and lack of impairment which [Mother's husband] displays would be impossible for someone who is dependent on alcohol.' It appears the only significant difference of the two assessments was that [Mother] was not a collateral in the second evaluation."

Mother begged the family court officer and Judge Johnson for a court-ordered chemical dependency evaluation of her husband. The family court officer refused. Judge Johnson read the family court officer's report. He did not order a chemical dependency evaluation of Mother's husband. He decided it was all right for the baby's father to care for her while he was drinking.

Sex With Animals

Dennis J. Murphy, Pennington County Judge
Minnesota Court of Appeals, Judges Roger M. Klaphake, Randolph W. Peterson, David Minge

Case Summary

Their 23 years of marriage often had been troublesome, especially so in the latter years. One day in the last year of their marriage, her husband came in from the barn on their farm. There was blood on his clothes in his groin area. A few minutes later she observed him urinating blood. She reminded him of his heart condition (he had a pacemaker) and urged him to let her take him to the hospital immediately. At their last meeting with the doctor, he said her husband had a clogged valve. He adamantly refused.

Acting on a hunch, she asked, "Have you been fooling around with the animals?" "Yes," he said. In fact, he regularly had been having sex with a calf.

She remembered that years ago she found her oldest son, now 21 years old, in the barn having sexual relations with a calf. She wanted to do something about that but he would not let her. Now, she realized, her son may have imitated her husband.

She had had enough. Within a week after the incident she left her husband and, with her 12-year-old son, fled to a woman's shelter. It was not enough to get away from him. He tracked her down at her place of work and physically assaulted her. This happened in front of a security camera.

More terrified of him than ever before, she sought and got an order for protection. The judge in that proceeding appointed a guardian ad litem (GAL) to provide a recommendation on who should have custody of the parties' younger son. This guardian ad litem conducted a thorough investigation, which included several interviews. She came to the conclusion that the boy's father was practicing bestiality and recommended that custody of the minor child be awarded to his mother. The judge in that proceeding awarded temporary custody of the boy to his mother.

Close in time, the boy's father started a separate court proceeding for a divorce. He asked for temporary and permanent custody of his younger son. Without receiving any evidence or even conducting a hearing, and despite the first guardian ad litem's investigation, report and recommendation, Judge Dennis J. Murphy, Chief Judge of Minnesota's Ninth Judicial District, changed temporary custody from the boy's mother to his father. He appointed a new guardian ad litem to conduct a new investigation and make a new report.

The second guardian ad litem investigated and submitted her report in which she recommended that the boy's mother have custody of him. In testimony, she told the judge that she had investigated allegations that the boy's father and older brother had been having sex with animals, had been told by witnesses that this was true, and believed these allegations were credible.

The judge said he would interview the boy privately in his chambers to learn his preference. This is illegal. A Minnesota law, Minnesota Statutes § 518.166, prohibits private interviews between a judge and a child. The guardian ad litem, the boy's mother, and the boy's doctor objected. They said the boy was unusually immature for his age, that he was of borderline intelligence, and that putting him in the middle might severely damage him emotionally. Angrily, the judge agreed not to interview the boy privately and dismissed the second guardian ad litem. Then the judge awarded custody of the boy to his father.

He awarded all of the couple's property, including the farm and home, to the husband except for $16,000 cash and some personal items of small value that he awarded to the wife. She used all of the money to pay her lawyer for his services.

The wife appealed to the Minnesota Court of Appeals. The brief submitted on her behalf informed appeals court Judges Klaphake, Peterson and Minge of the guardian ad litem's testimony about the father's bestiality. They still denied the appeal. In an interview, the wife provided documentary evidence that her younger son at age of 15-years old regularly has sex with animals. His psychological and emotion conditions are poor.

Additional Information and Comment

There were two hearings, each before a different judge, on the issue of custody of their minor son. The first hearing was in the order for protection case brought by the boy's mother. The judge in that case presided over a hearing in which both parties were represented by a lawyer. Each side testified and submitted evidence at that hearing. The judge found that the husband had committed acts of domestic abuse against his wife and granted her custody of their minor son.

A doctor testified in the second trial before Judge Murphy concerning the capacity of the 12-year-old boy to express a useful preference on custody. In his testimony, the doctor told Judge Murphy that the child had a poor perspective of reality. He testified further that the boy was emotionally immature and could easily be influenced by the way things were presented to him. The court asked the doctor if interviewing the child would have a significant emotional impact; the doctor believed that it would. In answer to a question by the wife's lawyer, the doctor said the child's preference should not be a factor in making a custody determination.

Despite the doctor's testimony, Judge Murphy awarded custody to the boy's father because, he said, the boy wanted to be with him. He based his decision on hearsay testimony – what someone said the boy had said some time in the past. Yet, Judge Murphy had this to say about hearsay testimony:

> Judge: Okay, We're going to take our break now. Before we take our break, since it's conceded by the respondent that TJ is going to tell me that he wants to stay with his dad, I'm not going to interview him.
>
> On the other hand, you should understand that everything that's been said here that they claim TJ said is now hearsay and I may well disregard it. That's the

> flip side of the coin. Okay. I'll be right back. Take me about -
>
> Wife's Lawyer: Your Honor. I guess I don't quite follow. You're saying that everyone agrees that TJ wants to live with his dad but it's going to be hearsay so you're not going to interview the child?
>
> Judge: I'm not going to interview the child. All these things he said about his father or his mother, all the rest of this, is hearsay, is it not? He's not going to testify, so it's hearsay.
>
> Husband's Lawyer: Does that mean anything that people testify that TJ has said, you'll disregard it?
>
> Judge: I'll probably disregard it unless there's some verification.
>
> Wife's Lawyer: So his preference isn't coming in?
>
> Judge: Preference is coming in because it's conceded. Okay?

The undeniable fact is that preference was not conceded by the wife or anyone else – only what the child had said in the past.

The second guardian ad litem appointed by Judge Murphy was an experienced lawyer. As the basis for his decision to dismiss her and disregard her recommendations, Judge Murphy wrote:

> "Since the trial of this matter, this Court, as Chief Judge of the Ninth Judicial District, has discovered that the appointed guardian ad litem, has taken neither the guardian ad litem course required by the state of Minnesota for guardian ad litems, nor the custody evaluator course."

There was no testimony or evidence submitted by anyone concerning the guardian ad litem's training. Judge Murphy got his information ex parte – from someone other than the parties and their witnesses in court. It is illegal and forbidden for a judge to get and use information in a court proceeding not received in court in the presence of the parties. In other words, he went to his own private sources to get information to justify his decision to discharge the guardian ad litem.

He disregarded the guardian ad litem's recommendations, he said, because, "It is the Court's opinion that the guardian ad litem became fixated on the charges of bestiality on the part of the Petitioner, which the Court finds to be without merit."

Except for the guardian ad litem and the doctor, there was no testimony by any professional person on what was in the boy's best interests. There was no neutral investigation of the allegations that the husband and his oldest son practiced bestiality other than those made by the discharged guardian ad litem and her predecessor.

Yet, Judges Klaphake, Peterson and Minge of the Minnesota Court of Appeals came to the conclusion, "Because the district court did not abuse its discretion or clearly err in its findings on the child's best interests, in rejecting the recommendations of the GAL that the child reside with appellant, or in rejecting appellant's allegations of improper conduct as unsubstantiated and based on unreliable hearsay, we affirm."

THE JUDGE WHO SQUELCHED FREE SPEECH

Michael J. Davis, Federal District Court Judge

Case Summary

Greg Wersal, a Twin Cities' lawyer, wanted to run against an incumbent Justice on the Minnesota Supreme Court. He wanted to become one of the seven Minnesota Supreme Court Justices.

As part of his campaign, Wersal criticized the Minnesota Supreme Court. In one campaign handout he stated that the Minnesota Supreme Court "has issued decisions which are marked by their disregard for the Legislature and a lack of common sense." Wersal criticized a decision that excluded from evidence confessions by criminal defendants that were not tape recorded, asking if people should "conclude that because the Supreme Court does not trust police, it allows confessed criminals to go free?"

He criticized a decision by the Minnesota Supreme Court that struck down a state law restricting welfare benefits and said it is "the Legislature which should set our spending policies." Wersal called a decision by the Minnesota Supreme Court that required public financing of abortions for poor women "unprecedented" and a "pro abortion stance."

Minnesota state government officials contacted Wersal. They told him he was violating a rule made by the Minnesota Supreme Court. The rule made it illegal for a candidate for judge or justice to state his or her views on disputed legal or political issues.

According to the Minnesota Supreme Court, the reason for the rule is to ensure that judges and justices have open minds on all issues. The officials who contacted Wersal threatened to take away his lawyer's license if he kept trying to tell voters his positions on disputed legal or political issues. It was all right, according to these officials, for Wersal to criticize the Minnesota Supreme Court and its decisions as long as he agreed to do nothing to change them.

Afraid of losing his license and right to be a lawyer, Wersal withdrew as a candidate for Justice. He sued in federal district court asking that the rule prohibiting him from speaking on disputed legal or political issues be set aside. Wersal argued that it was unconstitutional because it limited free speech.

Lawyers representing the State of Minnesota told Federal District Court Judge Michael J. Davis that the limits on what a candidate for judge or justice could say were necessary to protect the due process rights of parties in court. They said it assured that justices and judges would be impartial and open minded. Judge Davis agreed. He ruled that Mr. Wersal could not tell voters his views on disputed legal or political issues if he was a candidate for judge or justice.

Wersal appealed to a federal appeals court. By a vote of two to one it upheld Judge Davis. Wersal then appealed to the United States Supreme Court. In a 5-4 decision (the U.S. Supreme Court has nine justices), it told Judge Davis and the appeals court they were wrong. Candidates for political office, including candidates for judge or justice, have the constitutional right to tell voters their positions on disputed legal and political issues.

Greg Wersal returned to private practice and is still working for reform of the judicial election process. He is unsure whether he will again be a candidate for judge or justice.

Additional Information and Comment

U.S. Supreme Court Justice Anthony Scalia announced the court's decision in Republican Party of Minnesota v. White. Here is a portion of the court's opinion (footnotes and citations omitted):

> "Before considering the constitutionality of the announce clause, we must be clear about its mean-

ing. Its text says that a candidate for judicial office shall not 'announce his or her views on disputed legal or political issues.' Minn. Code of Judicial Conduct, Canon 5(A)(3)(d)(i) (2002).

"We know that 'announc[ing] ... views' on an issue covers much more than promising to decide an issue a particular way. The prohibition extends to the candidate's mere statement of his current position even if he does not bind himself to maintain that position after election. All the parties agree this is the case, because the Minnesota Code contains a so called 'pledges or promises' clause, which separately prohibits judicial candidates from making 'pledges or promises of conduct in office other than the faithful and impartial performance of the duties of the office,' ibid.-a prohibition that is not challenged here and on which we express no view.

"As the Court of Appeals recognized, the announce clause both prohibits speech on the basis of its content and burdens a category of speech that is 'at the core of our First Amendment freedoms'-speech about the qualifications of candidates for public office. The Court of Appeals concluded that the proper test to be applied to determine the constitutionality of such a restriction is what our cases have called strict scrutiny; the parties do not dispute that this is correct. Under the strict scrutiny test, respondents have the burden to prove that the announce clause is (1) narrowly tailored, to serve (2) a compelling state interest. In order for respondents to show that the announce clause is narrowly tailored, they must demonstrate that it does not 'unnecessarily circumscrib[e] protected expression.'

"The Court of Appeals concluded that respondents had established two interests as sufficiently compelling to justify the announce clause: preserving the impartiality of the state judiciary and preserving the appearance of the impartiality of the state judiciary. Respondents reassert these two interests before us, arguing that the first is compelling because it protects the due process rights of litigants, and that the second is compelling because it preserves public confidence in the judiciary. Respondents are rather vague, however, about what they mean by 'impartiality.' Indeed, although the term is used throughout the Eighth Circuit's opinion, the briefs, the Minnesota Code of Judicial Conduct, and the ABA Codes of Judicial Conduct, none of these sources bothers to define it. Clarity on this point is essential before we can decide whether impartiality is indeed a compelling state interest, and, if so, whether the announce clause is narrowly tailored to achieve it.

A

"One meaning of 'impartiality' in the judicial context-and of course its root meaning-is the lack of bias for or against either party to the proceeding. Impartiality in this sense assures equal application of the law. That is, it guarantees a party that the judge who hears his case will apply the law to him in the same way he applies it to any other party. This is the traditional sense in which the term is used. See Webster's New International Dictionary 1247 (2d ed.1950) (defining 'impartial' as '[n]ot partial; esp., not favoring one more than another; treating all alike; unbiased; equitable; fair; just').

"We think it plain that the announce clause is not narrowly tailored to serve impartiality (or the appearance of impartiality) in this sense. Indeed, the clause is barely tailored to serve that interest at all, inasmuch as it does not restrict speech for or against particular parties, but rather speech for or against particular issues. To be sure, when a case arises that turns on a legal issue on which the judge (as a candidate) had taken a particular stand, the party taking the opposite stand is likely to lose. But not because of any bias against that party, or favoritism toward the other party. Any party taking that position is just as likely to lose. The judge is applying the law (as he sees it) evenhandedly.

B

"It is perhaps possible to use the term 'impartiality,' in the judicial context (though this is certainly not a common usage) to mean lack of preconception in favor of or against a particular legal view. This sort of impartiality would be concerned, not with guaranteeing litigants equal application of the law, but rather with guaranteeing them an equal chance to persuade the court on the legal points in their case. Impartiality in this sense may well be an interest served by the announce clause, but it is not a compelling state interest, as strict scrutiny requires. A judge's lack of predisposition regarding the relevant legal issues in a case has never been thought a necessary component of equal justice, and with good reason. For one thing, it is virtually impossible to find a judge who does not have preconceptions about the law. As then Justice REHNQUIST observed of our own Court: 'Since most Justices come to this bench no earlier than their middle years, it would be unusual if they had not by that time formulated at least some tentative notions that would influence them in their interpretation of the sweeping clauses of the Constitution and their interaction with one another. It would be not merely unusual, but extraordinary, if they had not at least given opinions as to constitutional issues in their previous legal careers.'

Indeed, even if it were possible to select judges who did not have preconceived views on legal issues, it would hardly be desirable to do so. 'Proof that a Justice's mind at the time he joined the Court was a complete tabula rasa in the area of constitutional adjudication would be evidence of lack of qualification, not lack of bias.' The Minnesota Constitution positively forbids the selection to courts of general jurisdiction of judges who are impartial in the sense of having no views on the law. Minn. Const., Art. VI, § 5 ('Judges of the supreme court, the court of appeals and the district court shall be learned in the law'). And since avoiding judicial preconceptions on legal issues is neither possible nor desirable, pretending otherwise by attempting to preserve the 'appearance' of that type of impartiality can hardly be a compelling state interest either.

C

"A third possible meaning of 'impartiality' (again not a common one) might be described as open mindedness. This quality in a judge demands, not that he have no preconceptions on legal issues, but that he be willing to consider views that oppose his preconceptions, and remain open to persuasion, when the issues arise in a pending case. This sort of impartiality seeks to guarantee each litigant, not an equal chance to win the legal points in the case, but at least some chance of doing so. It may well be that impartiality in this sense, and the appearance of it, are desirable in the judiciary, but we need not pursue that inquiry, since we do not believe the Minnesota Supreme Court adopted the announce clause for that purpose.

"Respondents argue that the announce clause serves the interest in open mindedness, or at least in the appearance of open-mindedness, because it relieves a judge from pressure to rule a certain way in order to maintain consistency with statements the judge has previously made. The problem is, however, that statements in election campaigns are such an infinitesimal portion of the public commitments to legal positions that judges (or judges to-be) undertake, that this object of the prohibition is implausible. Before they arrive on the bench (whether by election or otherwise), judges have often committed themselves on legal issues that they must later rule upon. More common still is a judge's confronting a legal issue on which he has expressed an opinion while on the bench. Most frequently, of course, that prior expression will have occurred in ruling on an earlier case. But judges often state their views on disputed legal issues outside the context of adjudication-in classes that they conduct, and in books and speeches. Like the ABA Codes of Judicial Conduct, the Minnesota Code not only permits but encourages this. See Minn.Code of Judicial Conduct, Canon 4(B) (2002) ('A judge may write, lecture, teach, speak and participate in other extrajudicial activities concerning the law . . .'); Minn.Code of Judicial Conduct, Canon 4(B), Comment. (2002) ('To the extent that time permits, a judge is encouraged to do so ...'). That is quite incompatible with the notion that the need for open mindedness (or for the appearance of open mindedness) lies behind the prohibition at issue here.

"The short of the matter is this: In Minnesota, a candidate for judicial office may not say 'I think it is constitutional for the legislature to prohibit same sex marriages.' He may say the very same thing, however, up until the very day before he declares himself a candidate, and may say it repeatedly (until litigation is pending) after he is elected. As a means of pursuing the objective of open mindedness that respondents now articulate, the announce clause is so woefully underinclusive as to render belief in that purpose a challenge to the credulous.

"Justice STEVENS asserts that statements made in an election campaign pose a special threat to open mindedness because the candidate, when elected judge, will have a particular reluctance to contradict them. That might be plausible, perhaps, with regard to campaign promises. A candidate who says 'If elected, I will vote to uphold the legislature's power to prohibit same sex marriages' will positively be breaking his word if he does not do so (although one would be naive not to recognize that campaign promises are--by long democratic tradition-the least binding form of human commitment). But, as noted earlier, the Minnesota Supreme Court has adopted a separate prohibition on campaign 'pledges or promises,' which is not challenged here. The proposition that judges feel significantly greater compulsion, or appear to feel significantly greater compulsion, to maintain consistency with nonpromissory statements made during a judicial campaign than with such statements made before or after the campaign is not self-evidently true. It seems to us quite likely, in fact, that in many cases the opposite is true. We doubt, for example, that a mere statement of position enunciated during the pendency of an election will be regarded by a judge as more binding-or as more likely to subject him to popular disfavor if reconsidered-than a carefully considered holding that the judge set forth in an earlier opinion denying some individual's claim to justice. In any event, it suffices to say that respondents have not carried the burden imposed by our strict scrutiny test to establish this proposition (that campaign statements are uniquely destructive of open-mindedness) on which the validity of the announce clause rests.

"Moreover, the notion that the special context of electioneering justifies an abridgment of the right to speak out on disputed issues sets our First Amendment jurisprudence on its head. '[D]ebate on the qualifications of candidates' is 'at the core of our electoral process and of the First Amendment freedoms,' not at the edges. 'The role that elected officials play in our society makes it all the more imperative that they be allowed freely to express themselves on matters of current public irnportance. It is simply not the function of government to select which issues are worth discussing or debating in the course of a political campaign.' We have never allowed the government to prohibit candidates from communicating relevant information to voters during an election.

, , , , .

"The Minnesota Supreme Court's canon of judicial conduct prohibiting candidates for judicial election from announcing their views on disputed legal and political issues violates the First Amendment. Accordingly, we reverse the grant of summary judgment to respondents and remand the case for proceedings consistent with this opinion.

"It is so ordered."

U.S. Supreme Court Justice Sandra Day O'Connor agreed entirely with Justice Scalia's opinion, but she had something she wanted to add. Minnesota and other states can avoid the problem that so concerned the Minnesota Supreme Court simply by changing the way judges are chosen. She wrote:

Justice O'CONNOR, concurring.

"I join the opinion of the Court but write separately

to express my concerns about judicial elections generally. Respondents claim that '[t]he Announce Clause is necessary ... to protect the State's compelling governmental interes[t] in an actual and perceived ... impartial judiciary.' Brief for Respondents 8. I am concerned that, even aside from what judicial candidates may say while campaigning, the very practice of electing judges undermines this interest.

"We, of course, want judges to be impartial, in the sense of being free from any personal stake in the outcome of the cases to which they are assigned. But if judges are subject to regular elections they are likely to feel that they have at least some personal stake in the outcome of every publicized case. Elected judges cannot help being aware that if the public is not satisfied with the outcome of a particular case, it could hurt their re-election prospects. See Eule, Crocodiles in the Bathtub: State Courts, Voter Initiatives and the Threat of Electoral Reprisal, 65 U. Colo. L.Rev. 733, 739 (1994) (quoting former California Supreme Court Justice Otto Kaus' statement that ignoring the political consequences of visible decisions is 'like ignoring a crocodile in your bath tub'); Bright & Keenan, Judges and the Politics of Death: Deciding Between the Bill of Rights and the Next Election in Capital Cases, 75 B.U.L.Rev. 759, 793 794 (1995) (citing statistics indicating that judges who face elections are far more likely to override jury sentences of life without parole and impose the death penalty than are judges who do not run for election). Even if judges were able to suppress their awareness of the potential electoral consequences of their decisions and refrain from acting on it, the public's confidence in the judiciary could be undermined simply by the possibility that judges would be unable to do so.

. . .

"In response to such concerns, some States adopted a modified system of judicial selection that became known as the Missouri Plan (because Missouri was the first State to adopt it for most of its judicial posts). See Croley, 62 U. Chi. L.Rev., at 724. Under the Missouri Plan, judges are appointed by a high-elected official, generally from a list of nominees put together by a nonpartisan nominating commission, and then subsequently stand for unopposed retention elections in which voters are asked whether the judges should be recalled. Ibid. If a judge is recalled, the vacancy is filled through a new nomination and appointment. Ibid. This system obviously reduces threats to judicial impartiality, even if it does not eliminate all popular pressure on judges. See Grodin, Developing a Consensus of Constraint: A Judge's Perspective on Judicial Retention Elections, 61 S. Cal. L.Rev.1969, 1980 (1988) (admitting that he cannot be sure that his votes as a California Supreme Court Justice in "critical cases" during 1986 were not influenced subconsciously by his awareness that the outcomes could affect his chances in the retention elections being conducted that year). The Missouri Plan is currently used to fill at least some judicial offices in 15 states. Croley, supra, at 725-726; American Judicature Society, supra.

"Thirty one other States, however, still use popular elections to select some or all of their appellate and/or general jurisdiction trial court judges, who thereafter run for re-election periodically. Ibid. Of these, slightly more than half use nonpartisan elections, and the rest use partisan elections. Ibid. Most of the States that do not have any form of judicial elections choose judges through executive nomination and legislative confirmation. See Croley, supra, at 725.

"Minnesota has chosen to select its judges through contested popular elections instead of through an appointment system or a combined appointment and retention election system along the lines of the Missouri Plan. In doing so the State has voluntarily taken on the risks to judicial bias described above. As a result, the State's claim that it needs to significantly restrict judges' speech in order to protect judicial impartiality is particularly troubling. If the State has a problem with judicial impartiality, it is largely one the State brought upon itself by continuing the practice of popularly electing judges."

THE ROAD TO NOWHERE

Thomas P. Schroeder, Becker County Judge
Gretchen P. Thelmony, Becker County Attorney's Office

Case Summary

Two neighbors, one on the north side and the other on the south side of what they thought was the boundary between their farms, had been on friendly terms for years until they made a discovery. Two surveys revealed that the north side family owned the road to and driveway of their south side neighbor. In a neighborly spirit, the north side owner offered to give his neighbors property rights that extended to the center of the road and driveway, and to do so without charge except for the cost of preparing new legal descriptions and recording them at the office of the county recorder.

At first, that was acceptable. But after talking with a lawyer, the south side family demanded more. They wanted all of the road, all of the driveway, and some of the land his neighbor used to pasture his cattle. The families wound up in court.

The south side family became the plaintiffs. They were represented by a part-time county attorney who knew the judge. (She later became a full-time attorney in the Becker County Attorney's Office.)

To keep their cost of litigation low, the defendants represented themselves at the first and second hearings. They were disasters. At the first hearing, the judge literally screamed at them, "You're not here, this isn't happening." He made it impossible for the defendants to represent themselves.

At the second meeting in court, the judge screamed insults at the defendants and then gave the plaintiffs everything they asked for – by default. He said the defendants had not paid the court filing fee, which was not true, because they had as was documented by an entry in the court record and by a receipt the plaintiffs showed the judge.

More importantly, even if they had not paid the fee, that cannot be the basis for a default judgment. Failing to pay the court filing fee is not a legitimate basis for a default judgment. The judge knew that, or certainly should have. All that matters is that an answer to the complaint be served on the plaintiffs within 20 days, and that had been done. The judge was dishonest.

Following a trial, the judge again gave the plaintiffs everything they wanted. The plaintiffs' lawyer even wrote the judge's decision for him!

The Minnesota Court of Appeals reversed the judge's decision. It called the decision "clearly erroneous" and "not supported by the evidence." It ordered the judge to amend his findings of fact. It said the judge could, in his discretion, receive new evidence.

At the first hearing after he got the case back from the court of appeals, the judge said, "Well, before I hear anything, I just want you to know I am going to rule in favor of the plaintiffs, and why don't you guys just get a couple cases of beer and settle this thing around a bonfire."

Knowing that they were going to win left the plaintiffs with no incentive to settle, and the parties proceeded to a second trial. At that trial, the judge took some additional evidence – more recollections by the plaintiffs on where the boundary was.

As promised, the judge's decision was for the plaintiffs. This time he gave the plaintiffs more of defendant's land than he had given them the first or second times. An appeal was made to the Minnesota Court of Appeals a second time.

Additional Information and Comment

For years, two families thought that the boundary between their two farms in Becker County, Minnesota, was a township road that ended at a T, and beyond that point, by a fence to a Y junction. At the Y, the road to the left led to the north property which was owned by a family that later became the defendants in a lawsuit over the boundary. From the Y, the road ran to the east a short distance and then turned to the south property, which was owned by the family that became the plaintiffs in the lawsuit.

A fence that began at the Y where the angle lines joined into one line marked what the parties had thought was the continuation of the boundary between their properties. The first 570 feet of the fence was in place and had been accepted as the boundary. The first 250 feet of the fence ran parallel to the road and then jogged to the south for a short distance to a point where it was followed by open land because a portion of the fence after that point had been removed. After the open land the original fence was intact.

For more than 20 years, until the late 1990s, the defendants used and maintained the land north of the fence and perceived boundary. The plaintiffs used and maintained the land south of it. Relations between the parties were friendly during those years. Beginning in the 1980s, the defendants, with the plaintiffs' permission, even pastured cattle on some of the land both parties thought belonged to the plaintiffs.

In 1992, the plaintiffs had their property surveyed in connection with refinancing. To their surprise, they discovered that their driveway was on the defendants' property and that the defendants owned a portion of the property south of what everyone thought was the boundary. They did not reveal this information to the defendants.

In 1997, the defendants had the land surveyed and learned then that the driveway to the plaintiffs' home was their property. In a neighborly spirit, the defendants offered to give the plaintiffs the land on their side of the center of the township road and the end of their driveway if the plaintiffs would pay the expenses of preparing the legal description and action to implement the transfer. The plaintiffs hired a surveyor to prepare the needed legal description.

Then the plaintiffs met with their lawyer. After this meeting, plaintiffs told defendants they wanted more than just to the center of the township road. They wanted all of the road and then some. They wanted 2.25 acres of defendants' property including land that the defendants had been using to pasture their cattle. They said they would sue to get what they wanted, and they did.

After the default judgment, the defendants hired a lawyer – one they were told was among the best in the business. He persuaded the judge to rescind the improper default judgment against the defendants and reopen the case. At the trial he represented the defendants.

The issues in the case were: (1) adverse possession and (2) practical location of a boundary line. Adverse possession is one way a person can acquire land. To get ownership by this method, a person must prove that he actually lived on or used the land openly, without permission, exclusively, notoriously, which means for everyone to see, and adversely to everyone else. Adverse possession consists of actual possession with intent to hold solely for the possessor to the exclusion of others as shown by the exercise of dominion over the land. It includes using the land for himself or for profit. If a person lives on or uses the land in this way for a minimum period of continuous years he becomes the owner of the land. In Minnesota, the minimum period is 15 years.

Practical location of a boundary line is a form of adverse possession. If two adjoining landowners consider and act on the basis that a certain line between the land they own is the boundary between them, that line becomes the boundary.

The testimony and physical evidence at trial proved beyond anyone's doubt that each party possessed and used the property on their side of what they thought was the boundary. Thus, the plaintiffs proved that they had possessed, used and maintained the portion of the road from the Y to their home and their driveway. Therefore, the court of appeals said, the trial court was right in ruling that they may have been entitled to some of the land they claimed, but not to what the district court gave them.

The trial judge obviously was wrong according to the appeals court when he gave the plaintiffs land that was on the defendants' side of the incorrect boundary line. The defendants had maintained and used this land to pasture their cattle and grow crops. The defendants had even used land on the other side of the perceived boundary line to pasture cattle. There simply was no evidence of adverse possession of this land by the plaintiffs the appeals court said. Judge Schroeder was clearly erroneous.

Establishing a boundary line by practical location depends on the evidence. There was no dispute concerning the two portions of the fence still in place. The problem was the middle space where the fence had been removed. Everyone agreed that there had been a jog in the boundary line after the Y. The question was, where did it jog to?

The defendants submitted an old aerial survey that showed the actual fence when it was complete. Not even the plaintiffs disputed the defendants' assertion that they had used the land on their side of the perceived boundary line for farming and grazing. Numerous witnesses testified to the fact of a jog in the perceived boundary line from the Y through the open area to where it joined the balance of the original fence. Even the plaintiffs and their witnesses agreed there had been a jog in the fence. But they also vaguely remembered that the fence had been where the judge decided it had been.

At the first trial, the judge found as a fact that the boundary line in the open area was a straight line from the end of the first segment of the fence that was past the driveway to plaintiffs' home to the second segment of the remaining fence. This gave the plaintiffs a portion of what had always been considered the defendants' land that defendants had used for pasture and crops.

The court of appeals said there is nothing to support this result. Everyone agreed there had been a jog in the fence toward plaintiffs' home. Instead of a boundary with a jog, Judge Schroeder had substituted a straight line. Clearly, the appeals court said, this was erroneous.

After he got the case back from the appeals court, Judge Schroeder said he would fix the problem. He now found as a fact that there was a jog in the fence – toward defendants' home. He based this new result on plaintiffs' new recollections of where the removed fence had been. Based on his new finding of fact, the plaintiffs now had more of defendants' land.

THE BIG SURPRISE

Karen Asphaug, Dakota County Judge

Case Summary

After a builder went into bankruptcy, the bank that loaned money to the builder to finance the construction of a home foreclosed its mortgage. The home, which was being built for a senior couple, was redeemed by four subcontractors who had filed mechanic's liens on the home. They became co-owners of the not-quite-finished home. Plumber became one of the owners.

The co-owners completed construction of the home and the senior couple for whom the home had been built moved in on a lease. At the same time, three of the co-owners sued to have Plumber's ownership interest declared invalid on the basis that his mechanic's lien had been defective. Plumber countersued for damages on the basis that the other co-owners had breached the agreement all had signed, wrongfully depriving Plumber of his share of the rent paid by the senior couple. The first trial dealt only with Plumber's interest in the home.

The judge ruled in the first trial that Plumber's mechanic's lien had been valid and that Plumber had an ownership interest in the home. The second trial was supposed to be about Plumber's counterclaim. It was scheduled to begin on a Monday. Late in the afternoon on the Friday before trial, the lawyer for the other three co-owners raised a new issue: he claimed that the ownership percentage of each co-owner should be determined by the dollar amount of their liens, and said that would be one of the issues tried at the trial on Monday. Plumber's position was that all their interests were equal because each had paid the same amount at the redemption sale.

At the beginning of the trial on Monday, Plumber told the judge that he was not prepared to try the new issue raised by the opposition lawyer on Friday and had not had time to subpoena witnesses or prepare exhibits to submit into evidence. Plumber asked the judge to either postpone the trial or try just the issues originally scheduled for trial.

The judge refused to give Plumber more time or prevent his opponents from trying the new issue. She began the trial and ruled in favor of the three co-owners on the new issue by awarding them much higher ownership interests than Plumber. Almost a year later and after much more expense, the Minnesota Court of Appeals reversed the judge on the basis that one business day notice of raising a new issue was lack of due process. Eventually, Plumber was paid the $15,517 claim secured by his mechanic's lien – four years after the work had been completed and at a cost far higher in amount than his claim.

Additional Information and Comment

After it began to look like he might not be paid for the plumbing fixtures he had installed in a home under construction, Plumber filed a mechanic's lien on the home. If the holder of a mechanic's lien is not paid what he is due, he can go to court and ask a court to order sale of the property that was liened.

To file his mechanic's lien, Plumber went to the county Office of the Registrar of Titles. He asked a clerk there to inform him of the legal description of the home he wanted to lien because that legal description had to be stated on the mechanic's lien form. The clerk made a mistake and gave Plumber the wrong legal description. She told him it was lot 2, block 1; actually it was lot 1, block 1.

Plumber wrote the incorrect legal description he had been given in the space reserved in the mechanic's lien form for that information. Then, just to be sure, he also wrote in the street address. As it turned out, that was very important. Then, Plumber turned the mechanic's lien over to the clerk and paid the required fee to have it recorded.

Other subcontractors who had provided labor and materials in the construction of the same home also filed mechanic's liens.

However, all of them typed in the correct legal description.

About three months later, the general contractor failed financially and disappeared. The bank that had loaned the general contractor money to build the home foreclosed on its mortgage and had the sheriff sell the home at a foreclosure sale. The senior couple who had paid the general contractor a large sum of money to build the home for them hired a lawyer from a big Minneapolis law firm, a specialist in property law. Their dream of a retirement home had become a nightmare.

Liens against a home are ranked in priority. If a mortgage, which is a type of lien, is filed first, it comes ahead of mechanic's liens that are filed later and generally is the first lien that is enforced. The bank that had the mortgage interest in the home enforced it by arranging for the foreclosure sale. After a foreclosure sale, there is a "redemption" period. During the redemption period, the original owner, the general contractor in this case, can redeem the property by paying the bank what it is due.

If the original owner does not redeem the property, those who have the next priority liens can enforce theirs. In this case, the mechanic's lien holders had the liens that were next in priority. It became their turn to become the owner of the property by redeeming it – paying the mortgage bank what was owed on the mortgage loan.

Just before the redemption period came to an end, Plumber, now represented by a lawyer, discovered the mistake in the legal description in the mechanic's lien he had filed. To correct the mistake, he prepared and filed an amended mechanic's lien that stated the correct legal description.

The time arrived when the subcontractors could purchase the home on the basis of their mechanic's liens. When more than one subcontractor wants to redeem a home, they often cooperate and contribute proportionately to the total needed to redeem the property. This is what Plumber wanted to do. But the three other subcontractors who also wanted to redeem the home refused to work together with Plumber. They had been told by the lawyer who represented the senior couple that there was a way to get Plumber out of the picture without paying him anything.

The result was that all four subcontractors each paid the sheriff the full amount owed the mortgage bank. That made each subcontractor a co-owner. It also left the sheriff with four times the amount needed to redeem the home. It was a mess.

Now, the lawyer for the senior couple sprang his surprise. He went to court and asked it to cancel Plumber's ownership interest because his mechanic's lien had been filed too late. A mechanic's lien must be filed within 120 days after the subcontractor's last work on the project. Plumber had filed his first mechanic's lien within 120 days, but the amended mechanic's lien with the correct legal description came after that time period.

Plumber filed a motion for summary judgment. Such a motion can be filed when there is agreement on all the facts and all that is needed is to apply the law to these facts. Plumber asked the court to dismiss the claim that his mechanic's lien had been no good. After all, he told the judge, the sheriff had taken his money and named him one of the four owners. None of the other subcontractors or the senior couple had objected to Plumber's mechanic's lien before the redemption, nor had anyone paid Plumber for his labor and materials. And most importantly, Plumber argued, was a Minnesota law, Minnesota Statutes § 514.74, that states, "In no case shall the liens given by this chapter be affected by any inaccuracy in the particulars of the lien statement."

Minnesota Statutes § 514.74 had been interpreted by court decisions to mean that any mistake in a mechanic's lien could be corrected as long as the mechanic's lien statement identified the property it was liening. By writing in the street address of the home involved, Plumber had met that condition. Since his first mechanic's lien was timely and specifically identified the home being liened, Plumber argued that his mechanic's lien was valid.

In response, the lawyer from the big law firm argued that Minnesota Statutes § 514.74 was applicable only to abstract property, not torrens property. Since the home was torrens property, he argued, Plumber's mechanic's liens were invalid because the lien with the correct legal description had not been filed within 120 days.

Abstract and torrens property refer to the two different systems in Minnesota (and other states) of recording documents that pertain to units of real estate. The property in some areas is abstract property. In other areas it is torrens property. When a property is abstract property, all documents that affect the property are recorded independently of each other. To find out what liens apply to a particular parcel of real estate, you must conduct a search by the legal description.

The torrens system is the newer system. There is a certificate for each parcel of real estate with a unique certificate number. Each document that affects or relates to a particular parcel of real estate is listed in the certificate for that parcel.

Plumber's motion for summary judgment came before Judge Thomas M. Murphy. He told Plumber his mechanic's lien was no good and said he would rule in favor of the senior couple and grant them summary judgment, if they had moved for summary judgment.

A few weeks later, the senior couple, through their big law firm lawyer, moved for summary judgment. This time the case came before another judge – Richard G. Spicer. He denied the senior couple's motion for summary judgment and said in his opinion Plumber's mechanic's lien was good. He told the big law firm lawyer that he often disagreed with Judge Murphy and said, "Don't you wish you were in front of Judge Murphy?" (In the first judicial district, where Plumber's case was venued, a case rarely is assigned to a particular judge as it is in most of the 10 judicial districts. Instead, cases come before a judge who is assigned to hear matters on the day they are scheduled to be heard.)

These events set the stage for the third hearing when yet another judge ruled in Plumber's favor. She made her decision on the basis that Plumber should be paid for his labor and materials.

More than four years after Plumber performed his work, the four co-owners resolved the matter and the home was sold to a person not involved in Plumber's case. The senior couple paid many tens of thousands of dollars to the general contractor who disappeared, and many to the big law firm lawyer. They lost all that money and wound up without a home.

The Cops From Hell

John R. Rodenberg, Brown County Judge
Jason Fairbairn, Brown County Deputy Sheriff
Peter McGarry, Sleepy Eye Police Officer
Tim Brennen, Brown County Sheriff
Jeremy Brennen, Brown County Deputy Sheriff
Melanie D. Cook, Minnesota State Trooper
Jered D. Peterson, Assistant Brown County Attorney
James R. Olson, County Attorney Brown County
Jill Hady, Brown County Probation Officer

Case Summary

(Note: In order to tell this story, certain dialogue between the parties has been created. The author does not claim that these are the actual words spoken; only that they represent the gist of the conversations between parties.)

It was dark outside in Sleepy Eye, Minnesota, at about 7:00 p.m. on October 17, 2003. Gene, a 78-year-old senior citizen, drove his pickup truck on his way home, having picked up dinner for himself and his wife. A neighbor rode with him. She did not drive. Gene often gave her rides.

Gene and his friend had visited friends at a senior citizen's home before going to a take-out restaurant for some broiled chicken to take home. Gene's wife had stayed home. She had severe Parkinson's disease and could not care for herself independently.

Just after they left the restaurant, Gene told his friend he had to use the bathroom. He had taken medication for an infected bladder and had to get to a rest room quickly. He stopped at a familiar place.

Before resuming their trip, they chatted with acquaintances, and Gene briefly greeted a caged dog. Then they left.

A short distance after they turned onto the highway a vehicle drove up very close to the rear of Gene's pick-up truck. Bright light flooded the truck's interior. It produced a blinding glare that made it impossible to see. Gene began braking to stop.

Suddenly, the trailing car, a police car, pulled alongside Gene and forced his truck off the road. Gene brought his truck to a stop, but not before going over the curb and just missing some steel poles.

Brown County Deputy Sheriff Jason Fairbairn came to Gene's door and demanded to know if he had been drinking. "No," Gene said.

The officer ordered Gene to get out and walk. Gene replied that he had difficulty walking. "Well," Officer Fairbairn said, "where's your walker, where's your cane, where's your wheel chair, how do you get into your house? You don't look damn crippled to me." After more demands that he get out and walk, Gene said he wanted to talk to a lawyer.

"Show me your driver's license," the officer demanded. Gene reached for his wallet and the officer became angry. When Gene held up his wallet, the officer slapped it away so hard that it slammed up against the windshield. The officer tried to open the door, but it was locked. He reached in and opened it from the inside, then grabbed Gene's head and pulled it back. From a holster, the officer took a taser (electric shock device) and told Gene he was going to taser him.

"You attack me and now you are going to shoot me?" Gene said, horrified. "I tell you I have a weak heart." Gene had an irregular heartbeat for which he took medication.

Saying it would not hurt his heart, the officer shot Gene with his taser. That rendered Gene helpless, which is what a taser is supposed to do.

Gene collapsed in severe agony. Officer Fairbairn pulled him from the vehicle and slammed him to the cement. While he lay face down, his arms up toward his head, the officer ordered him to get up. When he didn't, he kicked him in the ribs. He then tasered Gene again, this time in the left forearm. Gene went stiff and then motionless.

Back-up officers arrived, including Brown County Sheriff Tim

Brennen. Four officers yanked Gene up and started slamming him around, banging him up against the truck. After several minutes, Gene's knees buckled and he fell to the ground. Then they dragged him off to a squad car.

Gene wound up in the hospital. Color pictures show the taser marks and the severe injuries he sustained. (These pictures are in our website, mncourtreform.org, in the "Horror Cases" section. Discretion advised.)

Gene and his friend are willing to take lie detector tests to prove their description of what happened. Of course, the police versions of what happened differ markedly from the version given by Gene and his friend.

Authorities charged Gene with resisting arrest and attacking five officers. He was given 30 days in jail. When he told Judge John R. Rodenberg that his wife had Parkinson's disease and needed him at home, the judge replied, "she will have to care for herself."

Additional Information and Comment

Officer Jason Fairbairn's report of events at the scene where Gene was arrested states:

> "REPORT: On 10 17 2003, at approximately 1900 hours, I, Deputy Jason Fairbairn, Brown County Sheriff's Office, noticed Minnesota license C13H977 weaving within its lane on Main Street East and Fifth Avenue NE in Sleepy Eye. Upon further observance I noticed CBH977 had several items hanging from the rear view mirror. Upon further observance I noticed the vehicle was extremely close to the curb on Main Street East and 7th Avenue NE. The vehicle then struck the curb and came back into its lane of traffic.
>
> "At which time I activated my lights and the driver of the vehicle turned over and drove up into a boulevard over the curb and into the parking lot of the

Family Dollar store located on Main Street East in Sleepy Eye.

"Upon approaching the vehicle I identified myself and informed the driver why I was stopping him. At that time the driver said that I had no right to stop him and the only reason why he drove up over the boulevard was due to the red lights of my squad car.

"I then asked the driver for his driver's license at which time he replied, 'why?' I then informed him that I was detaining him to investigate this traffic stop at which time the driver said I had no right for his driver's license.

"While speaking with the driver I noticed his eyes were bloodshot, glassy, his face was flushed, and there was a strong odor of alcohol coming from the vehicle. I asked the driver if he had been drinking and he replied, 'hell no.' I then asked the passenger, who was later identified as [name omitted], dob: [omitted] [address omitted] in New Ulm, MN, if she'd been drinking. She replied, 'no, I haven't.'

"I then asked the driver if I could see his driver's license, at which time the driver took his wallet out of his back right pocket, opened it and started to search for his driver's license. I quickly noticed that his driver's license was in the front part of his wallet, however, the driver was searching in the back part of his wallet for the license. After a roughly 30-second search of his wallet, the driver located his driver's license, took it out and handed it to me and said, 'There's my goddamn driver's license.'

"At which time I identified the driver as [Gene], dob: [omitted], [address omitted] in Lafayette, MN 56054. I then asked [Gene] again if he had had anything to drink prior to driving the vehicle at which time he replied, 'Hell no.'

"I then asked [Gene] where he was traveling to; he replied, 'home.' I then asked [Gene] where home was and he replied, 'Lafayette.' I asked [Gene] if he was a diabetic and he replied, 'no.' I then asked [Gene] if he would step from the vehicle so I could have him perform Minnesota Standardized Field Sobriety tests. [Gene] then replied, 'No, I'm not getting out of the vehicle to do those goddamn tests.'

"I then informed [Gene] that if he was to get out of the vehicle and pass the tests, I would send him on his way. However, due to the amount of alcohol I was smelling, his motor skills by fumbling through his wallet, his driving conduct, his eyes being bloodshot and red, and his face being flushed, I informed him that I would have to investigate this traffic stop further. At which time [Gene] advised me he was not getting out of the pickup because his legs did not work.

"I then asked [Gene] how he was able to operate the vehicle if his legs did not work and he replied, 'It's none of your goddamn business.'

"I then informed [Gene] that I had not seen a walker, cane, or a wheel chair in the back of his pickup or even in the back seat of the pickup. [Gene] replied again, 'It's none of your goddamn business'.

"I then informed [Gene] that I would have to have him get out of the vehicle to perform field sobriety tests. [Gene] once again said, 'I can't, my legs don't work.' I then asked [Gene] how he was able to get into the pickup, he once again replied, 'It's none of your goddamn business.'

“While speaking with [Gene] I noticed several times that he was moving his legs in the vehicle, pushing his body up by using the floor, and I noticed several times [Gene] pushed his body up when I would ask him the previous questions.

“I then informed [Gene] that there was a Standardized Field Sobriety test that could be performed without using your legs, at which time [Gene] said, ‘I’m not doing any of those goddamn tests.’

“At this time [Gene] stated, ‘Since you have no reason to stop me, I’m going to leave.’ At which time I asked [Gene], ‘Is there anything I could say or do that would get you to exit your vehicle?’ [Gene] replied, ‘No.’ I then opened the door of the truck, leaned over with my left hand to take the keys out of the ignition, fearing that [Gene] might leave with the vehicle, and for my safety and his. At this time [Gene] grabbed my left arm and I then stepped back and grabbed [Gene]’s left arm in an arm bar, my left hand on his wrist and my right hand just under his arm pit.

“I then noticed [Gene]’s right arm raise with a closed fist and he swung across his body towards me. At which time I let go of [Gene]’s arm and stepped back and [Gene] followed through with a punch missing me, however, his weight had him coming out of the vehicle at which time he slid down the front part of my legs as I backed up towards the left side, rear-end side of the pickup where he landed on the ground by my feet.

“At which time I asked [Gene] if he was alright and if he needed assistance getting up at which time he replied, ‘Get away from me, get away from me.’ I then asked [Gene] if he could get up or if he needed my assistance at which time he said, 'I don't need any help.' [Gene] then got up and once again started to climb back into the vehicle.

"At this time I informed [Gene] to please stay out of the vehicle. He turned around, raised his right fist again, at which time I activated my taser and struck [Gene] with the taser in the left wrist and left abdomen. A five-second shot was applied. [Gene] fell back into the truck seat at which time Officer Pete McGarry arrived at the scene after hearing me radio for assistance. Trooper Melanie Cook also arrived along with Brown County Sheriff Tim Brennan.

"After the shock had expired I asked [Gene] to please step from the vehicle and put his hands on the back of the truck at which time he did. At this time Sheriff Brennan handcuffed [Gene] and we escorted him to the back of the squad car. Of all the officers at the scene, we all agreed that [Gene] had a very strong odor of alcohol coming from him and he was very irritable and belligerent.

Upon securing the vehicle I approached [Gene's friend] and asked her if she had been with [Gene] the entire night. [She] replied, 'Yes, we were getting chicken and heading back to Lafayette.' I then asked [Gene's friend] if she had anything to drink tonight with [Gene] at which time she replied, 'I didn't have anything to drink at the bar.'

"I then asked [Gene's friend] if [Gene] had anything to drink at the bar; she replied, 'I don't know.'

"I then asked [Gene's friend] why she did not drive [Gene]'s vehicle if he had been drinking and she replied, 'I don't drive other people's vehicles.' [sentence omitted]

"[Gene's friend]'s eyes were bloodshot, glassy, her speech was slurred, and she had a mild alcohol odor to her. At this time I asked [Gene's friend] if she would be willing to give a statement in reference to the incident; she replied, 'No.' [Gene's friend] then informed Trooper Cook she was going to be going to a [name omitted]'s house in Sleepy Eye at which time Sheriff Brennan informed me to transport [Gene] to the Brown County LEC and read him the Implied Consent Advisory.

"The vehicle was secured by Deputy Jeremy Brennan and Sleepy Eye Officer Pete McGarry and towed to Brown County Sheriff's impound lot by [name omitted] of Sleepy Eye, MN.

"Upon arriving at the Brown County Law Enforcement Center, [Gene] was read the Motor Vehicle Implied Consent Advisory. The Implied Consent was started at 1950 hours and ended at 1956 hours. [Gene] informed this officer that he did not understand what was just read to him at which time I asked if he wished to consult with an attorney, he said, 'No.' I then asked [Gene] if he understood that refusal to take a test is a crime, he replied, 'Yes, I understand that.' I then asked [Gene] if he understood the Implied Consent Advisory, he replied, 'No.'

"Then I asked [Gene] if he would take a breath test and he replied, 'no, I will not answer that question.' [Gene]'s reason for refusing was that he stated he hadn't been drinking. [Gene] informed this deputy during the Implied Consent reading that his head was hurting from the fall he had taken during the arrest and that he'd like to see a doctor.

"At this time I informed [Gene] I would be taking him to the New Ulm Medical Center as soon as we finished the Implied Consent. Upon viewing [Gene]'s head there were no visible scratches or bruises of any sort. He did not complain of his head hurting on the car ride to New Ulm from Sleepy Eye and he did not complain of his head hurting from the squad car to the intoxilizer room.

"Upon completing the Implied Consent [Gene] was transported to the New Ulm Medical Center where he was seen by [name omitted], his regular physician. Dr. [name omitted] informed this deputy that [Gene] was fine, he had no scrapes or bruises of any sort on his body or on his head. She did state that he had a heart condition, however, was fine with the medication that she was giving him and would be able to go to the Brown County Evaluation Center for the detoxification.

"Dr. [name omitted] also stated to this deputy, along with Deputy Jeremy Brennan, that [Gene] had a very strong odor of alcohol coming from him and looked intoxicated. Dr. [name omitted] also informed this deputy of [Gene]'s history with alcohol. Dr. [name omitted] also informed the Brown County Evaluation Center of the patient's needs and okayed him for admission to detoxify at the Brown County Evaluation Center.

"At this time I transported [Gene] to the Brown County Evaluation Center for the safety of himself and others. I also informed [Gene] that his truck was at the Brown County Sheriff's impound lot and that upon his release from the Brown County Evaluation

Center he could pick up his vehicle after paying the required fee.

"On 10-18-2003, at approximately 2015 hours, I, Deputy Jason Fairbairn, received a phone call from [Gene's friend] asking me when she could pick up [Gene]'s truck. I informed [her] I could not release the truck to her unless [Gene] had given the Brown County Sheriff's Office written permission at which time [she] informed me that she had a written note from [Gene] allowing her to pick up his truck. I then informed [Gene's friend] that I could release the vehicle at 2030 hours, due to the fact that I was 15 minutes away from New Ulm. She then informed me that she would rather pick it up on 10-19-2003 sometime during the mid afternoon hours.

"While speaking with [Gene's friend] I asked her if she had been drinking with [Gene] the night of the arrest and she replied, 'No, I didn't have anything to drink at the bar.' I then asked [Gene's friend] if [Gene] is always uncooperative towards law enforcement and she replied, 'no, he just doesn't like to take orders when he's been drinking.' I then asked [Gene's friend] if she was willing to give a statement of the incident that occurred during the traffic stop; she replied, 'No.'

"Prior to [Gene]'s truck being released, an inventory was taken. All of his belongings were recorded. [Gene] also had a large amount of money on him at the time of the arrest. At the scene the money was counted to be $194. Upon this deputy transporting [Gene] to the Brown County Evaluation Center during his inventory there, [Gene] also had $194.

"On 10-19-2003, [Gene]'s pickup was released to [Gene] and [Gene's friend]."

Gene and his friend deny that they had any alcohol to drink on the day he was arrested. Several people who saw Gene and his friend before he was arrested say they saw no evidence that either had consumed any alcohol or acted other than normal. Gene and his friend deny that he was asked to take a sobriety test at any time before he was arrested and taken away.

The report of Minnesota State Patrol officer Melanie D. Cook states:

> "On Friday, October 17, 2003, at approximately 1900 hours, I, Trooper Melanie D. Cook, was northbound on MNTH 4 just North of USTH 14, in the City of Sleepy Eye, MN, when I heard radio traffic from Deputy Jason Fairbairn. Deputy Fairbairn was on a traffic stop at the Family Dollar Store parking lot and was requesting assistance from Sleepy Eye Police Officer Peter McGarry. I responded to his location. Officer McGarry arrived a short time before I did. When I arrived I observed a White Ford F150 pickup, license number CBH 977, parked in front of Deputy Fairbairn's squad car. Both vehicles were in the Family Dollar Store parking lot. I observed Deputy Fairbairn with a male on the driver's side of the pickup truck near the bed of the truck. As I approached Deputy Fairbairn was trying to get the male to follow his directions and stay turned away from him and against the truck. Deputy Fairbairn had used his Taser and appeared to have the male under control. Officer McGarry was nearby as well. I observed a passenger in the vehicle and approached the passenger's side of the vehicle. I observed a female on the passenger's side of the vehicle. She was eating some food and I asked her if she had her driver's license or any identification on her? I identified her by Minnesota Picture Driver's license as [Gene's friend]. I asked that [she] remain in the vehicle.

"I walked back to the rear of the truck and observed Deputy Fairbairn asking the male to stop moving around. The male was not following deputy Fairbairn's instructions. Sheriff Tim Brennen arrived and took the male's left arm and asked that the male follow Deputy Fairbairn's instructions. Sheriff Brennen advised [Gene] that he was going to jail. As Sheriff Brennen and Deputy Fairbairn were putting handcuffs on the male his trousers fell down and his watchband broke and the watch fell to the ground. After the handcuffs were placed on the male I gave the watch to [Gene's friend]. Deputy Fairbairn placed the male in the rear seat of his squad car.

"[Sentence concerning Gene's friend omitted.] I was given the male's Minnesota picture driver's license and asked if I could run a check on him. He was identified as [Gene]. [Gene]'s driving privileges were valid with one driving while impaired in 1973 and one in 1978. [Sentence omitted concerning Gene's friend] and a tow was ordered for the truck. [Gene's friend] was asked if she had someone that she could call and have come and pick her up. She said that she did and went into the Family Dollar store to use the telephone. Once [she] was done she exited the store and ran across Main Street. I observed her run toward Jubilee Foods and then back to across from our location. I approached her and asked her if she was able to get a hold of someone to come and get her. She stated that she was waiting for a [name omitted] to arrive.

"I approached Deputy Fairbairn's squad car where Deputy Jeremy Brennen and Deputy Fairbairn were standing. I was near the rear passenger side door when Deputy Brennen opened the door to talk with [Gene] and I could smell a strong odor of an alcoholic beverage coming from the rear seat. Deputy

> Brennen asked [Gene] if he would blow into a Preliminary Breath Test and [he] refused.
>
> "My video camera recorded portions of audio and video upon my arrival. In reviewing my video tape I noticed that the camera was aimed straight ahead and didn't show [Gene].
>
> "The vehicle was towed by [name omitted] to Brown County impound lot in New Ulm MN."

Gene's friend denies that she sat in the car eating food while the officers were with Gene.

THE YOUNG MUMMY (6 YEARS OLD)

Plaintiffs' Trial Lawyers

Case Summary

An engineer returned home from work and drove his station wagon slowly into the driveway of his comfortable home in the suburbs. As he eased his way into his driveway, he carefully watched his neighbor's 6-year-old son who was on his neighbor's lawn astride a bicycle with training wheels. He was near the driveway but seemed in control. After his vehicle stopped, the engineer heard a soft "thump" from the rear. He got out and walked to the rear of his vehicle. He saw the bicycle leaning against the right rear fender of his vehicle. The boy was standing nearby with a frightened expression on his face.

The engineer looked at the area of impact. He found no damage. While he was making this examination, the boy's parents came out of their home and walked over to their son. After a minute, they turned to the engineer and told him how sorry they were. The engineer asked about the boy. He is fine, they told him. There was no sign of any injury. Just the same, the engineer said, we must take him to the hospital to be certain there was no injury. The boy's parents said that would not be necessary, but the engineer insisted and all set out for the hospital. After an examination, hospital personnel declared the boy fine and all returned to their homes.

The next day, the engineer returned home from work. He pulled into his driveway, stopped, and got out. He glanced toward his neighbor's yard. The boy again was on his lawn, but much nearer to the front door of his home. This time he sat in a wheel chair. Bandages covered him from his head to his feet. All you could see were his eyes, nose and mouth. His parents came out of their home and walked over to the engineer. "You hurt our son very badly," they told him, "when you ran over him yesterday. We are going to sue you." And they did.

Legal papers soon were delivered to the engineer, one entitled a summons and the other a complaint. The complaint said terrible things about the engineer, falsely accused him of many things that were untrue, and demanded a huge amount of money. The engineer promptly contacted his insurance company, which was one of the biggest and best.

The lawyers provided by the engineer's insurance company did not seem concerned. That bothered the engineer. Even more bothersome were the humiliating questions he had to answer in what were called "interrogatories," quite a few if you count all the parts of each question, and the intense questioning of him at his deposition when he had to sit calmly while his neighbors' lawyers harassed him.

Eventually, the insurance company settled the case, paying his neighbor $5,000. He could not understand this since it was clear the boy had not been injured. The insurance company lawyers told him it was cheaper and smarter to settle than go to trial. He protested that a settlement hurt his reputation. That does not matter, the insurance company lawyers replied.

Additional Information and Comment

The engineer had immigrated to the United States from Pakistan. He was grateful for the success he had achieved in his new country as a result of a good education and hard work. Life in America was good for him and his family and they had made a good adjustment, although there were some things about his adopted country he still had not figured out.

He had never been involved in a court case. Always cautious, he followed all laws and rules religiously, drove very conservatively, and never, never exceeded the speed limit. Taking any chance was foreign to his nature.

Until his contact with the insurance company lawyers, the engineer had no reason to question the legal system. Programs that he occasionally watched such as LA Law, Law and Order, and The Practice, and commercials telling viewers that "we mean business" – gave him the impression that the country's legal system was reasonable, and reliably produced justice, even if that was challenging sometimes.

His perception began to change the day he received a fat package from the insurance company lawyer. One of the documents it contained was a very long list of questions called "interrogatories." The questions called for a huge amount of information that to him seemed totally irrelevant to the alleged injuries suffered by his neighbor's son, which, as everyone knew, were none. His opponents wanted to know all about his health, work, recreation, hobbies, what he watched on television, his income and expenses, how much alcohol he drank, what medications he took, what crimes he had committed, and on and on and on.

Another document called "request for production of documents" was just as onerous. His adversary wanted copies of his tax returns, pay stubs, check register, medical records, job performance evaluations, employment records, military records, insurance policies, automobile service and repair records, and many other documents that would take a long time to find and copy. This was ridiculous, he said to himself, because there was no injury. The hospital report proved it.

A third document in the package was "request for admissions." It was a long list of statements. He was required, the document said, to "admit or deny" each statement. If he did not do so within 30 days, the document said, all the statements would be admitted even though they were both absurd and almost entirely untrue, such as he was not watching, was sick, had been drinking alcohol, drove too fast, worried about money, and on for pages.

It took several tries to get the insurance company lawyer on the telephone. That probably was fortunate because some of his anger had dissipated. Still, he was very irate.

"What is the meaning of this?" he demanded to know. "It will take me days," he told the insurance company lawyer, "to answer all this. There is no reason for me to have to do this," he continued, "because there were no injuries. Why doesn't someone tell them to go away?"

The insurance company lawyer explained that this was "discovery," a standard part of lawsuit procedure. The rules required compliance by all parties.

"Discover what?" the engineer retorted. "Nothing happened. There is nothing to discover."

Eventually mollified and convinced there was no alternative, the engineer completed the responses and provided them to the insurance company lawyer. Although not a drinking person, he felt he needed a stiff one after he finished his responses.

But the worst was yet to come. A few weeks later, the insurance company lawyer sent him a letter in which he said he had received a notice of taking deposition. The engineer had to be at the office of the other side's lawyer on a certain day at a certain time to give his deposition – his answers under oath to questions asked him orally by the lawyer who represented his neighbors and their son.

The engineer appeared at the scheduled time at the designated place. A court reporter asked him if he swore to tell the truth and the engineer said, "Yes." The opposition lawyer began to ask questions. He asked the engineer about his job satisfaction. "What does that have to do with this lawsuit," the engineer wanted to know? "This is discovery," the opposition lawyer replied. "Your answer might lead to discoverable evidence." The engineer told the opposition lawyer what he had told the insurance company lawyer, there was nothing to discover. "There was no evidence because there had been no injury," the engineer explained. "We checked it out at the hospital. He was okay," the engineer continued. "Don't you understand?" the engineer asked.

When the lawyer asked the engineer about his personal finances with his neighbor sitting next to him, the engineer told him, "None of your damn business." After the insurance company lawyer and the other lawyer argued for a while, the engineer reluctantly agreed to provide the requested information, but only on condition that it not be disclosed to his neighbor.

After two hours, the engineer had had enough. He stood up and said, "I'm tired of this bullcrap. I'm leaving!" After his neighbor's lawyer told him he would call the judge if he did and the judge might send him to jail, the engineer, thoroughly exasperated, sat down and endured more deposition.

About an hour later the neighbor's lawyer asked the engineer to tell him about his sex life with his wife. "That's it," the engineer exploded. "Go to hell!" and he stalked out of the room.

The insurance company lawyer scrambled after him down the hall. "They're calling the judge right now," he said. "You'll be sorry if you don't go back." Beaten and subdued, the engineer went back and endured hours more of deposition.

After his deposition, the engineer stopped watching television programs about courts and the law.

THE GODZILLA CONSPIRACY

Joan N. Ericksen (formerly Joan Ericksen Lancaster), Federal District Court Judge (formerly a Minnesota Supreme Court Justice)
James H. Gilbert, former Minnesota Supreme Court Justice
Jonathan Lebedoff, Federal District Court Magistrate
Ronald J. Meshbesher, Criminal Lawyer

Case Summary

One of the most extraordinary websites on the internet is: www.geocities.com/CapitolHill/6641/fbi_chronology.html. This website describes incredible wrongdoing by three of Minnesota's leaders in the legal field: former Minnesota Supreme Court Justice James H. Gilbert, former Minnesota Supreme Court Justice Joan N. Ericksen (formerly Joan Ericksen Lancaster), now a U.S. District Court Judge, and renowned criminal lawyer Ronald Meshbesher.

In this case, a U.S. government agency charged a person we will call Mike with mispricing rare coins. After an investigation, the agency found Mike had done nothing wrong and gave him a complete clearance. What happened during the investigation is nothing less than criminal.

Mike hired Ronald Meshbesher and James H. Gilbert, then a partner in the Meshbesher law firm, to represent him for a fee of $100,000. Mike was not able to pay Meshbesher and Gilbert right away because the federal agency froze all of Mike's business and personal assets, even though he had not been convicted of anything – or even indicted. Lawyer Gilbert and the federal agency arranged for the appointment of a receiver. Then they worked with the receiver, who, without any legal right to sell Mike's property, sold off his assets at prices far less than what they were worth, and at considerable profit to the receiver. Eventually, court authorities discharged the receiver, but as far as is known he never suffered any penalty.

One result of the fraudulent sales was that Gilbert was in an awful spot. If Mike discovered his role in arranging for the fraud, he and Meshbesher could be liable to Mike for a lot of money. Employees of the federal agency also were at risk. If the mishandling of Mike's assets became known, careers could be lost.

At the time of the agency investigation, Joan Ericksen was an Assistant U.S. Attorney. She was assigned to the case and worked with the employees of the federal agency. At a secret meeting, these employees gave Ericksen confidential information they had obtained from Mike even though they had promised in a contract they would never reveal it to anyone. Ericksen used this information first to locate all of Mike's assets and freeze them, and then to drive Mike and his company into bankruptcy.

This $38 million involuntary bankruptcy was first filed in January 1992. It still is open to this day, 12 years later. Normally, an involuntary bankruptcy is speedily processed and closed.

By withholding information and other deceit, Ericksen got Mike indicted. During this process, she lied to federal judges. Gilbert lied to Mike in a letter in which he said he had informed a judge about the fraud of the receiver who illegally sold off Mike's assets.

Mike caught on to the dishonesty and unethical conduct of Gilbert and Meshbesher, who joined in representing Mike in the criminal case. He found other lawyers and wanted to hire them to replace Gilbert and Meshbesher. But the U.S. District Court Judge in the case would not let him replace Gilbert and Meshbesher. He disregarded Mike's objections and denied Mike's motion to substitute new lawyers to represent him, and then re-appointed Gilbert and Meshbesher to represent Mike in the trial, even though Mike had fired them. To cover up this horrendous injustice, the judge put Mike's motion and evidence "under seal" so the public could not see it.

Gilbert and Meshbesher represented Mike at trial. They refused to subpoena many witnesses who would have proven Mike was innocent of any crime until it was too late to enforce the subpoenas. They and Ericksen, who prosecuted the case for the government, withheld a huge amount of information and documents that never were made known to the jury. Mike lost everything, including his marriage. The jury convicted Mike of the crimes the federal agency found he had not committed. He spent five years in a federal prison. Gilbert and Meshbesher were paid more than $400,000, most of this from the proceeds of the fraudulent sales, for their legal services.

Additional Information and Comment

Mike is a well-educated man. Until lawyers and judges ruined his life, he was a successful man with a wife and three children. He earned a Ph.D. in education with a minor in Japanese business history, taught for several years, and was a school administrator.

During his youth, Mike studied coins as a hobby and later went into the rare coin business, first part time, then full time. He was not a rare coin broker – a person who locates rare coins and arranges for coin sales, but never owns the coins sold. Mike purchased coins and owned them until he sold them.

Mike became an expert in grading rare coins. This became very useful after the rare coin industry changed the way it graded coins. Mike had a knack for finding and purchasing coins that increased in value.

Mike's coin business became very successful. During a six-year span, his business had more than $50 million in sales. He operated internationally and became wealthy. He created pension accounts for his family and all his company's employees, with assets of near $1 million.

The U.S. Internal Revenue Service audited his business once. It found Mike's business in full compliance with all accounting rules. At first there was a claim for back taxes based on internal transfers of funds from business to personal accounts, but it was dropped. There were no fines or penalties.

Then the U.S. Federal Trade Commission (FTC) stepped in. It questioned how Mike's business determined the value of the coins he sold. The FTC had found that some rare coin dealers were using the new valuation system to induce unsophisticated investors to purchase low quality coins.

At the beginning of its investigation of Mike's business, the

FTC froze all of his and his wife's business and personal assets. The agency told them that it would approve reasonable requests for funds to pay business and personal expenses. Acting through the U.S. Postal service, government agents made an armed raid of Mike's business office and seized almost all business records and many personal records.

Two days after the raid, Mike and his wife hired lawyer James H. Gilbert to help them. They agreed to pay $100,000 as the initial retainer, subject to the FTC's approval.

During the next four days, Gilbert negotiated an agreement with the FTC to release $50,000 that could be used for living expenses and some other purposes. To get the $50,000 released, Mike and his wife agreed to an extension in the freeze of their assets, subject to the condition that no one other than Mike could sell or transfer any of those.

Despite the agreement, the FTC refused to release any funds to Mike and his wife. This put them into extreme financial straits that threatened to ruin their business. Without FTC approval, they could not even ship rare coins already bought and paid for by Mike's customers.

Because the FTC would not release the $50,000 it had promised to release, Mike had to make emergency arrangements. With the FTC's approval, he pledged assets to two coin dealers as collateral for loans that were to be paid back in 30 days. As consideration for one loan, Mike gave a competitor access to his customer list and promised to consider him as a possible supplier of rare coins in the future.

The coin dealers who promised to loan money to Mike never did send him any money, yet they took ownership of the assets Mike had pledged as collateral. Gilbert did nothing to enforce the loan agreements or prevent the two dealers from defrauding Mike and getting his assets for nothing.

Mike and his wife were financially devastated by the frauds of the two dealers, which were fully known to the FTC and Gilbert. The FTC's refusal to release the funds Mike and his wife needed to survive forced them into a situation in which they were vulnerable to fraud. Gilbert had negotiated some of the transactions that resulted in Mike and his wife losing hundreds of thousands of dollars. But instead of protecting Mike and his wife and fighting to recover the assets that were stolen from them, Gilbert, together with the FTC, forced Mike and his wife to accept appointment of a receiver to control their assets.

Gilbert and the FTC chose and agreed on the receiver who assumed control of Mike's and his wife's assets. Despite the provision of the freeze agreement that no one other than Mike could sell or transfer any of his assets, and then only with FTC approval, the receiver appointed by Gilbert and the FTC sold hundreds of thousands of Mike's and his wife's assets.

The receiver also illegally sold several millions of dollars in coins that had been paid for by customers and were waiting for shipment, and ERISA pension assets that were Mike's and his wife's personal property. He paid much of the proceeds from these sales to Gilbert for his legal fees, and pocketed a large amount for his fees. He was discharged by court order for cause 90 days after he was appointed. Despite being fired for criminal misconduct, he has been paid more than $100,000 since then during the 12 years of the drawn-out bankruptcy.

Six months after its investigation began, the FTC entered into a settlement agreement with Mike and his wife. The settlement agreement states that Mike and his wife did nothing wrong. According to the agreement, everything Mike did in his rare coin business, including how he graded rare coins, was completely legal. This settlement agreement was approved by a federal judge and is included in a civil federal court file, 4-91-438.

Despite the FTC's conclusion that Mike did nothing wrong, the U.S. Attorney for Minnesota got Mike indicted for alleged crimes, including some based on the loss of assets that were the result of mishandling by Gilbert and the FTC. At the trial, the government produced witnesses who testified that they had paid Mike for rare coins they never received. Neither Joan Ericksen, the Assistant U.S. Attorney who prosecuted the case against Mike, nor Mike's purported lawyers, Gilbert and Meshbesher, allowed the jury to find out why Mike's customers had not received the coins they purchased from Mike. They were never informed that the FTC would not let Mike ship them. Nor was it made known to the jury that the FTC and Erickson let the receiver illegally dispose of assets that had been sold to customers and then use the proceeds to pay Gilbert and Meshbesher.

The jury was not told about the settlement agreement and the FTC investigation that cleared Mike of any wrongdoing. Gilbert and Meshbesher refused to introduce it at trial.

Gilbert and Meshbesher refused to subpoena witnesses who could have revealed the frauds of the receiver and coin dealers that prevented Mike from fulfilling his business obligations. In this manner, the lawyers arranged the conviction of Mike for stealing and defrauding his customers.

With Ericksen standing silent during the trial, Gilbert and Meshbesher denied under oath that any conflicts existed. But since then, two letters were discovered, written months before the trial by their law firm, in which the firm admits conflicts that should have kept them from representing Mike. These letters show that Mike had an absolute defense to all charges in the indictment. They demonstrate that Gilbert should have been called as a witness to prove that Mike had nothing to do with the mishandling of assets.

These letters also show that Ericksen withheld crucial evidence from the judge and jury to cover up her and Gilbert's misconduct. In short, Mike was not allowed to chose the defense lawyers he wanted. He was sent to prison and his family stripped of their assets to cover up the wrongdoing of federal officials and his original lawyers.

Overwhelming evidence of Gilbert's and Meshbesher's crimes against Mike and his family, and their unethical behavior, and the complicity of the federal judge who presided at Mike's trial, are contained in two federal court files. People who want to see these files must pay $45 per file to have them retrieved from storage. The last time a news reporter examined the case files, Mike's accusations against his lawyers still were sealed, more than seven years after the trial. Until docket file 69 is unsealed by a judge, the public will not know that Mike would have been proven innocent if the lawyers he wanted had been allowed to prove that the indictment and trial were tainted.

This is almost the perfect crime, but it is not over. New lawyers who are working on Mike's case have uncovered those letters and a bankruptcy tax return that proves who really stole the frozen assets. These documents could be the smoking guns that turn the Godzilla Conspiracy against its real perpetrators – if a federal judge addresses this evidence.

The Purloined Heart

Larry G. Jorgenson, Pennington County Judge (retired)

Case Summary

A man, Shafted, and his female significant other had cohabited with each other for more than seven years. During the sixth year, they purchased a farm and herd of cattle. They registered the property in both names. One day during their final year together, he was given a restraining order she had obtained unilaterally before the judge heard any of Shafted's evidence. It accused him of physical and mental abuse, and ordered him to leave the farm and stay at least one mile away. In a later court action, she asked the court to award her all of the property owned by both of them.

At the trial, no one corroborated her testimony that he had abused her, even though her teenage daughter had resided with them and never had complained. She did not testify. There was no evidence of any injury or physical abuse or of medical or psychological treatment. Somehow, the judge determined that everything she said was true and everything Shafted said was not.

Shafted worked full time during the day and had paid the mortgage and property tax payments and all the insurance premiums. His companion made monthly payments to her mother on the amount they borrowed for the down payment. While they were living together, he paid more than $1,700 for new appliances: a washer, dryer, freezer and stove.

Minnesota law, Minnesota Statutes § 513.075, clearly precludes a person who is cohabiting with another to whom he or she is not married from obtaining any property of the other unless there is a signed, written contract. If this was not the law, a person could leave a relationship and take with him or her property owned by his or her former companion even if the other person never agreed to give up property he or she owned.

With respect to real estate jointly owned by unmarried persons, the rule is that the property must be sold and the net proceeds divided equally. Under the law, Shafted was legally entitled to thousands of dollars he could have used to rebuild his life.

The judge disregarded the law. He awarded her the farm, cattle, home, all appliances and everything else except one box of items he awarded to Shafted. He even ordered Shafted to pay $2,500 to her mother even though he had never benefited from anything charged to her mother's charge account, or charged anything to it, except for two charges he made at his companion's request when he picked up her vehicle from the repair shop.

At trial, she told the judge that the value of the farm was only $25,000 and there was no net equity. An expert real estate appraiser testified that the value was $35,900. Eventually, she listed the property for sale after the parties separated for $48,000. The judge accepted her low valuation for the purpose of dividing the parties' property.

Shafted declared bankruptcy. At age 48, all he had was a box of possessions and a broken heart.

Additional Information and Comment

In Minnesota, unmarried men and women who live together do not get an ownership interest in the property owned by his or her partner in the absence of a written contract, even if the partner who does not have an ownership interest actually paid for an item of property. For example, if the man in such a partnership buys a home in his name only and the woman pays all the mortgage, tax and insurance payments, she gets no ownership interest in the home. If the couple separate, he gets the home free and clear of any claim by her.

This rule is stated in Minnesota Statutes § 513.075:

> If sexual relations between the parties are contemplated, a contract between a man and woman who are living together in this state out of wedlock, or who are about to commence living together in this

> state out of wedlock, is enforceable as to terms concerning the property and financial relations of the parties only if:
>
> (1) The contract is written and signed by the parties, and
>
> (2) Enforcement is sought after termination of the relationship.

Minnesota Statutes § 513.076 states as follows:

> Unless the individuals have executed a contract complying with the provisions of Section 513.075, the courts of this state are without jurisdiction to hear and shall dismiss a contrary to public policy any claim by any individual to the earnings or property of another individual if the claim is based on the fact that the individuals lived together in contemplation of sexual relations and out of wedlock within or without this state.

In Shafted's case, title to the farm and herd of cattle was in both their names. Under the statute quoted above, his companion was not entitled to the share of their jointly-owned property that was in his name. Shafted's lawyer explained this very clearly in a memorandum to the judge in which he wrote:

> "When individuals cohabitate with the knowledge and understanding that they are not married, the relationship is a meretricious one. Carlson v. Olson, 256 NW 2d 249 (Minn. 1977). By statute, the validity of a marriage requires it to be a civil contract between a man and a woman to which the consent of the parties, capable in law of contracting, is essential. See, Minn. Stat. § 517.08.
>
> "A common law marriage is one in which a man and

a woman have lived together and held themselves out as a husband and wife, but the marriage was not contracted pursuant to the statutory requirements. The law specifically states that marriages after April 26, 1941, that do not conform to the legal requirements are null and void. As of that date, common law marriages in the State of Minnesota were not recognized as legally binding marriages. See, Minn. Stat. § 517.01. Parties who cohabitate with one another with the knowledge that they are not legally married have limited rights. The law provides that men and women who cohabitate with one another do not acquire rights by virtue of their cohabitation, unless they specifically contract for such rights. See, Minn. Stat. § 513.075 and § 513.076.

"Without a specific written contract no claim can be made by one cohabiter against the real or personal assets of the other cohabiter, or against the income of the other cohabiter without a specific contract enabling the court to grant such relief. Id.

"It is extremely clear that the Court does not have Jurisdiction to award the relief set forth in the Court's May 6, 1999 Judgment. There exists no specific written contract and plaintiff cannot be allowed to make a claim against the real or personal assets of the defendant or against the income of the defendant without a specific contract enabling the Court to grant such relief. The legislature established a clear public policy position in adopting Minnesota Statute § 513.076."

Judge Jorgenson ignored the law and awarded Shafted's companion all ownership of the farm, the herd, and the appliances. The facts proved by Shafted were that he had paid over 71 percent of the amounts paid for the farm, herd and appliances. He should have been awarded 71 percent of their value, not zero.

THE JEKYLL AND HYDE MOTHER

John B. Van de North, Ramsey County Judge
Sandra Warner, Guardian Ad Litem

Case Summary

Judge John B. Van de North knew Mother was doing an excellent job of raising her six-month-old daughter who was in her custody. Judge Van de North personally saw the infant at trial when she sat on Mother's lap while Mother was on the witness stand. He heard substantial evidence that Mother was raising her daughter by herself in her own apartment. Yet, he found "grave and weighty reasons" why Mother was unfit to parent her other child, a three-year-old son. He awarded custody of him to an almost 60-year-old single foster mother who was unrelated by blood to the boy.

At age 18, just after she gave birth to Son, Mother was unsettled. She lived in a noisy, messy apartment, moved often, partied more than she should have, and used marijuana and alcohol in more than moderation. She came from a dysfunctional home, had not completed high school, and worked only occasionally. Her large family helped care for Son and because of that he always had been healthy, well-fed and clothed, watched, and kept safe and happy.

But Ramsey County child protection was concerned. A child protection worker started a proceeding in Ramsey County Juvenile Court to make sure Son was protected. Mother put Son in foster care for a short time, but decided to get him back and the child protection worker helped Mother retrieve Son from the foster home.

The child protection worker wanted Mother to be evaluated and Mother agreed. She went to a psychologist selected and paid for by

Ramsey County, who gets 90 percent of her business from Ramsey County social workers and rarely makes findings or recommendations not agreeable to the agency. The psychologist found that Mother was mildly retarded, immature, aimless and irresponsible and recommended against Mother having custody of Son. Two other evaluators, again selected and paid for by Ramsey County, came to the same conclusions.

At about that time, Mother settled down. She was not happy with her life style. She went back to school, began training to be a commercial cook, stopped all use of alcohol and drugs, and lived responsibly. She became much more mature. Mother proved all of that at trial.

In the meantime, the foster mother who had cared for Son decided she wanted him permanently, along with the financial assistance she received. She started a lawsuit in Ramsey County Family Court and asked that she be given permanent custody of Son. She persuaded the court to give her temporary custody. Later, the court dismissed the juvenile court action and went forward in the family court lawsuit which meant there were no child protection workers involved to help decide what was in Son's best interests.

After she got Son, the foster mother shut Mother out of his life except for one hour per week of visitation at the foster mother's home. Mother's visitation with Son was supervised by the foster mother who did everything she could to hassle and anger Mother. The foster mother refused to allow Son to have any personal contact with any of Mother's extended family.

Meanwhile, Mother became pregnant and gave birth to her second child. She found a nice apartment that had two bedrooms, one of which was reserved for Son. In preparation for trial, Mother located a highly respected and qualified Ph.D. psychologist who conducted psychological and parenting evaluations of her.

Trial in the foster mother's lawsuit began 14 months after the first set of evaluations. Two attractive law school seniors from the University of Minnesota Law School Clinic represented the foster mother. They batted their eyelids, flashed their legs and said sweet nothings to Hizzoner. That proved to be far more important than the facts, the law, or even the best interests of Son.

All of the first set of evaluators told Judge Van de North that they had not had any contact with Mother for more than a year, knew nothing about her current circumstances, attitude, condition, or living arrangements, or of the training and schooling she had received, or her current state of mind. The Ph.D. psychologist who had just evaluated Mother testified that Mother was fully capable of parenting Son even though she still needed some therapy, principally anger management to cope with how she felt in not having Son and the problems she encountered when she was allowed to visit with him.

Judge Van de North disregarded evidence that the almost 60-year-old foster mother, who walked with a cane and who would be 70 when Son became 13, already could not keep up with or always control Son. Evidence of Son twice needing stitches to close wounds, incidents of dangerous substances within Son's reach, and a speech impairment Son developed after he began living with the foster mother were ignored.

Nor did Judge Van de North think it was significant that Son was not allowed to see his sister or extended family or was constantly torn by the tension between Mother and the foster mother, or the argument over who was his "mother." In his opinion, Judge Van de North said that giving Son to the foster mother would give Mother more time to be a good parent to her daughter.

Additional Information and Comment

Minnesota law is very clear about what it takes to justify separating a child from his or her biological parents and giving custody to a third person who is not blood related to the child. It takes huge justification. The law in Minnesota is that a natural parent is:

> " 'presumed to be a fit and suitable person to be entrusted with care of child or children born to and belonging to them. The burden of disproving this presumption rests upon those who challenge it.' [citations omitted] The natural parent is entitled, as a matter of law, to custody of a minor child unless 'there has been established on the [parent's] part neglect, abandonment, incapacity, moral delinquency, instability of character or inability to furnish the

> child with needed care, * * * or unless it has been established that such custody otherwise would not be in the best interest of the child.' Although the presumption favors appellant, it may be overturned if there are 'grave and weighty' reasons to separate a child from his or her natural parents." (Custody of N.A.K., 649 N.W. 2d 166) (Minn. 2002)

A third person who is seeking custody of a child from his or her natural parent has the burden of proof. In this case, the foster mother had to show "grave reasons" before custody of Son could be taken from Mother. To justify transfer of custody to her, the foster mother was required to prove that Mother was unable to parent her son. Because depriving a natural parent of his or her child is an "extremely grave matter," a court is required to authorize such a transfer only when the evidence clearly mandates such a result.

Finally, the evidence that allows a court to give a natural parent's child to a third person must be current. The court is required by law to base its decision on conditions as of the time of the trial.

At her trial, Mother proved beyond a doubt that she was properly parenting her six-month-old daughter. There was no evidence to the contrary. The foster mother did not present evidence of poor parenting of the six-month-old daughter because she had none.

Seven people, Mother, two members of her family, and four friends who knew her well, testified that Mother had always taken good care of her son with the help of her family and currently was taking superb care of her daughter.

The most the foster mother proved was that, at age 18, there were times when Mother was unsettled. She would leave her son with her mother or grandmother for relatively short periods of time. But the evidence was that the boy always was well cared for, happy and well adjusted. The judge acknowledged that Mother had changed and progressed. She had gone back to school, was getting trained, had stopped all use of alcohol and drugs, and greatly matured, and had religiously visited her son to the extent she was allowed.

Most significant of all, it was crystal clear to Judge Van de North that Mother deeply loved her son and earnestly wanted to raise him. She flatly told Judge Van de North in testimony that she would willingly do whatever was required to regain custody of her son.

That was not enough for Judge Van de North. The evidence that she was now properly raising her daughter simply was irrelevant. He could not see that it is idiotic to rule that a parent who is properly raising a six-month-old child is unable for "grave and weighty" reasons to raise her three-year-old son.

Judge Van de North chose to disregard the law. In his decision he mouthed the rule that a determination of a person's ability to parent a child must be based on conditions at the time of trial, and then proceeded to do the opposite. Time after time in his decision, he cites evidence more than one-and-one-half years old as the evidence that supported his decision. Repeatedly in his decision he cites the results of four evaluations made more than one-and-one-half years earlier, well before Mother matured and rehabilitated herself, as the basis for his decision to give permanent custody of the boy to a blood stranger.

Judge Van de North minimized the testimony, report and recommendations of the Ph.D. psychologist, who was far more qualified and experienced than any of the other evaluators, that Mother was capable of parenting her son, had made significant progress, and with some additional treatment, which Mother said she was willing to get, could independently parent her son. He rejected her conclusion that Mother was capable within a period of months of completing the treatment she needed to get.

Judge Van de North openly acknowledged that Mother's mother, grandmother and other members of her family were willing to help Mother raise her son. No, Judge Van de North ruled, that was not enough. A third person blood stranger would be better for him than his own family. It was not significant at all that this stranger despised Mother and her family to the extent of not allowing any contact with them except Mother, and, with respect to her, only one hour per week in the foster mother's home. It also was not significant that the foster mother was determined to destroy any bond between Mother and her son and require that the boy call her his mother.

This case is an example of a nice, pleasant, simple-minded judge deliberately breaking the law to get a result that he had decided on despite the law. After all, Mother had an IQ of 76. She simply could never be a fit person to have custody of and raise her son.

The Infant Trade

Michelle Hatcher, Assistant Hennepin County Attorney
Diane Kassler, Hennepin County Child Protection Worker
Myron S. Greenberg, Hennepin County Juvenile Court Judge
Christine Litsey, Guardian Ad Litem
Eric S. Rehm, Attorney for the Guardian Ad Litem

Case Summary

Mother had a good upbringing in a comfortable home in Chicago, Illinois. She married at a young age and soon had four beautiful, healthy children. Then her tragedies began.

Her husband abandoned her and their children. Unable to both care for her young children and support herself, and without child support, she became homeless. The county put her children in foster care. Eventually, it terminated Mother's parental rights to her four children on the basis that she could not provide a home for them.

Mother fled to Minnesota. Her fifth child was the product of a relationship. Then, tragedy struck again. At age 3, her child died in a fire in Mother's apartment. It was an accident, but Mother had been negligent. Hennepin County prosecuted Mother for negligent homicide. Mother was sentenced to a long term of probation. Again, she had lost everything. She had nothing. In weakness, she turned to alcohol and drugs.

That was a probation violation. Mother went to jail for two years followed by additional years because of additional probation and system violations. She came out the last time penniless, homeless, without any of her children, and with no one to turn to.

But she came out with something else. She was determined to

turn her life around. Weeks and then months of intensive drug abuse counseling led to complete abstinence from alcohol and the use of illegal substances. Participation in individual and group counseling conducted by psychologists resulted in a new sense of respect for herself. Confidence in her future replaced the grieving over past losses. Reaching out to people who could and wanted to help her became a habit. She no longer feared the future, she was determined to conquer it.

She entered into another relationship and became pregnant. Hope soared in her heart. Life for her again had meaning. She was going to give birth to a daughter.

But even before this child was born, a Hennepin County Child Protection worker intervened. The child went directly from the hospital to a foster home.

From the beginning of her intervention, there was no doubt in the child protection worker's mind. Mother could never have custody of her latest child. After all, her parental rights to four children had been terminated, she had been in jail two times, and had a history of alcohol and drug abuse. There was no point in even trying to re-unite Mother and her youngest child. Besides, the foster parents had fallen in love with Mother's child and wanted to adopt her. The child protection worker began a proceeding in Hennepin County Juvenile Court to terminate Mother's rights to her youngest child.

But this time, Mother refused to give up or fail again. She continued intensive counseling from an independent woman's drug rehabilitation service and faithfully abstained from alcohol and drug use. She got more therapy from a reputable therapist. She undertook career training. Eventually, with the help of a housing counselor, she rented a nice apartment, even if it was on the third floor of a building that had no elevator. And she conceived another child by the same companion who fathered the child in foster care.

Months of weekly tests showed that Mother consistently was alcohol and drug free. She demonstrated a pattern of responsible living. A highly respected psychologist issued a parenting evaluation that reported Mother was a changed person who was coping with life and was capable of parenting her daughter. But the child protection worker held her ground. Mother could not have custody of her daughter.

The child protection worker vainly tried to persuade Mother to give up her daughter. The foster parents, the child protection worker told Mother, lived in a very nice home in Plymouth, could raise the child in comfort and provide her with luxuries, and even give her a college education. Wasn't that better than living in poverty? Mother was not persuaded.

Hennepin County withdrew all its support services and told Mother she was on her own. Mother still did not quit or relapse. She fought on.

As trial drew near, the child protection worker and Assistant Hennepin County attorney tried again. They produced a report from a county laboratory that Mother, who faithfully took drug detection tests at the laboratory twice a week as required, had a trace of illegal drugs in her blood. But Mother, who also had faithfully taken drug detection tests at a private agency, disputed the report.

Now desperate, the child protection worker made an offer. If Mother would agree to give up her daughter for adoption by the foster parents, she could keep her soon-to-be born child. Otherwise, the child protection worker threatened, she would take that child at birth.

Mother won the battle over her unborn child. She was allowed to take her new son home. In February 2004, Hennepin County agreed to reunite Mother and her daughter. For more than one-and-one-half months, Mother cared for her two children. But Hennepin County was not finished. Acting on false charges against her, Hennepin County took her two children from her custody and placed them with the foster parents who wanted to adopt her daughter.

The county filed another petition to continue their effort to terminate Mother's parental rights to her children. Another trial – the fourth was held. The judge has not yet issued his decision.

Additional Information and Comment

Mother's obstinate refusal to see the light angered the child protection worker and assistant county attorney. Mother would not listen to them or do as they directed. They see themselves as trained professionals who know what was best for Mother and her children.

As everyone knows, the child protection worker, assistant county attorney and Guardian Ad Litem reasoned to themselves, they were good people who were trying to help Mother and her children. Mother should know and respect that. That was especially applicable to Mother's lawyer. He was hurting Mother and her child by waging a futile battle against Hennepin County. If he really wanted to help Mother, they told him, he should persuade her to quit wasting everyone's time. In return, they proposed, they would let Mother visit her children periodically.

All their friendly persuasion failed to work. Mother and her lawyer would not give up. The child protection worker, assistant county attorney, with the support of the Guardian Ad Litem, the Guardian Ad Litem's lawyer, and the foster parents of Mother's child, took off the gloves. In front of Judge Myron S. Greenberg, the assistant county attorney made an oral motion the very day that Mother turned down the county's then latest entreaty.

They asked Judge Greenberg for approval to stop all county services for Mother: no more tests for alcohol and drug usage so Mother could not prove she was free of substance abuse; no more visits with her daughter; no more transportation services; no more efforts by Hennepin County to do what the law required – help Mother reunite with her child. The assistant county attorney told Judge Greenberg it was not necessary to wait for trial. He could take the county's word for it that Mother had no case.

The assistant county attorney did not give Mother's lawyer any notice of her motion. Under court rules, before a judge can rule on a party's motion, the party making the motion must send the motion being made in writing to the other party or parties. This must be done a specific number of days in advance, usually 14 days. This gives the party receiving the motion time to prepare a reply and send it to the judge before the hearing. The assistant county attorney did not bother to do that.

She made the motion orally on the spot. Judge Greenberg refused the request of Mother's lawyer for a written motion by the county, a statement of the reasons for its request, and a reasonable opportunity to prepare and submit a response. Judge Greenberg ruled on the spot – motion granted.

Hennepin County could not understand Mother's continued refusal to quit in the face of overwhelming odds. She did not seem to understand that when Hennepin County speaks, she must listen.

Then the county got a break, or so it thought. It received a report from a unit of the Hennepin County Medical Center that the result of a drug detection test showed a trace of an illegal substance. It was barely enough to constitute drug abuse. Now, the child protection worker and assistant county attorney had Mother. A trial was not even necessary. Mother should quit, they told the new judge and Mother's lawyer.

Mother pointed out that her actions on the day of the alleged drug use were inconsistent with drug abuse. That very day she had visited her daughter under the child protection worker's supervision. The child protection worker did not detect anything amiss. Earlier the same day, Mother had been with a services provider who helped her purchase items for her new apartment. He had not observed anything unusual.

Even more significant, Mother pointed out, is that a drug addict cannot stop after a little bit of the drug. The addict's system will not permit that. An addict's craving for more of the substance after he or she consumes a small quantity is irresistible. That meant the report the county was relying on was contrary to reality.

Rather than give Mother the benefit of the doubt and conduct a further investigation into the validity of the report, the child protection worker and assistant county attorney accepted it at face value. Their mission was not to be fair or reasonable; it was to take Mother's children from her and place them with someone else.

Insanity in Wonderland

Kathleen Gearin, Ramsey County Judge
Annemarie Suchta, Ramsey County Family Court Officer
Minnesota Appeals Court Judges Bruce Willis,
Robert H. Schumacher, G. Barry Anderson
Minnesota Supreme Court Appeal denied by Justice Alan Page

Case Summary

A couple in their late 20s were the parents of two children, a girl, 8, and a boy, 10. The children's maternal grandmother, who had abused the children's mother when she was a child in her home, wanted custody of her grandchildren. She made false charges that her daughter and son-in-law had abused their children and asked Ramsey County Child Protection to investigate. Based on these charges, she persuaded a judge to give her temporary custody of the children.

Ramsey County Child Protection started a CHIPS proceeding, which is heard in juvenile court. There never was an evidentiary hearing in this proceeding and no finding of any child abuse.

The grandmother started and for several years pursued a family court proceeding by filing a petition in which she asked that custody of the children be transferred to her. As part of the proceedings in a family court case, the judge appointed a Family Court Officer to investigate and submit a report. The judge dismissed the juvenile court case. This ended the participation of the child protection workers.

Dismissing the juvenile court case had another consequence. It is required in juvenile court proceedings that child protection workers prepare a case plan and do everything possible to keep a family together. That was not done in this case because that rule does not apply in family court proceedings.

The Family Court Officer investigated. In her report, she repeated the grandmother's charges, which were never verified in any earlier court proceeding, and recommended that custody of the children be permanently transferred to their grandmother. She disclosed her recommendation to the children's parents in a telephone conversation the week before the custody trial. When they protested and said they would hire a lawyer to fight against the recommendation, she told them a lawyer would do them no good in court.

Judge Gearin gave the parents only four days notice of the trial that cost them custody of their children. Two business days before the trial, the parents got the Family Court Officer's report and recommendation.

When the trial began, Judge Gearin asked the parents if they had a lawyer. They said no. Judge Gearin did not ask if they wanted a lawyer. In later proceedings, she ruled that there was no requirement to provide a lawyer for them if they were too poor to pay for one even if custody of their children was at stake.

If the case had been continued in juvenile court, a lawyer would have been appointed to fight for the parents. A law requires this in juvenile court cases, but not in a family court case. Both the juvenile court and family courts are in the same building in Ramsey County and its judges hear both types of cases.

The children's parents tried to be their own lawyers at trial, but they did not know what they were doing. They did not know the procedures, how to ask questions, what questions to ask, what the law was, or how to prove their case.

Judge Gearin awarded permanent custody of the children to their maternal grandmother and stubbornly refused to change her mind even after she was given a psychologist's report that, while she was in her grandmother's custody, the girl regressed to the state of an 18-month-old infant and had been sexually abused.

Additional Information and Comment

The grandmother had never liked her son-in-law and did not get along with her daughter. They were not raising her grandchildren like she wanted them to. The charges she made of child abuse resulted in a CHIPS (Child In Need of Protection) proceeding in juvenile court, but not in transfer of custody of the children to her as she wanted. She hired an attorney and started a family court proceeding in which she asked for custody of the children. An Assistant Ramsey County Attorney persuaded the judge to dismiss the juvenile court proceeding.

The children's parents had no money to pay a lawyer to represent them. However, after they learned of the family court officer's recommendation, they decided they would borrow what they needed to get a lawyer. They decided against that after the family court officer told them it would do them no good in court so they tried to represent themselves.

Judge Gearin allowed the trial to go forward even though it was obvious the children's parents did not know what they were doing and could not defend themselves. Here are examples of how the children's mother conducted the case:

> [Concerning the Guardian Ad Litem's report]
>
> > The Judge: All right. What about the parents? Mr. and Ms. [parents' last name], what's your position on this?
> >
> > [Mother]: I disagree with it. I've had these kids since the day they were born, especially my daughter. I've taken care of her. I mean, I –"
>
> [Mother's examination of the Guardian Ad Litem]
>
> > [Mother]: Okay. I don't know where to begin.
> >
> > The Judge: Okay.
> >
> > By [Mother]:
> >
> > Q: I don't know – March 1st was an incident that I had concern for you. How did you get to know what

happened that day?

A. I – I don't know what you're referring to.

Q: Where my daughter had supposedly put – fell down on the stairs. Did you – how did you come up with this?

A. Can you tell me which page you're referring to?

The Judge: Page four.

[Mother]: Page four.

The Judge: It says, March 1st she notes that [name of daughter] supposedly fell down stairs, bit her – half her tongue off. [Daughter] went to school the next day only to go to the hospital again because her mouth was still bleeding and the nurse said she threw up a pool of blood.

[Mother]: That's it.

A. Okay. That is under the category of my interview that I had with [Grandmother], so this is information provided to me by [Grandmother].

The Judge: Okay. That's what she got. Within the context, that would be – if you read it, the whole page, that's what [Grandmother] told her.

[Mother]: And my understanding to you is, I told you this – I told you what happened that day, too, supposedly, but it didn't get in the documents. My mom has no knowledge what happened that day.

The Judge: Okay, that's an argument. That's an argument.

[Mother]: Okay. Refer to, because –

The Judge: Right.

[Mother] – the statement that you put in there from my mom is incorrect. I mean, I'm the one.

The Judge: No. No. No. No. No. No. What she put in is what your mother told her. It's correct that that's what your mother told her.

[Mother]: Okay.

The Judge: She didn't put it in as that's how it happened.

[Mother]: Okay. My statement – excuse me, my statement is incorrect. I was there when it happened. She did not fall and hit a chair. She fell down the stairs and that's what I told you. So my statement on this is incorrect on how it was.

[Mother's examination of a witness for the parents]

[Mother]: Well, this is [Daughter's] Godfather, so she's – he's been around since [Daughter]'s been newborn and since [Son]'s been little.

So go ahead, I don't know what you want to tell her.

The Judge: Did you ever see anything at either house that concerns you with regards to the children?

The Witness: No.

The Judge: Pardon?

The Witness: They're doing fine.

By [Mother]:

Q. I don't know, the last incident that supposedly she fell on the ice, did she not fall on the ice, did she not fall on the ice? You were there, I wasn't.

A. I and [children's father] were both there and it was a narrow path and she slipped on the ice and she went down head first into the ice. It was a pure accident.

The Judge: All right.

[Mother]: I don't know what else to ask.

The Judge: Pardon?

[Mother]: I don't know what else to ask. He's been around a long time. I don't know. This was his best friend. And then when me and him met, then we just kind of all went together, so – I mean, he's been there since I've had both the kids, but –

[Mother's self-testimony]

The Witness: I don't know where to begin. I don't know.

I don't know. There's a lot of different accusations in the report that I don't approve of.

The Judge: In the past, however, [Parents] requested the children had lived with [Grandmother] during child protection involvement. During such times the children lived with [Grandmother] several weeks to several months.

Are you saying that's not true?

> The Witness: Nope. They lived with her one time this past year for two weeks, both of them. That's the only –
>
> The Witness: Well, there's a lot of different things in here. I don't know how to justify it. But I'd just like to say, since I've had my kids I've gone through a lot. You know, I'm not saying I'm perfect by no means. I mean, my mom and dad beat the hell out of each other and that was okay, you know, so – they didn't mentally abuse us, but they did each other and we witnessed a lot of this. My husband's family's the same way. And you'll – I got to say with this case is I've done a lot of changes. I've grown up a lot since I've had my daughter.
>
> I don't know what to say. I've done a lot of stuff with these two kids and I can't see losing my kids because she's trying to take them away from me.

After they lost the trial and their children, the parents retained a lawyer to get them back. The lawyer asked Judge Gearin to grant the parents a new trial. He argued that the family court officer had misled the parents when she told them that a lawyer would do them no good. He also argued that the trial was not fair to the parents or their children because the parents were not capable of trying a case in court.

Judge Gearin refused to order a new trial. She chose to believe the family court officer's testimony that she did not remember telling the parents that a lawyer would do them no good. As to the argument that the parents should have been represented by a lawyer, Judge Gearin said that is not essential in family court proceedings. If the parents wanted a lawyer, it was their responsibility to get one.

Judge Gearin did not bother to comment on the lack of adequate notice of trial in accordance with the rules of procedure, or her failure to inform the parents that they would be given time to get a lawyer if they wanted one. As far as Judge Gearin was concerned, her mind and the case were closed. The grandmother had been given permanent custody. What was in the best interests of the children was no longer relevant.

The children had serious emotional problems while they were living with their grandmother. They saw counselors regularly. The counselor for the boy told his parents that he should be in their custody, that conditions at his grandmother's home were hurting him. But the psychologist, an employee of the Wilder Foundation that gets millions of dollars of business from Ramsey County, refused to provide a report or recommendation to the judge, or get involved in trying to help get a change of custody. The Wilder Foundation would not let him.

Nor did it matter to Judge Gearin that the boy's health was deteriorating at his grandmother's home. That was likely due to the heavy use of tobacco at his grandmother's home, which resulted in respiratory problems.

Even the report of the girl's regression to the state of an 18-month-old infant and sexual abuse of her failed to move Judge Gearin. She ordered an investigation, but dropped the matter because a report was never submitted to her.

The Minnesota Court of Appeals, Judges Bruce Willis, Robert H. Schumacher, and G. Barry Anderson, denied the parents' appeal. They did not care that the parents did not have and could not afford a lawyer at the trial over the custody of their children, could not represent themselves effectively, and permanently lost custody of their children. They said the parents should have asked for a "continuance." The Supreme Court of Minnesota also denied the parents' appeal. They did not give a reason for doing so.

THE SUSPICIOUS TRUNK LOCK

Russell Platzek, Falcon Heights Prosecutor

Case Summary

Just after midnight on a Thursday night, police of the City of Falcon Heights turned on their flashing lights and stopped an automobile. Falcon Heights is an almost all-white suburb of St. Paul, Minnesota. Three young black men sat in the car.

In their report, the officers wrote that they stopped the automobile because it had a "suspicious trunk lock." In fact, the automobile, which was more than 20 years old, had no trunk lock. It had been removed, "punched out," apparently because there was no key to the trunk lock. To open the trunk, a person had to stick a finger in the hole and lift the latch.

One of the occupants of the car was charged with probation violation. There was a warrant for his arrest because he had not reported to his probation officer as often as required. He hired a lawyer who argued that the stop was made because of racial profiling.

The court ruled that the police stop violated the United States Constitution because a suspicious trunk lock is not probable cause for stopping and searching an automobile. Although he won, the cleared defendant could not recover any of the hundreds of dollars he paid his lawyer. The city prosecutor was fully paid for his work in defending the illegal act of the Falcon Heights police. The officers who made the illegal stop were never penalized or punished.

Additional Information and Comment

In a memorandum to Judge M. Michael Monohan, Russell Platzek, City of Falcon Heights Prosecutor, made this argument:

ISSUE

(1) Whether the officer had a reasonable, articulable suspicion justifying the stop of the motor vehicle in which Defendant was a passenger.

. . . . .

A. THE ARRESTING OFFICER HAD REASONABLE ARTICULABLE SUSPICION TO STOP THE SUBJECT MOTOR VEHICLE

"In order to stop a person or vehicle, an officer must be able to point to 'specific and articulable facts which, together with reasonable inferences from those facts, reasonably warrant the intrusion of a citizen's personal security.' State v. Encholm, 290 N.W.2d 780, 783 (Minn. 1980). The quantum of facts necessary to justify such a stop is minimal; investigatory stops have been upheld where the basis for the stop was the observation of expired license plates (Pennsylvania v. Mimms, 434 U.S.106 (1977)), of a beer can on the vehicle's roof (United States v. Parham, 458 F.2d 438 (8th Cir. 1972)), of defective signals State v. Curtis. 190 N.W.2d 631 (1971)), of a stopped car with its driver staring out in a stupor (State v. Hodgman, 257 N.W.2d 313 (Minn.1977)), of a car with its license plate attached by baling wire (State v. Barber, 241 N.W.2d 476 (Minn. 1976)), of slow, erratic driving with the possibility of a curfew violation (State v. Wicklund, 205 N.W.2d 509 (Minn.1973)), or of furtive actions or flight (City of St. Paul v. Vaunhn, 237 N.W.2d 365

(1975)). An officer's suspicion need not be correct in order to be a reasonable basis for a stop. Id.

"To explain the standard applied to the basis for stops, the Minnesota Supreme Court has quoted, approvingly, from People v. Ingle, 36 N.Y.2d 413, 420, 369 N.Y.S.2d 67, 74, 330 N.E.2d 39, 44 (1975):.

"It should be emphasized that the factual basis required to support a stop for a 'routine traffic check' is minimal. An actual violation of the Vehicle and Traffic Law need not be detectable. For example, an automobile in a general state of dilapidation might properly arouse suspicion of equipment violations. All that is required is that the stop be not the product of mere whim, caprice, or idle curiosity. It is enough if the stop is based upon 'specific and articulable facts which, taken together with rational inferences from those facts, reasonably warrant (the) intrusion.'" (italics added.) Barber, 241 N.W.2d at 477.

"Recently, the Minnesota Supreme Court has held that a stop based on a broken side window, covered with plastic, was not based on 'reasonable articulable suspicion.' State v. Britton, 604 N.W.2d 84 (Minn. 2000). In that case, the Court observed that broken car windows are a 'fact of urban life.' Id. at 88. Car windows, wrote the Court, can be broken 'by accident or ... by an owner who locked his keys in the vehicle.' Id. While recognizing that 'wholly lawful conduct might justify the suspicion that criminal activity is afoot' (Id. at 89), the Court observed that any car with a broken window may be stopped under the State's theory. Id. The Court also indicated that it did not consider this decision to overrule the Barber decision (regarding the license plate attached by wire.)

"The instant case is easily distinguishable from Britton. The Minnesota Supreme Court in Britton was clearly concerned about the nature of the irregularity observed, which admitted of common, innocent reasons for broken auto windows. The Court was concerned about the high likelihood of police stopping innocent drivers whose side windows had been broken accidentally, or by owners who had locked their keys inside the vehicle. These concerns are not present when the police stop a vehicle with a punched out trunk lock. The probability of a trunk lock being accidentally punched out is nil; similarly, the possibility of a trunk lock being punched out by an owner who is locked out of the vehicle is extremely remote. A vehicle's owner would break a window to enter a locked vehicle, not the trunk.

"This stop, based on the observation of the punched out trunk lock, offers significantly stronger indicia of criminal activity and is much less likely to result in the stopping of innocent drivers. As such, it satisfies the minimal standard for reasonable articulable suspicion."

Judge Monohan rejected Mr. Platzek's argument. He informed Mr. Platzek that he was wrong. In his decision, Judge Monohan wrote:

"Law.

"A stop is lawful if it is 'based upon reasonable and articulable suspicion of ongoing criminal activity.' State v. Britton, 604 N.W. 2d 84, 89 (Minn.2000). Police are allowed to conduct limited stops to investigate suspected criminal activity if they can 'point to specific and articulable facts which, taken together with rational inferences from those facts, reasonably warrant that intrusion.' Terry v. Ohio 392 U.S. 1 (1968). An investigatory stop must be justified by some objective manifestation that the person stopped is, or is about to be, engaged in criminal activity, United States v. Cortez, 449 U.S. 411, 417 (1981), and the officer must be able to point to something objectively supporting that suspicion. Britton, 604 N.W. 2d at 87. In making this determination, the courts review the events surrounding the stop and consider the totality of the circumstances in determining whether the police had a reasonable basis for the stop. State v. Victorsen, 2001 WL 410380 (Minn.App. 2001).

"Decision.

"Here, the basis for the stop was the lack of a trunk lock and the officer's conclusion that it looked suspicious. The officer did not articulate why it looked suspicious. The State argues that, based on the officer's training and experience, he could reasonably believe that the lack of a trunk lock pointed to the possibility of a stolen vehicle. But, the State introduced no evidence supporting this speculation. Given that lack of evidence, the State has not met its burden of establishing that the stop was made for the purpose of investigating possible criminal activity."

The Cursed Home

David M. Duffy, Hennepin County Judge
Citizens State Bank of Gaylord, Minnesota

Case Summary

A Family (Mother, Father, four children) who moved from another state to Minnesota, went looking for a home. They found one in the Minneapolis, Minnesota area that the estate of a deceased woman had put up for sale. The woman who had occupied the home had been an avid collector of African artifacts.

People who lived nearby spoke of strange goings on in the home. The home was filled with strange objects – wildly painted statues of animal-like figures with human parts, mystical paintings, writings in incomprehensible languages, twisted shapes having no recognizable pattern, and bizarre items of clothing. It was said that some of these objects came with a curse. It also was said that the walls of the home had secrets. But Mother and Father were God-fearing people who were very religious. They did not believe in curses.

The deceased woman's son (Son) was the representative of the estate and acted on its behalf. He met with Mother and Father and they agreed on a price and all the terms of sale of the home. He told Mother and Father that a bank, the Citizens State Bank of Gaylord, Minnesota (Citizens Bank), had a mortgage on the home but that he had conferred with the bank and it had approved the sale of the home at the agreed upon price.

Normally when people buy a home, the buyers and sellers sign a purchase agreement. This is because the law requires that an agreement to buy or sell a home or land (called "real property") must be in writing. Mother and Father prepared a purchase agreement, signed it, and sent it to Son. He responded that he could not sign it. He said there were some title problems that had to be taken care of, but that they would be fixed soon.

Father told Son that the period of temporary housing provided to Father by his new employer had expired. For this reason, Family would have to look for another home if they could not move in right away. Son agreed to a "move in" agreement. It stated that Family could move in immediately while action was being taken to complete the purchase agreement. A sentence in the move-in agreement said that it was an amendment to the purchase agreement Mother and Father had signed. Son signed the move-in agreement.

Family moved in. They spent thousands of dollars to clean and fix up the home. A large number of friends and relatives helped them. Together, they added more than $20,000 value to the home.

Thirteen days after Family moved into the home, Son sent Family a letter in which he demanded that they move out within ten days. When Family rejected this demand and demanded instead that Son proceed with the sale he had agreed to, Son started an unlawful detainer action to have the sheriff throw them out of the home. Son told Family he wanted more money than he had agreed to accept for the home.

What Son had not told Family is that all the money Family had agreed to pay for the home would go to Citizens Bank. It turns out Son was a figurehead for Citizens Bank. Although it had approved the sale and the sale price, Citizens Bank wanted more money for the home than it and Son had agreed to.

Family fought back in court. They argued that the parties had a written agreement that contained all the terms for the sale of the home to Family. Bank hired two large Minneapolis law firms to fight Family. Minneapolis Judge David M. Duffy ruled against Family. In his decision he said that neither Son nor Citizens Bank had been obligated to clear up the title problems, as they had promised to do and which could have been done in about 90 days.

He ruled that refusing to honor the sales agreement unless Family agreed to pay more money was legal. He did not see any fraud on the part of Son and Citizens Bank in allowing Family to move in and greatly improve the home before telling them 13 days later to pay more money for the home or move out.

Judge Duffy said the purchase agreement was unenforceable even though the move-in agreement, which was signed by both Son and Family, specifically said it was an amendment to the purchase agreement signed by Family. Judge Duffy said it was irrelevant. He could not see the connection.

Family had to move out of the home and find another home. They lost all of the thousands of dollars they had spent to fix and improve the home, and the value of their work and the work of their friends, as well as thousands of dollars they spent for lawyer fees.

Additional Information and Comment

There are two general categories of contracts: written and oral. Both are equally valid and, with exceptions, enforceable, although an oral contract can be far more difficult to prove than a written one.

For some kinds of transactions, a law referred to as the statute of frauds requires that a contract be in writing. The chief characteristic of a statute of frauds is a provision that no claim can be enforced or lawsuit maintained unless there is a written note or memorandum signed by the person against whom the claim is made. The object of a statute of frauds is to close the door to numerous possible frauds and perjuries. Originally, the name of this kind of statute was statute of frauds and perjuries.

A contract for the purchase of a home or land is subject to a statute of frauds. In Minnesota, the statute of frauds for a contract to buy a home or land is Minnesota Statutes § 513.05. It states:

> 513.05. Leases; contracts for sale of lands
>
> Every contract for the leasing for a longer period than one year or for the sale of any lands, or any interest in lands, shall be void unless the contract, or some note or memorandum thereof, expressing the consideration, is in writing and subscribed by the party by whom the lease or sale is to be made, or by the party's lawful agent thereunto authorized in writ-

> ing; and no such contract when made by an agent shall be entitled to record unless the authority of such agent be also recorded.

Although a contract for the purchase of a home or land must be in writing, there is no particular form. The law is very lenient in this respect. A simple note or memorandum satisfies the statute of frauds as long as the statute's requirements are met: (1) what is being sold must be positively identified; (2) the price, called consideration, must be specified; and (3) the writing must be signed by the person who is making the sale or leasing the property.

The note or memorandum can be made up of more than one writing if their connection is clear without the need for oral testimony. For example, a note would satisfy the statute of frauds if it said, "I, John Jones, agree to sell my home at 1234 Jensen Way, Somewhere, Minnesota, the legal description of which is: lot 3, block 3, Happy Way Estates, Dakota County, Minnesota, to Steve Smith for the price quoted in my letter dated July 4, 2004 to Steve Smith," and the note or memorandum was signed by John Jones.

Of course, it is preferable to be much more thorough in documenting a transaction as important as buying and selling a home. That is why many pre-prepared forms are used in real estate transactions. One of these forms is called a purchase agreement. It is the form typically used to document an agreement by a buyer to buy a home from a seller.

The essential facts in the case of "The Cursed Home" are simple. On behalf of his mother's estate, Son agreed to sell her former home to Family for $142,000. Son, with the knowledge and approval of Citizens Bank, which had a mortgage on the home, informed Family that there were some title problems, but also assured Family that these problems would be resolved and the sale would proceed.

Because Family, who had moved to Minnesota from Colorado, had exhausted the temporary housing provided by Father's new employer, they informed Son and Citizens Bank that they had to complete the sale/purchase quickly or look for another home. Son and Citizens Bank agreed that the Family could move into the home while title problems were cleared, and Citizens Bank even provided funds so that Family could enter and inspect the home.

Family moved in and, as they had informed Son and Citizens Bank in writing, made significant improvements to the home to make it livable. Thirteen days after they moved in, Citizens Bank and Son decided to terminate the move-in agreement and ordered them to leave the home within seven days. To enforce their decision, Son, with the knowledge of Citizens Bank, brought an unlawful detainer action against Family. Son then sought a higher price as a condition of not proceeding with the unlawful detainer action.

Citizens Bank retained two large Minneapolis law firms to represent it, perhaps thinking this would overwhelm the young family and their one-person law firm. Family refused to buckle. They asked for a trial. The unlawful detainer case was assigned to Judge Allen L. Oleisky.

Before the trial, Son moved for summary judgment in the estate's favor. When the facts in a litigation are clear and are not disputed, a court can immediately issue a judgment based on those facts. When there are genuinely disputed facts, a court cannot grant summary judgment. It must receive and consider testimony and evidence to establish the facts before it can make a ruling.

Son argued that there were no disputed facts. There was no signed purchase agreement, he said, and without a signed purchase agreement Family had no right to stay in the home. The move-in agreement gave him the right, Son said, to terminate it if there was not going to be a purchase agreement.

Family argued that there were many disputed facts. One was whether or not there was a purchase agreement. Son had signed the move-in agreement which stated that it was part of the purchase agreement – it was an amendment to the purchase agreement. From the purchase agreement and the move-in agreement a person could easily establish all the terms of sale. In addition, Family told Judge Oleisky, there were many facts that indicated misrepresentation, fraud and inequitable dealing.

Judge Oleisky denied Son's motion for summary judgment. In his opinion he wrote:

> "The [Family] have brought an action in Hennepin County District Court, File No. CT-00-002561, seeking specific performance of the purchase agreement

> that they claim existed between the Estate and themselves. In that action, the presiding court will necessarily have to resolve a number of the issues that are also present in the Estate's unlawful detainer action. For instance, that court will have to determine if a purchase agreement existed between the parties as the [Family] claimed it did. If that court finds that a purchase agreement did exist and determines that specific performance is a proper remedy, then the sale of the Property to the [Family] will proceed. It is also possible that that court will find that equity demands that the sale proceed even if a purchase agreement did not exist."

After the decision in the unlawful detainer action, Son turned matters over to Citizens Bank because, he said, the estate had no financial interest in the outcome. Citizens Bank began negotiating directly with Family. It repeatedly told Family they would have to pay substantially more for the home than the originally agreed upon price. Family repeatedly told Citizens Bank it could not pay the additional tens of thousands of dollars it demanded even if Family was willing to do so.

Family pushed to get to trial in the case they had started to get specific performance – a court order directing Son and Citizens Bank to proceed with the original sale. Family felt confident that a jury would quickly see through Son's and Citizens Bank's deceit.

Citizens Bank did not want a jury trial. They instructed their lawyers to move for summary judgment before Judge Duffy who was the judge in the Family's specific performance lawsuit.

Judge Duffy granted summary judgment in favor of Citizens Bank and ordered Family to move out of the home in a few days. He said there were no disputed facts. He distinguished the conclusion he reached from that reached by Judge Oleisky as follows:

> "The reasons Summary Judgment was denied at that time were that:
>
> "1. The UD action would determine only present

possessory rights and would not bar subsequent actions involving title or equitable rights of the parties (See, July 18, 2000 Order of Judge Oleisky) and,

"2. The [Family's] action was pending before Judge Duffy and then Judge Duffy later found a purchase agreement did exist, [Family] would then have to move back into the Property after having been ordered to leave it. id., at 3."

It is obvious, of course, that the facts before Judge Oleisky that he found to be disputed were the very same facts before Judge Duffy.

Judge Oleisky is one of the few honest judges in Hennepin County. Judge Duffy is dishonest. His dishonesty besmirches the reputation of every judge in Minnesota. Good judges are hurting Minnesota and themselves by tolerating judges like Judge Duffy.

Other Horror Case Digests

Below are very brief digests of other horror cases. In the future, they will be summarized in greater detail in our next book or in our website at: www.mncourtreform.org.

The Family Room Floor

Ann Leslie Alton, Hennepin County Judge

A housewife convinced Judge Alton that she should not have to pay anything for a concrete floor installed by a concrete contractor and was entitled to collect over $10,000 from the contractor. She told Judge Alton that she always planned to have a bare concrete floor in her over $300,000 home so her children could come in the patio door without dirtying the carpet. The concrete floor was not as smooth as she wanted and she convinced Judge Alton the floor would be replaced – in the future.

The Slippery Verdict

Michael F. Fetsch, Ramsey County Judge

A jury found that a trucking company defrauded a truck driver by misrepresenting the condition of a truck it sold to the driver and awarded the driver damages to compensate him for his losses. Judge

Fetsch threw the verdict out and made the truck driver go through another expensive jury trial because he didn't agree with the way the driver was going to report the damages awarded him in his income tax returns.

THE CABINETMAKER WHO WAS TOO PATIENT

Thomas R. Howe, Scott County Judge

A cabinetmaker who installed cabinets worth thousands of dollars in a model home constructed by a new home builder waited patiently for his money until the model was sold. As requested, the cabinetmaker re-worked the cabinets periodically to repair damage after walk-throughs. Even though he filed his mechanic's lien on time and met all legal requirements, Judge Howe denied the cabinetmaker any recovery because he owed the lawyer for the bank (who took over the home builders' interest) a favor.

THE UNBELIEVABLE MINISTER

Robert H. Lynn, Hennepin County Judge

Judge Lynn disregarded the sworn deposition testimony of an ordained minister who testified that when he was a construction worker before he became a minister he saw a painter and his helper perform painting services during a certain month, which made the painter's mechanic's lien timely and enforceable. Judge Lynn, who was mad at the painter's lawyer, didn't believe the minister or the painter and his helper and threw the case out without even a trial.

THE MEANINGLESS PROMISE

M. Michael Monohan, Ramsey County Judge
Mark D. Thompson, Deputy General Counsel, Metropolitan Council

A subcontract between a small concrete company and a company that was the general contractor for a public works project of the

Twin Cities Metropolitan Council stated that, by law, the general contractor was obligated to pay its subcontractors within ten days after the general contractor was paid by the Metropolitan Council. The concrete company asked the Metropolitan Council for help after the general contractor refused to pay for work performed by the concrete company, and accepted and paid for by the Metropolitan Council (the general contractor wanted a discount). Judge Monohan agreed with the Metropolitan Council that all the law required was to put the promise in its contracts; there was no obligation to enforce the promise.

JUDGE ROULETTE

Thomas M. Murphy, Dakota County Judge

Different judges can decide the same question differently as this case shows. Whether you win or lose does not always depend on what is right but who the judge is. In this case, a Plumber filed a mechanic's lien (a legal document that states a claim against real estate) to secure a claim for money due him. Plumber had installed plumbing fixtures in an expensive newly constructed home. Because of a mistake by a county clerk, the mechanic's lien stated the wrong legal description, but also stated the correct street address. Although a law says mistakes in a mechanic's lien should be ignored as long as you can identify the property, Judge Murphy told Plumber his mechanic's lien was no good and that he would rule for the other side if that side moved for judgment. The other side moved for judgment but the case went before a different judge. That judge said Judge Murphy was wrong and ruled against the other side. The case then went before a third judge who ruled in favor of Plumber. She said it was only fair that Plumber be paid for his labor and materials. It took three judges and three years and lots of lawyer time and court costs for a judge to arrive at that conclusion concerning a claim for $15,517.

Judge Obstinacy

Michael V. Sovis, Dakota County Judge

To get the $15,517 due him as described in the case before this one, Plumber had to appear in court many times – some because the judge he was in front of was unreasonable and obstinate. Both parties in the lawsuit filed claims against the other. Plumber's claim was called a "counterclaim" because it came after the other side filed a claim against Plumber. The claims of all the parties normally are considered in the same trial because they usually are closely connected. During the time leading up to trial, there were arguments between the parties concerning discovery – the process of getting information and documents from each other to prepare for trial. Plumber moved for an order directing the other side to answer his discovery requests in accordance with the rules so he could obtain evidence to support his counterclaim. Judge Sovis denied Plumber's motion and even denied him the right to have his counterclaim heard at trial. Judge Sovis gave no reason for his rulings and did not explain why he ignored a court rule that gave Plumber the right to discovery. In a later hearing, another judge reached the opposite result and ruled that the other side had to obey the rules and respond to Plumber's discovery requests. He also scheduled trial on Plumber's counterclaim. Because of Judge Sovis, there were two trials instead of one and Plumber had to wait months more and spend more for lawyers to have his counterclaim decided. Judge Sovis never explained why he disregarded court rules.

The Little Boys Who Hated Their Fathers

Joanne M. Smith, Ramsey County Judge

Their start in life was troubled. They had the same mother, but different fathers. Each father was a quadriplegic bound to a wheelchair. Mother was mentally retarded and unable to provide any care for her children. She discontinued all contact with their fathers. But the two little boys, ages four and six, had each other. And they had loving maternal grandparents who took them into their homes and parented them, even though grandmother had to quit work because it was too much for her. It was a warm home and the boys were normal and happy except for one problem: visitation with their fathers. Each father demanded that his son spend full weekends with him in his apartment as well as many holidays. This, after all, was their right, even if neither provided any monetary or other support for his son. Each boy hated spending time with his father and visitation greatly upset him. Their grandparents suggested visitation by both fathers in family settings such as picnics, trips to the zoo, a visit to a children's theater or museum, etc. A respected child psychologist who met extensively with both boys, and even the family court officer, recommended supervised visitation only in view of each father's circumstances in non-threatening settings. None of that was satisfactory to the fathers or Judge Smith. Even though it created a serious financial burden on the grandparents, and whether or not it hurt the boys or brightened their lives, she ordered separate visitation for each father including visitation at a children's safety center at a cost of $50 per session with the grandparents providing all transportation – a 50-mile round trip that, with visitation time, took four hours each time.

Part II

Major Problems

Do you think our courts and legal system have problems? If so, we would very much like to know what you think they are. With your permission, we may include your comments in our next book.

Send your comments:

By e-mail: dalenathan@usfamily.net

By mail:

Dale Nathan
PO Box 211284
Eagan, MN 55121

Chapter 1
Lack of Accountability

Unlike any other member of our society, a judge can intentionally and wrongfully hurt or damage a person, and not be liable for a cent in damages or suffer any other consequence. There is nothing you can do about it. No matter how unjust his decision, or how wrongfully he hurts you, there is no consequence to the judge as a result of an official act in a court proceeding.

JUDICIAL IMMUNITY

Under the rule of "judicial immunity," judges are protected against any liability for damages, or any liability at all for that matter, in cases within their jurisdiction. When you are before a judge in a case, and he has the jurisdiction (legal power) to make a ruling concerning you, he is not liable for anything he does to you, even if it is terribly wrong or even evil. Judges made up this rule to protect themselves. It was never passed by Congress or the Minnesota legislature, or any state legislature.

The rule is that a judge is never liable for damages for anything he does in court, even if the action is in bad faith, as long as he had jurisdiction – the power to make a ruling.[1]

Judicial immunity is based on the old, even ancient, proposition that the king (or queen) could do no wrong.[2] They were untouchable. Sometimes, they were considered divine. When judges took over decision-making power, they carried forward the invincibility enjoyed by kings and queens. However, the rationale changed.

No judge has claimed, as far as we know, that he or she is divine, although some judges appear to think he or she is omniscient. Rather, judges explain in decisions, they must be free from potential liability so they can make decisions fearlessly. They say it will compromise their independence to make the right decision if there is potential liability. To reach the independence judges say they need, cases explain, judges must be free to commit evil deeds, abuse people, act irresponsibly, conspire against those who appear before them, and, literally, do anything they want or choose to do to anyone who becomes subject to their judicial power.[3]

The doctrine of judicial immunity is not immutable. It can be changed. The Minnesota legislature has the power to abrogate judicial immunity if it chooses. It can change the law so that judges, prosecutors, and other public officials are accountable for their intentional wrongdoing.

A Wisconsin case shows that judicial immunity can be re-fashioned. In a Wisconsin court case, Candee v. Egan, 267 N.W. 2nd 890 (1978), a Wisconsin court ruled that under a Wisconsin law, Wisconsin Statutes Section 256.24, a judge can be "held personally liable to any party injured for any willful violation of the law in granting injunctions and appointing receivers, or for refusing to hear motions to dissolve injunctions and to discharge receivers." In its decision, the Wisconsin Supreme Court said:

> "Ordinarily a judge is immune from suit for damages, even when his acts are willful. [citations omitted] However, sec. 256.24 plainly abrogates this doctrine of immunity with respect to willful violation of the law in granting injunctions and in appointing receivers." (267 N.W. 2d at 898)

Judicial Immunity Lets Judges Hurt People Without Consequence

A relatively recent (1994) Michigan court case illustrates the extreme emotional damage a judge can inflict on people and still go unpunished because of judicial immunity. One of the plaintiffs in Cameron v. Seitz,[4] a single, divorced woman, began working for the defendant, a Michigan probate court judge, as his secretary. Before long, Seitz, married at the time, took a romantic interest in Cameron. He showered her with gifts, most of which she returned, paid for a trip by her and her son to Disney World, told her how much she meant to him, and hinted that he was thinking of divorcing his wife after the next election. Although he never made sexual advances towards her, he repeatedly suggested that she not remarry.

Her strenuous efforts to stave off Seitz's overtures were futile. Over Seitz's protests, Cameron dated her eventual husband, who was a youth counselor in the same probate system in which Seitz was a judge. When he learned about Cameron's new relationship, Seitz was furious. He left voice mail messages for her in one of which he said he "threw up" when he heard of her engagement. He sent her emotional notes one of which described "how crushed and hurt and devastated" he was when he was told about the engagement, and another in which he wrote that her engagement made him "really goddamn sick and disappointed – more than you can possibly know."

Seitz turned hostile toward Cameron's fiancée. He cited him for incompetence, complained to his supervisors, refused to recognize him in court, and rejected his recommendations. Cameron had had enough. She quit her job as Seitz's secretary and took a job in another county department at a pay cut of $8,000. She explained her reasons in a letter to Seitz in which she wrote:

> "I would like to indicate that I take exception to the statement on your tape that you took me from being a 'pregnant hill ape' and made me the 'sophisticated lady' that I am today. I am not and never have been a hill ape, and the lady I am today was created by me, and certainly not by yourself."

Cameron and her husband sued Seitz for violation of their civil rights. A jury found in their favor and awarded them $188,800 in damages. The trial court judge awarded the Camerons $72,000 for lawyer fees as allowed by the federal civil rights law.

A three-judge federal appeals court reversed. Seitz, they held, was immune from liability under the doctrine of judicial immunity. They threw out the jury award and reversed the order that reimbursed the Camerons for their lawyer's fees. The tens of thousands of dollars the Camerons paid their lawyers went for naught.

Because of judicial immunity, a judge can take your children away from you, put you in jail, lie about you, give your money away, take all your property intentionally for the purpose of destroying you, and get away with it. As long as it is part of a legitimate legal proceeding before the judge, he can do whatever he wants.

This rule is stated most clearly in a federal case known as Ashelman v. Pope,[5] where the court wrote: "Judges and those performing judge-like functions are absolutely immune from damage liability for acts performed in their official capacities. . . . Judicial immunity applies however erroneous the act may have been, and however injurious in its consequences it may have proved to the plaintiff. . . . Such immunity applies even if it leaves 'the genuinely wronged defendant without civil redress against a prosecutor whose malicious or dishonest action deprives him of liberty.' [citation omitted]" (793 F.2d at 1075)

Even "a conspiracy between judge and prosecutor to predetermine the outcome of a judicial proceeding, while clearly improper, nevertheless does not pierce the immunity extended to judges and prosecutors."

In a famous case, Stump v. Sparkman,[6] a judge wrongfully ordered that a mildly retarded 15-year-old girl be secretly sterilized. The judge told her that her appendix was being removed. Despite this outrageous deception, the U. S. Supreme Court decided the judge could not be held liable.

According to the Ashelman case, the reason judges must have total absolute immunity regardless of what they do is "to ensure independent and disinterested judicial ... decision-making." In reality, judges have made themselves dictators. They can do what they please without fear of paying for the damage or hurt they cause.

This obviously is not beneficial to our society. No one should have the power to hurt others intentionally or through gross negligence. As Lord Acton observed, power corrupts; absolute power corrupts absolutely. Charles Caleb Colton, the noted English epigrammatist, said, "Power will intoxicate the best hearts as wine the strongest heads. No man is wise enough, nor good enough to be trusted with unlimited power."

JUDGE IRRESPONSIBILITY

Because they are not accountable in damages or consequences

for what they do as a judge, judges are free to do as they please. As the horror cases illustrate, they can choose to be unjust. They can order the absurd, like awarding custody of a 12-year-old boy to a father who has sex with animals and who resides with the boy's brother who also has sex with animals.

If he is so inclined, a judge like Judge Van de North in the case of "The Jekyll and Hyde Mother" can find "grave and weighty" reasons why a mother is completely unfit to parent her three-year-old son while recognizing that she is properly parenting her six-month-old daughter.

Judges can be dense, in fact, very dense, like those involved in the case of "The Desperate Mother." One judge wanted her to produce witnesses to the physical abuse she suffered at the hands of her alcoholic husband. Because her husband did not beat her in front of witnesses and there were none, judges refused to give her any temporary help and approved a settlement that gave her husband all the parties' money and property and gave her a pittance for support for herself and her child.

The judges in that case could not fathom why she had a money problem simply because her student immigration status prevented her from working and supporting herself. Finally, the judge who granted the divorce decree decided that $100 per month was enough for her to support herself and her child the 40 percent of the time she had custody.

From the above, it is obvious that judges do not have to exercise common sense. A judge like Judge Clark in the case of "The Young Sex Perverts" can, as he chose to do, condone the racism of and conduct by a child protection worker that caused a family unimaginable grief and suffering and resulted in a sexual assault on and probable rape of a 12-year-old-girl. The judge also had the power to severely penalize the lawyer who represented the mother in that case because the lawyer spoke out against the obnoxious behavior he saw and disclosed it to the public.

Judges need not worry about their misconduct in court. They can issue a gag order and cover it up. No one will know. The public, who knows very little about judges anyway, will continue to be uninformed about what really happens in our courts.

Because they are immune from liability for damages or other

penalty for what they do in court, judges can, with disdain, destroy businesses, rob people of their money and property, and ruin the lives of defendants by convicting them of crimes they did not commit. A judge can find a defendant guilty out of spite, or because of race or religion, or nationality, and the most a defendant can hope for is a reversal of the conviction – after months or years of agony.

Loss of pay is not a concern for judges. They get their pay regardless of the quality of their decisions. Nor are they concerned that there will be bad publicity. The media does not report mundane cases however unjust in outcome – unless a star athlete or other dignitary is involved.

To justify the result a judge decides he wants, he can distort or twist or omit facts, or even lie as Judge Bruce Willis did in the case of "The Young Sex Perverts."

Loss of their job has not worried most incumbent judges – at least in the past. Generally, they are unopposed for re-election and have the advantage of being designated the incumbent if there is a challenge. Very few voters know anything about judges on the ballot seeking re-election. In general elections every other year, one-fourth to one-third of voters do not even bother to cast votes for judges in elections. Judges expect to be re-elected to their office until they retire, which they usually do well before an election so the governor can appoint a replacement.

Judges have no incentive to do the very best job they can of making just decisions other than their conscience. If they are dedicated to justice, it is voluntary.

Prosecutors and Government Officers Also Are Immune

Like judges, prosecutors are absolutely immune from liability or consequence based on their official acts. A prosecutor can charge a person with a crime with no evidence, and even out of spite, without worry. He can vigorously pursue an obviously meritless case and demand that the defendant plead guilty to some crime even when he knows the defendant is innocent of any wrongdoing. He can even conspire with the judge to wrongfully convict a person of a crime, and get off scot-free.

Like judges, prosecutors have no incentive to act responsibly toward defendants. In fact, the incentive is to get a conviction for something in every case as in the case of "The Suspicious Trunk Lock." That creates the impression of success and promotes re-election or reappointment.

Public employees such as child protection workers, family court officers, and guardians ad litem, and others also are immune from liability based on their official acts. A child protection worker like the one in the case of "The Infant Trade" can, without worry, make the outrageous demand that a mother give up her infant daughter as a condition of being allowed to keep her unborn baby. Regardless of the anxiety and suffering she causes, the child protection worker is untouchable. And if a judge dared to punish her or the agency, he risks incurring the wrath of the public employees' union who, unlike the public, has real clout.

Police officers can brutalize a 78-year-old man as in the case of "The Cops From Hell" and, as a practical matter, avoid any consequence. They know that judges do not believe defendants over police officers. And they know that their union will provide lawyers for their defense in the rare case when a defendant has or gets the resources to pursue legal action.

Like judges, prosecutors and government agency workers, police officers can act irresponsibly without penalty, although only a small percentage do.

Judges, prosecutors, government agency workers, and police officers have too much power. They need to be accountable for their actions like everyone else in the United States of America. This can be accomplished without impinging on judge independence. Chapter 11 in Part III proposes reforms that can achieve this.

Chapter 2
Judge Selection and Re-Election

Who can become a judge? The answer: only a lawyer can become a judge. Why? The Minnesota Supreme Court made this a rule of law based on its interpretation of the Minnesota Constitution.[7] The Minnesota Constitution requires that a judge be: "learned in the law."[8] According to the Minnesota Supreme Court, only lawyers are learned in the law.

There are two ways a lawyer can become a judge: by election or by appointment. The governor is the person who appoints a lawyer to be a judge. A lawyer can seek to be elected to the office of judge. A petition with the required number of signatures[9] must be filed with the Secretary of State and a fee must be paid. That is the easy part. The hard part is the campaign – almost always against an incumbent judge. It is well known that judges retaliate against a lawyer who challenges an incumbent and loses. Because of this, very few lawyers challenge incumbent judges.

Appointed Judges

Almost all Minnesota judges begin their career as a judge by appointment. Unlike the federal process, there is no requirement in Minnesota that an appointment to be a state court judge be confirmed. (A person nominated by the President to be a U.S. judge must be confirmed by the U.S. Senate.)

Until a few years ago, becoming a Minnesota state judge was a highly political process. This proved an observation by Judge Curtis Bok: "It has been said that a judge is a member of the bar who once knew a governor." That is not always true. Sometimes you have to know a legislator as well.

Governors often appoint individuals who support their campaigns, support legislation the governor wanted or are powers in the governor's party. That changed somewhat in 1990 when the Judicial Merit Selection law[10] became effective. It created a commission to review applications from lawyers who want to be appointed a judge. The commission also evaluates the candidates and sends a list to the governor of the individuals the commission believes are the best candidates for appointment. However, the governor is not required to appoint a candidate recommended by the commission. He can ignore the commission's recommendations and appoint whomever he wishes.

The commission is part of the governor's office. It consists of at-large members and members from each of the ten state judicial districts. Most of its members are appointed by the governor. The remaining members are appointed by the Minnesota Supreme Court.

A lawyer who wants to be considered by the commission must complete and submit an application to the commission. Then, a candidate typically gets as many friends and associates as he or she can to write to the commission on his or her behalf. In other words, he does everything he can to get the commission to include his name as one of the three individuals recommended to the governor.

No one can say for certain if it helps under the current process to be a member of the governor's party. However, Governor Perpich appointed mostly DFL judges and Governor Carlson appointed mostly GOP judges. Under the current system, it is clear that judges may not be selected on the basis of merit. They may be selected because of a political connection.

Selecting Judges by Election

Election of judges by voters as occasionally occurs in Minnesota is not an effective way of choosing people who most likely will make the best judges. Few voters have the time or expertise to evaluate candidates for judge. The little information that is provided, primarily in political advertisements financed largely by lawyers and law firms, is not reliable or properly researched.

Newspaper articles occasionally provide additional information about a candidate's qualifications, but the value of this information depends on the ability and biases of the reporter. Newspaper editorials that recommend a particular candidate are almost always based on answers to a questionnaire and a short interview of each candidate.

Candidates for judge do not campaign or present themselves to the voters like candidates for governor or the Minnesota House of Representatives or Minnesota Senate. Candidates for those offices seek out voters and make speeches to them. They tell voters what they stand for. Judges do not campaign in that manner. Until recently, candidates for judge could not even tell voters their positions on political issues. A rule of the Minnesota Supreme Court prohibited that.

In reality, Minnesota's voters do not select their judges. It is customary for incumbent judges to resign far enough in advance of an election to permit the governor to select his replacement. The governor and judges of Minnesota do not trust the voters to select judges.

Judge Re-election

The current system for re-electing (or retaining) judges is as deficient as the process for the initial selection of judges. Most voters know nothing about the incumbent judges whose names appear in a ballot. Still worse, in almost all cases the incumbent judge has no opponent. Such an election is a farce and a sham. Before voters can cast an informed and meaningful vote, they need to know the performance records of the judges who want to be re-elected.

Currently, such information is not available. The information that is available is very limited. It does not normally include information from interviews with a candidate for judge. Voters are not told what lawyers and people who appeared before these judges think about them. It does not include an analysis of the decisions the judges made. Voters are not told about decisions that were reversed by an appeals court. No report is made on the quality of each judge's decisions.

Lack of information and knowledge about incumbent judges who seek re-election probably are the reasons one-fourth to one-third of Minnesotans who vote in an election do not bother to vote for or against incumbent judges.

Re-election of judges is just as much of a sham in almost all states of the United States, although, as discussed in Chapter 13 in Part III, some states actually do circulate information to voters at election time on the performance of judges who are on the ballot. Veteran *Wall Street Journal* writer Max Boot called the judicial branch of government "the least accountable branch" of government in America in his book, *Out of Order: Arrogance, Corruption, and Incompetence on the Bench* (Basic Books, 1998). He gave this appraisal of judge elections:

> "The default position that most people adopt is simply to vote for the incumbents. Term limits proponents often bemoan the high re-election rate of congressmen; well, judges are voted out of office only slightly more often than Prince Rainier of Monaco, and their terms (often 10 to 15 years) rival that of the late, unlamented Romanian President Nicolae Ceausescu. To be exact, only one percent of judges who have faced retention elections have been removed by the electorate.
>
> "Obviously, voters don't do a great job of watching judges and judicial candidates. And who can blame them, when they have so many more important things to do, like eating, sleeping, and paying bills. So who oversees the third branch of government? Journalists occasionally take jurists to task, but the judges and their sympathizers in the legal community always scream that any outside criticism of a judge's ruling is tantamount to constitutional treason. Legislators also occasionally oversee the third branch of government, but, as you might imagine, a subject that doesn't grip their constituents doesn't hold much interest for most politicians.
>
> "Judges, then, are for the most part watched by . . . judges. Most states have some kind of judicial

> review commission, usually made up of judges, sometimes with lawyers and laymen also serving. Their proceedings are usually conducted in private, and the punishments they mete out are as rare as they are lenient. How could it be otherwise? Just imagine if the only check on butchers were other butchers, the only check on investment bankers other investment bankers. How much oversight would there be?"

Party Endorsement

Judge elections are not supposed to be connected with political parties. The rules require that they be nonpartisan. However, in 2000, some political parties endorsed some candidates for judge. All of the endorsed candidates lost.

Endorsement of candidates for judge by political parties is not appropriate or useful. It suggests that a candidate for judge will reflect the policies or initiatives of his party rather than fair and balanced interpretations and applications of the law. Voters might expect a DFL candidate to be a liberal big-spender who will make generous damages awards to clients of trial lawyers who heavily support the DFL party.

In contrast, voters might fear that a GOP endorsed candidate would be too tight-fisted or too favorable to big business. Simply put, neither politics nor political philosophy should be involved in judging.

Merit Selection of Judges

The process in Minnesota for selecting and retaining judges by election has become a sham. Voters are not really selecting judges or deciding if they should remain in office even though this is mandated by our constitution. A new process is needed.

United State Supreme Court Justice Sandra Day O'Connor recommended a process for selecting and retaining judges in a recent decision, Republican Party of Minnesota v. White.[11] She suggested selection of candidates for judge by a nonpartisan commission based solely on merit, and periodic retention elections limited solely to determining if a judge should remain in office.

For each judge vacancy, the commission submits a list of three nominees to the governor who must appoint one of those individuals to fill the vacant judge position. After a short period of service, the individual selected stands for election unopposed to determine if he or she should remain in office.

This system often is referred to as the Missouri Plan, which was the first state to adopt such a system. Systems like it are in effect in 15 states. It is described in Chapter 12 of this book as the system we should consider for Minnesota. Chapter 13 in Part III proposes a report card on judges who seek to remain in office so the voters have an informed basis for determining if a judge should be retained in office.

Chapter 3 Campaign Contributions for Judges

A Minnesota judge who wants to stay in office must run in an election at least once every six years. If there is no challenger, there is no need for campaign contributions. When the election is contested, that is, when someone challenges the incumbent judge, the judge needs to find a way to finance his or her campaign to avoid losing by default. A re-election campaign for a district court judge can cost $50,000 or more. The state-wide re-election campaigns for appeals court and Supreme Court judges can cost tens of thousands of dollars. There is no spending limit.

Money for Judge Elections

Typically, an incumbent judge facing a challenger creates a campaign finance committee just like candidates for executive and legislative offices. These committees hold fundraisers and solicit campaign contributions like those of other politicians running for office.

Campaign finance committees for judges raise as much money as they can. There is no limit on the amount they can raise. Nor is there any limit on the amount a law firm, lawyer or other person can contribute to a judge's re-election campaign.

The need to raise money to finance their election campaigns corrupts many politicians. Like other candidates who want to be elected to office, judges need campaign contributions. This need corrupts judges just as it corrupts other politicians.

Minnesota judges get over 80 percent of their campaign contributions from lawyers. Lawyers give judges campaign contributions for a reason. For most, the reason is to buy decisions favorable to them and their clients.

Judges need campaign contributions to win elections. To keep his cushy job with its power and prestige and fawning sycophants, a judge must be realistic and do what is necessary to get campaign contributions. He must sell decisions.

JUSTICE FOR SALE

Commentators including judges recognize this. They have said so in publications and programs such as The *Buying of the Bench;*[12]*Judicial Corruption Rampant*[13]*; Justice for Sale;*[14] *"On The Make: Campaign Funding and The Corrupting of the American Judiciary,"*[15] and *Campaign Contributions Corrupt Judicial Races.*[16]

United States Supreme Court Justice Sandra Day O'Connor is concerned about this problem. In the case of Republican Party of Minnesota v. White,[17] she noted the needs of judges for huge campaign contributions:

> "And campaigning for a judicial post today can require substantial funds. [citations – not included] [A study published in a law journal reported] in 2000, the 13 candidates in a partisan election for 5 seats on the Alabama Supreme Court spent an average of $1,092,076 on their campaigns).
>
> "[Another report stated] 'in 1995, one candidate for the Pennsylvania Supreme Court raised $1,848,142 in campaign funds, and that in 1986, $2,700,000 was spent on the race for Chief Justice of the Ohio Supreme Court.' . . . Yet relying on campaign donations may leave judges feeling indebted to certain parties or interest groups [citations not included]."

Justice O'Connor believes corruption of judges and the public's perception of a corrupt judiciary are the consequences of campaign finance through private contributions:

> "A study by the public interest group Texans for Public Justice found that 40 percent of the $9,200,000 in contributions of $100 or more raised by seven of nine Texan Supreme Court Justices for their 1994 and 1996 elections 'came from parties and lawyers with cases before the court or contributors closely linked to these parties.'
>
> "([A survey showed that] 76 percent of registered voters believe that campaign contributions influence judicial decisions). [Another survey showed] two-thirds of registered voters believe individuals and groups who give money to judicial candidates often receive favorable treatment."

Minnesota Supreme Court justices are no exception. They need large amounts of campaign contributions and they get them – over 80 percent from lawyers, many of whom appear before that court and another 10 percent from corporate moguls whose interests at times are before the justices. In 2000, the combined total spent by four Minnesota Supreme Court Justices to win re-election was $505,121.[18] Minnesota lawyers were not nearly as generous to those among them who challenged the incumbent justices. The combined total spent by the challengers (including their own money) was $23,583.

EFFECT ON JUDICIAL INTEGRITY

The buying of judge decisions, or the perception of that, is a major concern of many leaders of the legal community. An American Bar Association special task force called the problem major and recommended sharp limits on the amounts lawyers can give judges for their campaigns as well as full disclosure of such largess by lawyers and by the judges who accept it.[19]

The task force specifically condemned "pay-to-play" – the practice of lawyers contributing to the re-election campaigns of judges and other public officials and receiving lucrative appointments to perform services as trustees or members of a special commission. It strongly urged states, including Minnesota, to change the rules applicable to lawyers to prohibit the making of political contributions for the purpose of getting government work. Minnesota has not yet implemented any of the recommendations made by the ABA task force.

In a Public Broadcasting Station Frontline program entitled: "Justice for Sale,"[20] a media consultant revealed that many states have a system where elections for judges can be bought. Even some current judges call for campaign finance reform to limit money's influence in judicial races. The vast majority of respondents to a poll funded by the Hearst Corporation agreed "elected judges are influenced by having to raise campaign funds."

Judges routinely pretend they do not know who contributed to their re-election campaigns. But they do. In response to a question on whether judges were insulated from the fundraising process, a noted lobbyist for a major industry group said:[21]

> "Thin insulation, yes. The judge is not supposed to accept a check, not supposed to make the phone call, and, to my knowledge, they do not. Obviously, their campaign staffs are doing that. Do the judges know who the big donors are, or, the candidates know who the big donors are? Of course, everybody does. It's common knowledge as to who the big donors are and where the sources of funds are. Do they know after the fact who made the contributions? Of course they do. When PEG has made contributions, it's been acknowledged by the judicial candidate in a thank-you . . . ."

Law professor Kathryn Abrams described the corrupting effects of contributions to judge campaigns in a law review article:[22]

> "Using realist and post-realist conceptions of judging as a standpoint for assessment helps us to identify several factors that should raise concerns about the influence of judicial campaign contributions. First, the singularity, explicitness, and case-relatedness of the messages such contributions often com-

> municate distinguish them from the kind of complex, diffuse, non-case specific messages we have come to view as an acceptable consequence of judges' social formation or group-specific affiliations. Second, campaign contributions create in judges motives for action that are distinct from the socially shaped, yet largely internalized, normative visions through which judges seek to resolve the indeterminacies implicit in legal rules. Third, campaign contributions create pressures that cause judges to see their own interests as intertwined with those of a party in a case, rather than leading them to identify imaginatively with the positions of the parties. Finally, campaign contributions create mechanisms of direct control over members of the judiciary that move relations of representation with constituents forcefully in the direction of a legislative model."

The need of judges for campaign contributions can be greatly reduced and even eliminated. Adoption of a merit-based appointment process as proposed in Chapter 12 of Part III would eliminate election as a means of selecting new judges. Little, if any campaign funds would be needed if the re-election of judges is limited to determining whether or not a judge continues in office. If this were the case, there would be no challenger to run against. If election and/or re-election of judges continue, the reforms proposed in Chapter 14 of Part III for public funding of judge elections would end the campaign finance corruption now prevalent in Minnesota judge elections.

Chapter 4
$150 Gratuities (Gifts) for Judges

The judge who was about to preside over a trial struck the gavel on the sound block and said: "Before I begin this trial, I have an announcement to make. The lawyer for the defense paid me $15,000 to swing the case his way. The lawyer for the plaintiff paid me $10,000 to swing the case her way. In order to make this a fair trial, I am returning $5,000 to the defense."

A politician was on trial for political corruption. At the height of the trial, the prosecuting attorney bellowed from behind the prosecutor's table, "Isn't it true that you accepted a $5,000 bribe?"

The politician, who was on the witness stand, stared out the window as though he hadn't heard the question. Aware that the jury was listening intently, the prosecuting attorney repeated the question. The politician still did not respond.

Finally, the judge leaned over and said, "Sir, please answer the question."

"Oh," the startled politician said, "I thought he was talking to you."

Judges Can Accept $5,000 Gifts

In Minnesota, judges are not allowed to accept gifts of $5,000 in one lump sum – unless they report it to the Board on Judicial Standards. That makes such a gift legal. But Minnesota judges can accept as many gifts of $150 or less as they want without reporting them to anyone. This includes gifts of tickets to sports events, musical or theatrical events, use of a law firm's vacation lodge, expensive meals, and other favors commonly referred to as gratuities.

Minnesota's state court judges can accept gratuities of up to $150 in amount or value as many times per day as they want. There is no limit on the number of gratuities a person can give a judge or that a judge can accept. There is no law that prevents a judge from accepting a gratuity. If the gratuity is $150 or less, there is no requirement to report or tell anyone about it.

Unlike members of the state legislature and the executive branch of state government, it is legal for judges to take $150 gratuities. State law has nearly done away with the practice of lobbyists giving gifts to legislators and state executive personnel so that even a cheap lunch or cup of coffee for a legislator can put a lobbyist in jeopardy. However, judges made up a rule for themselves that allows them to accept gratuities and the Minnesota Supreme Court issued it as an official court order. The order is included in the "Code of Judicial Conduct." Canon 4, section 5, states that a judge can accept:

> "(h) any other gift, bequest, favor or loan only if the donor is not a party or other person who has come or is likely to come or whose interests have come or are likely to come before the judge; and if its value exceeds $150, the judge reports it in the same manner as the judge reports compensation in Section 4H."

Minnesota state court judges are not the only Minnesota judges who accept gratuities. United States judges take gratuities – big time. Abner Mikva, former member of congress, Chief Judge of the U.S. Court of Appeals for the District of Columbia, and White House lawyer for President Bill Clinton, had this to say about gratuities for federal judges, 27 of whom are based in Minnesota[23]:

> "Between 1992 and 1998, according to a report from the Community Rights Counsel, a nonprofit public-interest law firm, more than 230 federal judges took one or more trips each to resort locations for legal seminars paid for by corporations and foundations that have an interest in federal litigation on environmental topics.

"In the seminars devoted to so-called environmental education, judges listened to speakers whose overwhelming message was that regulation should be limited, that the free market should be relied upon to protect the environment, for example, or that the 'takings' clause of the Constitution should be interpreted to prohibit rules against development in environmentally sensitive places.

"Judges who attended the seminars wrote 10 of the most important rulings of the 1990's curbing federal environmental protections including one that struck down habitat protection provisions of the Endangered Species Act and another that invalidated regulations on soot and smog. In six of these cases, according to the report, the judge attended one of the seminars while the case was pending before the court. And, the report reveals, many judges failed to disclose required information about these seminars on their financial disclosure forms.

"If an actual party to a case took the judge to a resort, all expenses paid, shortly before the case was heard, the judge and the host would be perceived to be acting improperly even if all they discussed was their grandchildren. The conduct is no less reprehensible when an interest group substitutes for the party to the case.

"Of course it may be a coincidence that none of the seminars financed by private interests take place in Chicago in January or in Atlanta in July. It may be a coincidence that the judges who attend usually come down on the same side of important policy questions as those who financed the meetings. It may even be a coincidence that environmentalists are seldom invited to speak. But surely any citizen who reads about judges attending fancy meetings under ques-

> tionable sponsorship will have well-founded doubts about their objectivity.
>
> "I know one federal judge who has been on a dozen trips sponsored by the three most prominent special interest seminar groups. I remember at least two occasions where judges on judicial panels where I also served took positions that they had heard advocated at seminars sponsored by groups with particular interest in the litigation."

No Minnesota judge has ever been disciplined for accepting a gratuity with one exception. In the case of In Re Bartholet[24] a probate judge was disbarred because he received kickbacks of appraisal fees.

Many large law firms have lawyers who are designated entertainers. Their principal job is to wine and dine and entertain judges and public officials. These lawyers rarely if ever practice law. Most never represent a client or appear in a courtroom.

What is the justification for allowing judges to accept gratuities, particularly from lawyers and law firms? Perhaps judges are underpaid. Let's consider that.

There are three levels of courts in Minnesota.[25] They are the Minnesota Supreme Court, the state's highest court, the Minnesota Court of Appeals, the second highest court, and the district courts, sometimes called trial courts, which are the third-level courts.

Judge Salaries

The table that follows this paragraph shows what Minnesota judges are paid. Justices of the Minnesota Supreme Court receive the highest salaries. Court of Appeals judges are paid less than Justices of the Minnesota Supreme Court, but more than district court judges. As you can see, all judges are paid more than $116,000.

In addition, judges receive generous benefits. As state government employees, they are eligible for pensions, medical insurance, sick and vacation time, and other benefits. It is safe to say that judges are very well paid and do not need gratuities of up to $150 in value

Minnesota Supreme Court

Chief Justice and six Associate Justices
Hears appeals from all lower level courts.
Chief Justice – $146,920; Associate Justices – $133,564

Court of Appeals

Chief Judge – $132,144
15 Appeals Court Judges – $125,852
Hears appeals from all trial courts except in murder cases and appeals of unemployment awards decisions.

Special Courts

Workers' Compensation

Chief Judge – $122,211
5 Judges – $116,392
Hears appeals of workers' compensation decisions.

District (Trial) Courts

10 Judicial Districts
10 Chief Judges – $132,144
261 District Judges – $118,141
Hears civil, criminal and other cases.

Tax Court

Chief Judge – $122,211
2 Judges – $116,392
Hears appeals of Department of Revenue decisions.

to lead the good life.

Judges get their salary expense free. They do not have to pay rent for their office, salaries to their law clerks and court reporters, or any other expenses as lawyers do.

Higher Judge Salaries?

Some argue that the salaries of judges should not be higher than they are because they already are close to or more than the salary of the highest state official – the governor. The current salary of the governor is $120,303.

That comparison, however, is unfair. Governors serve a relatively short period of time – usually eight years in continuous terms, although a governor can serve longer because there is no limit in Minnesota on the number of times a person can be elected governor. After their term or terms as governor, it is common for them to earn substantial amounts on the lecture circuit and as directors on corporate boards.

Judges do not have these opportunities, although judges have resigned from time to time to enter private practice with a large law firm where he or she earns the hundreds of thousands of dollars mentioned below. Judges generally serve until they retire.

Although they can earn small additional amounts while in office from performing marriage ceremonies and giving lectures, the amount of this additional income is trivial compared to the after-office earnings a former governor can get. In fact, the total compensation a governor receives when his post-office income is considered is many times greater than that paid judges during their careers.

While it cannot be denied that judges are well paid, certainly compared to the average citizen, it often is argued that judges are not as well paid as lawyers in private practice. It is true that judges receive far less for their work than partners and even many associates in large firms. It is not uncommon for big firm partners to make $500,000 or even $1 million per year. As illustrated in the tobacco contingent fee lawsuits, many associate lawyers in a law firm make hundreds of thousands of dollars annually.

Even beginning lawyers in the top percentage of their class generally receive more in their starting salaries than judges. In comparison to big law firm lawyers and associates, and many other lawyers in private practice, Minnesota judges earn a paltry $116,000 to $146,000. Minnesotans want and expect their judges to be as smart and capable as the lawyers who appear in their courts, including those who make $500,000 or more a year. Do we expect lawyers who could make $500,000 or more per year to accept $116,000 to $146,000 for the privilege of serving the public?

Actually, compared to lawyers in general, judges are fairly compensated. According to data generated by the Minnesota Department of Economic Security in their Salary Survey,[26] the median pay for lawyers in the Twin Cities' seven-county metropolitan area in the fourth quarter of 2003 was $91,316. In all of Minnesota the median pay for lawyers was $85,825. Median means the middle. Fifty percent of lawyers earn more than the median amount, and 50 percent earn less. In comparison, the median pay of judges combined with magistrate judges, magistrates and referees was $103,487 in the Twin Cities' seven-county metropolitan area in the fourth quarter of 2003 and $104,667 for all of Minnesota.

Individuals in other occupations earn far more than judges. Athletes, coaches, entertainers, university presidents, school district superintendents, corporate executives, bank presidents, all typically receive compensation far more than $116,000 to $146,000 a year. Are not judges as important as these individuals? Should we not pay them commensurately? Why is it that we do not? Are gratuities the best way of paying judges the additional compensation they deserve?

Providing additional compensation to judges by giving them gratuities creates serious problems. It creates the concern that judges favor those lawyers who give them gratuities. Many lawyers believe that they have little chance for success in a lawsuit if they appear before a big city judge when the other side is represented by a big city law firm. The horror case, "The Cursed Home," may be an illustration of favoritism by a big city judge to two big city law firms who take good care of the judge in that case. How else can we explain the absurd decision the judge made?

Similarly, big city lawyers often fear they cannot get justice regardless of the merits of their case if it is before a small-town judge and a local lawyer is the opponent.

The obvious fact is that gratuities for judges is a bad idea, just as we recognized long ago that gratuities for legislators and officials in the executive branch of state government is a bad idea. We should abolish gratuities for judges and find other ways to pay judges fairly as proposed in Chapter 15 of Part III.

Chapter 5
Lawyers

"The only thing a lawyer won't question is the legitimacy of his mother."

W. C. Fields

Four surgeons were discussing their work during a coffee break. The first said, "I think accountants are the easiest to operate on. You open them up and everything inside is numbered." The second said, "I think librarians are the easiest to operate on. You open them up and everything inside is in alphabetical order." The third said, "I like to operate on electricians. You open them up and everything inside is color-coded." The fourth one said, "I like to operate on lawyers. They're heartless, spineless, gutless, and their heads and rear ends are interchangeable."

In one of Shakespeare's plays, *Henry VI*, a rebel named Dick proposes a solution to many of society's problems. He says: "The first thing we do, let's kill all the lawyers." (*Henry VI, Pt. II, Act IV, Sc. 2*) Dick's proposal may be too drastic to be implemented, but there are people, perhaps many, who share his opinion.

Lawyers have a bad reputation. Here is a sample of opinions of lawyers:[27]

> David Crombie, <u>The World's Stupidest Laws</u> (2000): It was so cold in Minnesota that the lawyers had their hands in their own pockets.
>
> Jean Giraudoux, <u>The Madwoman of Chaillot</u> (1945): You're an attorney. It's your duty to lie, conceal and

distort everything, and slander everybody.

Patrick Murray: A lawyer will do anything to win a case, sometimes he will even tell the truth.

Eugene E. Brussell: A lawyer is one who defends you at the risk of your pocketbook, reputation and life.

Will Rogers: People are getting smarter nowadays; they are letting lawyers, instead of their conscience, be their guide.

North Carolina Senator Elizabeth Dole to her husband, former U.S. Vice President Bob Dole: "Sometimes I think we're the only two lawyers in Washington who trust each other."

Charles Caleb Colton: A lawyer is a chimney-sweeper who has no objection to dirty work, because it is his trade.

U.S. Supreme Court Justice Oliver Wendell Holmes, Jr.: Lawyers spend a great deal of their time shoveling smoke.

Although many lawyers are ethical, honest and hard working, others, some say most, routinely evade, distort, posture, deceive and even lie. Often they are ruthless and unscrupulous. Low-income criminal defendants, especially minorities who cannot afford an expensive lawyer, typically have little chance in court, while those who have expensive lawyers often get light sentences or none at all. We know the problem: out-of-control lawyers. Some judges do what they can to level the playing field, but most are insensitive and indifferent to the behavior of lawyers, especially lawyers from big law firms that wield substantial power and influence.

Theoretically, lawyers who misbehave can be penalized by the judge who can assess monetary fines that officially are called sanctions. Court rules, primarily Rule 11 of the Rules of Civil Procedure, authorize a judge to assess a sanction if a court paper signed by an attorney is served on another party or put in the court file and the paper is not based on fact or a reasonable belief, or the purpose of the paper is "to harass or cause unnecessary delay or needless increase in the cost of litigation."

There also is a law, Minnesota Statutes § 549.211, that permits a judge to assess sanctions for similar reasons. In severe cases, a judge or anyone else can report a lawyer to the Minnesota Office of Lawyers Professional Responsibility which can discipline the lawyer. But rarely is a lawyer, particularly one from a big law firm, penalized when he or she evades, distorts, postures, deceives, or lies in court papers or in arguments in court, or when the lawyer makes what everyone knows is a ridiculous argument. Rarely does a judge even criticize a lawyer who engages in such tactics.

OFFICE OF LAWYERS PROFESSIONAL RESPONSIBILITY

The Minnesota state agency that receives complaints from individuals who believe a lawyer has mistreated them is the Office of Lawyers Professional Responsibility (Lawyer's Board). It is part of the judicial branch of state government. The Board reports to the Minnesota Supreme Court. Its power to provide relief to individuals who file complaints is very limited and it typically fails to provide a result that is satisfactory to the complaining person.

Individuals who file a complaint with the Lawyer's Board must provide a high level of proof of wrongdoing before it finds a lawyer guilty of an offense. It frequently rules that there was no "clear and convincing" proof of the alleged misbehavior. When there is a conflict between the lawyer's statements and the statements of the client, the Board almost always accepts the lawyer's version of what was said. It generally allows lawyers to get away with wrongdoing against clients.

The major reason for the failure of the Lawyer's Board to stamp out lawyer untruthfulness, dishonesty and other misbehavior is that its primary job is something else. It is to shield the image of judges, especially the Justices of Minnesota's Supreme Court. The Lawyer's Board is tough on lawyers who criticize judges – very tough.

The position of the Lawyer's Board and Minnesota Supreme Court is that lawyers do not have the right to freely criticize Minnesota's judges and justices even if they are public officials. They reject the notion that the right of freedom of speech guaranteed by the United States and Minnesota Constitutions gives lawyers the right to criticize them to the same extent that citizens have to criticize the president of the United States, the governor of Minnesota, and other United States and state government officials. They disagree with the observations of United States Supreme Court Justice Hugo Black in Bridges v. California, 314 US 252 (1941):

> "The assumption that respect for the judiciary can be won by shielding judges from published criticism wrongly appraises the character of American public opinion. For it is a prized American privilege to speak one's mind, although not always with perfect good taste, on all public institutions. And an enforced silence, however limited, solely in the name of preserving the dignity of the bench, would probably engender resentment, suspicion, and contempt much more than it would enhance respect." (314 US at 270-71)

Minnesota lawyer Gregory Wersal is an example of what happens to a lawyer who dares to criticize the Supreme Court of Minnesota. He had the nerve to publicly say the Minnesota Supreme Court was legislating rather than interpreting and applying the law. He lambasted the Minnesota Supreme Court for promoting abortion and making it easier to get. He committed the sin of running against an incumbent Supreme Court Justice and threatening to talk about political issues in his campaign.

Minnesota state officials wasted no time starting a Lawyer's Board proceeding to strip Wersal of his license to practice law. These events led to the case of Republican Party of Minnesota v. White[28] and a major defeat for the Minnesota Supreme Court.

One of the lawyers who works for the Lawyer's Board is Timothy Burke. He prosecuted the author of this book for criticizing judges. In his presentations and briefs he exaggerated, distorted, misrepresented and lied in ways that have disgraced the legal profession and given lawyers their bad reputation. He is an example of why the Lawyer's Board should be removed from the control of the Minnesota Supreme Court and made independent of the judicial branch of government. As proposed in Chapter 11, the Lawyer's Board should be free of the influence of judges.

Why Lawyers Act As They Do

Minnesota native son Warren E. Burger, who was Chief Justice of the U.S. Supreme Court for many years, said this about lawyers:[29]

> "Ours is a sick profession marked by incompetence, lack of training, misconduct and bad manners. Ineptness, bungling, malpractice, and bad ethics can be observed in court houses all over this country every day . . . these incompetents have a seeming unawareness of the fundamental ethics of the profession."

According to Chief Justice Burger, the prognosis is not good. On another occasion he said:

> "The harsh truth is that we may well be on our way to a society overrun by hordes of lawyers, hungry as locusts, and brigades of judges in numbers never before contemplated."

In fairness, it is not true that lawyers are inherently prone to dishonest and unethical conduct. The system drives lawyers to do what society considers repulsive.

Lawyers in private practice are in business. They need to earn money to support themselves and their families. To do this it is necessary to yield to the demands of the industry. If success requires a lawyer to give gratuities to judges, what practical choice does a lawyer have? Justice Sandra Day O'Connor pointed out that lawyers who contributed to the re-election campaigns of judges believe it improves their chances for success (see Chapter 3). Doesn't that tell lawyers that making such contributions is the smart thing to do?

Lawyers lie, distort, exaggerate and deceive in court papers and in court hearings to win their cases. Those who are the most accomplished in these tactics often win cases that lack merit. That is what clients pay lawyers to do – win, not necessarily get justice. For example, corporate executives who defrauded investors out of millions and even billions of dollars do not want justice; they want to get away with what they did. Lawyers are not paid to do what is right; they are paid to get their client what he wants. J. Pierpont Morgan, the well-known American financier, said: "I don't want a lawyer to tell me what I cannot do; I hire him to tell me how to do what I want to do."[30]

Ambulance chasing is profitable. That is reason enough for lawyers to practice it. Contingent fee lawsuits can make a lawyer wealthy. And while some lawyers may have taken a vow of poverty, it is a sure thing that most are engaged in America's highest priority activity – making money.

A class action lawsuit can make millionaires out of a small group of lawyers. Such suits are legal, and its easier to start one than get on Who Wants To Be A Millionaire. Moreover, lawyers convince themselves, these suits serve great social purposes, like gouging the automobile makers, toy manufacturers, pharmaceutical companies, and other big businesses who charge consumers such outrageous prices.

It may be that America's power structure best explains the despicable behavior of many lawyers that has given the profession such a bad reputation. Our nation's power barons, special interests, big businesses, politicians and other segments of our society, want control. Each has an agenda that it wishes to achieve. None of them likes opposition.

The power elite – those who have amassed huge fortunes and who control society – do not want to lose that. They want it to be difficult, even impossible, for people to challenge them. Making justice unaffordable and unavailable is a means of maintaining the ever-widening gulf between the rich and powerful, and the poor and defenseless. Lawyers are one of the keys to maintaining the status quo. Lying, distorting, posturing, delaying, are among the useful tactics in keeping challengers at bay.

Big businesses, even those who we now know defrauded stockholders of huge sums of money, want to make it hard for the little guy to get redress. Social workers and government agencies who wrongfully destroy families, or hurt or neglect children, do not want to be penalized for their wrongful actions. They want the agency to use its power to shield them. How the agency's lawyers do it is of no concern to these officials.

Police officers who practice racial profiling, or who cruelly brutalize a prisoner, want the government to defend their conduct. They want government lawyers to do whatever it takes.

The list of powerful people who use the law to protect themselves is endless. Theirs is the politics of greed and power.

If they choose to do so, judges have the power to prevent or make it largely unnecessary for lawyers to act as many now do. Years ago, there was a judge who would not tolerate lawyer misconduct. He refused to have his intelligence insulted or be played for a fool. And guess what? Lawyers rarely misbehaved before that judge, certainly not more than once. That judge was famous for his fairness and is still honored every year by an annual award in his name to the outstanding federal judge of the year – the Edward J. Devitt award.

If our current judges followed Judge Devitt's lead, maybe we wouldn't have reason to consider Shakespeare's suggestion. Lawyers should be held accountable for their misbehavior. Reforms that will make them accountable are proposed in Chapter 11, Part III.

Chapter 6
Lawsuit Expense

litigant n. A person about to give up his skin for the hope of retaining his bones.[31]

Sometimes a lawsuit is the only way to resolve differences. Sadly, few people can afford them. Lawsuits cost thousands of dollars, often tens of thousands of dollars. Only the wealthiest 10 percent of our population can afford to fund a major lawsuit. For the rest of society, justice is unavailable.

In his annual State of the Judiciary speech in 2001, California's Supreme Court Chief Justice said: "If the motto 'and justice for all' becomes 'justice for those who can afford it,' we threaten the very underpinnings of our social contract."[32] Claire Trevor said: "What a holler would ensue if people had to pay the minister as much to marry them as they have to pay a lawyer to get them a divorce."[33]

Except in contingent fee cases, lawyers generally charge by the hour for their work. The hourly rate in the Twin Cities for a high quality lawyer is at least $250 per hour. Many charge $350 per hour or higher. The hourly rate for a beginning lawyer or lawyer in a small firm is seldom less than $150 per hour.

Lawsuits take time – client meetings, fact finding, drafting court papers, interviewing witnesses, taking depositions (sworn testimony) of parties and witnesses, research, meetings with lawyers for the other party, negotiations, preparation for trial, trial – all require hours of effort. The total rarely is less than 100 hours for a case that goes to trial.

Law firms have high overhead expenses. Rent, payroll for secretaries and legal assistants, payroll taxes, employee health insurance, continuing legal education, janitorial service, copiers and copying service, fax machines, and many other business expenses are unavoidable and add significant cost to litigation. Like other professionals, prudent lawyers carry malpractice insurance, which costs many thousands of dollars per year.

Many lawyers require a retainer – an up-front payment – before they will even look at a case. Lawyers experienced in family and juvenile court matters (divorce, child custody) often require $5,000 to $10,000 before they will meet with a potential client.

Court fees, although small in amount compared to amounts for lawyer fees, nonetheless are significant. It costs $245 merely to open a court file. An additional $55 must be paid every time a person asks the court to take an action (by filing a motion). The person who starts a lawsuit does so by having papers personally handed to each opponent (called service of process).

Deputy sheriffs and police officers charge $50 to $100 or more, depending on the distance they must travel and time they must take, to serve the papers. Private process servers charge even more. A subpoena (court order requiring a person to attend a court hearing) costs $12 each. Additional money such as recording fees must be paid in some kinds of lawsuits such as a mechanic's lien action to recover what is due for work on a home.

One or more expert witnesses may be necessary for a trial to testify about such matters as the severity and effect of an injury, the value of a home or business or other property, what is in the best interests of a child, and other issues. Because of their special expertise and experience, expert witnesses are especially expensive – typically costing $5,000 to $10,000 even in ordinary cases.

To improve the chance for success at trial, most lawyers want to take depositions. A deposition is a scheduled meeting at which a person such as one of the parties to the lawsuit or a potential witness gives testimony under oath before a licensed court reporter who records the testimony. Transcripts of depositions almost always cost hundreds of dollars, sometimes thousands.

Even mediators and arbitrators, commonly referred to as "neutrals," are expensive – far beyond the financial resources of many Minnesotans. Experienced neutrals generally charge $200 per hour or higher. Preparation for and conducting a mediation or arbitration normally takes at least five hours.

So-called incidental expenses – postage, mileage, copies, travel, long- distance telephone, document processing – mount up. In big cases, they total hundreds or even thousands of dollars.

Most lawyers work during regular business hours. People involved in a lawsuit as a party usually have to take many hours from their job for meetings, attendance at court hearings and depositions, preparation of documents such as an affidavit (a sworn statement), and other events. This often is a major problem and can add even more thousands of dollars to the cost of a lawsuit in the form of lost income.

If a party wants to appeal a loss in the trial court, a $500 filing fee must be paid to the appeals court unless the person who wants to appeal qualifies as living at the poverty level. But the really big expense in appeals, after lawyer fees, is paying for a transcript of testimony at the trial. Such transcripts typically cost thousands of dollars.

An appeal also requires a $500 cost bond. This bond is to guarantee that the party who brings the appeal will pay at least $500 of the other party's appeal costs if the appeal is unsuccessful.

The party who is appealing may need to buy another bond known as a supersedeas bond. This bond is needed if the party who lost in the trial court wants to suspend the trial court's judgment or order. For example, suppose the party who wants to appeal was ordered to pay $50,000 to the other party and wants to delay having to pay that until after the appeal is decided. To get such a delay requires a supersedeas bond. This can be very expensive because it in effect guarantees that the party who won in the trial court will be paid.

Thus, to delay enforcement of a judgment for $50,000, a supersedeas bond for $50,000 would be required. In most cases, such a bond would require a deposit of $50,000 in cash, or the person buying the bond would have to provide collateral satisfactory to the bonding company to secure a $50,000 supersedeas bond. This is in addition to the cost of the bond.

A relatively new development that in some instances makes legal help affordable for the average Minnesotan is prepaid legal insurance. For a premium usually paid in monthly installments a person is entitled to the services of a lawyer and his or her firm. The services provided are adequate for most routine legal matters such as preparation of a will and review of a contract. It might cover real estate transactions such as buying a home, relatively minor criminal defense, and other consultations and representation that do not require large expenditures of time by a lawyer.

But the coverage often is limited to protect the law firm from having to provide representation in a major lawsuit which could bring financial devastation to the law firm. Rarely does such insurance cover the staggering expense of a major lawsuit. With further development and financial underwriting, legal insurance may become a viable option for getting all the legal services a person needs. Yet, as has medical insurance, it could have the effect of driving legal costs even higher.

Greater and more effective use of mediation and arbitration may eliminate much of the expense of a lawsuit. This is discussed in Chapter 16 – Make Justice Efficient, Affordable and Reasonable of Part III. Reforms that will reduce the expenses of litigation also are discussed in Chapter 16.

Chapter 7
Lawsuit Overload and Abuse

A post office patron entered a post office. While standing in line he noticed a richly dressed man at a work counter. On the counter was a very large stack of greeting card envelopes. The envelopes were bright pink in color and were plastered with hearts. The impressively attired man was placing a "love" stamp on each envelope. After he completed putting stamps on the envelopes, he took a bottle of perfume out of his posh briefcase. Then he spritzed the envelopes.

Unable to contain his curiosity, the patron walked over to the man and said: "I hope you don't mind my asking, but what you are doing appears to be very thoughtful and I wondered what it is." The well-dressed man said: "These are very nice valentine cards. There are over a thousand of them and I am going to mail them."

Choosing his words carefully, the patron said: "My word, you certainly have a lot of romantic relationships." "Oh no," the man said. "I don't know any of these people. None of them will know I sent them a valentine because I signed each one 'Guess Who.' "

"I don't understand," the patron said. "Why are you doing this?"

The well-dressed man replied: "I'm a divorce lawyer."

Over Two Million Court Files in 2003

More than two million cases, most of which concerned minor matters as described later in this chapter, were filed in Minnesota courts in 2003.[34] This is in addition to the unknown number of cases that were started but never filed with a court. (In Minnesota, a state court lawsuit can be started and resolved without filing it with a court.) Additional thousands of cases were filed in Minnesota's federal court called the United States District Court for the District of Minnesota. The population of Minnesota in 2003 was about five million. That comes to about one lawsuit for every two residents.

Our courts are choked with litigation. They are overwhelmed. Judges often focus on disposing of cases rather than deciding them on the merits. In many criminal cases, judges press defendants to plead guilty to something – anything to get rid of the case.

To cope with this overload, judges take shortcuts. A "plea bargain" is routinely accepted by judges even when a potentially dangerous defendant is set free or escapes with a light sentence. A plea bargain is a deal between the defendant, generally through his lawyer, and the prosecutor. The prosecutor agrees to dismiss some of the charges against the defendant if he or she admits guilt to other charges, which are always less severe in consequences.

Frustrated police officers often see defendants who committed assaults and other crimes, many times with weapons, get off with little or no jail time. Back on the streets, many of these individuals commit new offenses and hurt more victims and force police and prosecutors to repeat the cycle of arrest, booking, confinement and prosecution.

Our jails are filled to capacity. Ramsey County (St. Paul, Minnesota area) completed a new jail in 2003 to house its exploding prison population only to find when it opened that it was not big enough. It was overflowing in less than a month. New jails costing Minnesota taxpayers hundreds of millions of dollars still are needed.

Causes of the Overload

The overload is not difficult to explain. Unlike many, perhaps most, nations in the world, courts in America have become the institution that addresses and attempts to resolve most of what is perceived to be society's ills: drug/alcohol abuse, divorce and family controversies, victimless crimes (status offenses, runaways), failure to pay rent, etc.

As demonstrated by the case of "The Suspicious Trunk Lock," prosecutors pursue charges they know are without merit. Why not?

There is no penalty if they lose and winning increases their success rate and brightens their chance for continuing in office.

The prosecutor in the case of "The Suspicious Trunk Lock," lawyer Russell Platzek, should have been disciplined for prosecuting this case because he violated the Minnesota rules of ethical conduct for prosecutors, specifically Rule 3.8:[35]

> The prosecutor in a criminal case shall: (a) refrain from prosecuting a charge that the prosecution knows is not supported by probable cause.

He also violated a cardinal principle applicable to prosecutors included in the American Bar Association Model Rules of Ethical Conduct. Regrettably, this principle is not a part of Minnesota's rules applicable to prosecutors. Specifically, the rule Mr. Platzek violated is Ethical Consideration EC 7-13, which states:

> The responsibility of a public prosecutor differs from that of the usual advocate; it is to seek justice, not merely to convict. This special duty exists because: (1) the prosecutor represents the sovereign and therefore should use restraint in the discretionary exercise of governmental powers, such as in the selection of cases to prosecute; (2) during trial the prosecutor is not only an advocate but he also may make decisions normally made by an individual client, and those affecting the public interest should be fair to all; and (3) in our system of criminal justice the accused is to be given the benefit of all reasonable doubt.

Many suits for damages have a very shallow basis. There is little deterrent to asserting such suits and it is known that defending such cases can be very expensive. And there always is the possibility of loss in a jury trial. Many defendants decide it is smarter and cheaper to pay something to settle rather than fight the suit. Again, there is no effective deterrent, such as requiring the loser to pay the lawyer fees and litigation costs of the winning party.

Lawsuit abuse is a significant cause of the system's breakdown.

Such abuse in the form of outlandish damages awards is well known. You probably have heard of the elderly lady who won $2.7 million from McDonalds because the coffee she spilled on her lap was too hot,[36] and the $4.4 million awarded to a doctor against the dealer who had repainted a part of the BMW automobile it delivered to the doctor after repairing minor damage sustained in transit, even though the repair or refinishing were not visible.[37] They are only a few of the lawsuit jackpot winners.

Obviously, there should be limits on damages awards. They are needed not only to curtail outrageous demands and unjustified court filings, but also for consumer economy. It is you, the consumer, who reimburses McDonalds for the amounts they pay in damages. As pointed out by Peter W. Huber in *Liability: The Legal Revolution and its Consequences* (Basic Books, Inc., publishers, 1988), pages 3-4:

> "IT IS [sic] one of the most ubiquitous taxes we pay, now levied on virtually everything we buy, sell, and use. The tax accounts for 30 percent of the price of a stepladder and over 95 percent of the price of childhood vaccines. It is responsible for one-quarter of the price of a ride on a Long Island tour bus and one-third of the price of a small airplane. It will soon cost large municipalities as much as they spend on fire or sanitation services.
>
> "Some call it a safety tax, but its exact relationship to safety is mysterious. It is paid on many items that are risky to use, like ski lifts and hedge trimmers, but it weighs even more heavily on other items whose whole purpose is to make life safer. It adds only a few cents to a pack of cigarettes, but it adds more to the price of a football helmet than the cost of making it. The tax falls especially hard on prescription drugs, doctors, surgeons, and all things medical. Because of the tax, you cannot deliver a baby with medical assistance in Monroe County, Alabama. You cannot buy several contraceptives certified to be safe and effective by the Food and Drug Administration

(FDA), even though available substitutes are more dangerous or less effective. If you have the stomach upset known as hyperemesis, you cannot buy the pill that is certified as safe and effective against it. The tax has orphaned various drugs that are invaluable for treating rare but serious diseases. It is assessed against every family that has a baby, in the amount of about $300 per birth, with an obstetrician in New York City paying $85,000 a year.

"Because of the tax, you cannot use a sled in Denver city parks or a diving board in New York City schools. You cannot buy an American Motors 'CJ' Jeep or a set of construction plans for novel airplanes from Burt Rutan, the pioneering designer of the Voyager. You can no longer buy many American-made brands of sporting goods, especially equipment for amateur contact sports such as hockey and lacrosse. For a while, you could not use public transportation in the city of St. Joseph, Missouri, nor could you go to jail in Lafayette County in the same state. Miami canceled plans for an experimental rail-bus because of the tax. The tax has curtailed Little League and fireworks displays, evening concerts, sailboard races, and the use of public beaches and ice-skating rinks. It temporarily shut down the famed Cyclone at the Astroland amusement park on Coney Island.

"The tax directly costs American individuals, businesses, municipalities, and other government bodies at least $80 billion a year, a figure that equals the total profits of the country's top 200 corporations. But many of the tax's costs are indirect and unmeasurable, reflected only in the tremendous effort, inconvenience, and sacrifice Americans now go through to avoid its collection. The extent of these indirect costs can only be guessed at. One study con-

> cluded that doctors spend $3.50 in efforts to avoid additional charges for each $1 of direct tax they pay. If similar multipliers operate in other areas, the tax's hidden impact on the way we live and do business may amount to a $300 billion annual levy on the American economy.
>
> "The tax goes by the name of tort liability. It is collected and disbursed through litigation. The courts alone decide just who will pay, how much, and on what timetable. Unlike better-known taxes, this one was never put to a legislature or a public referendum, debated at any length in the usual public arenas, or approved by the president or by any state governor. And although the tax ostensibly is collected for the public benefit, lawyers and other middlemen pocket more than half the take."

A legal doctrine known as joint and several liability gives tort liability real clout. It is a legal doctrine that overburdens defendants with liability for damages. The doctrine allows a plaintiff to collect a disproportionate share of his damages from a deep-pockets defendant even if that defendant was only partly to blame for the plaintiff's injuries. It encourages plaintiffs to join a deep-pockets defendant to a lawsuit so the plaintiff can collect all the damages he is awarded.

For example, a jury might find that two of the defendants in a case were jointly responsible for the injuries suffered by the plaintiff. If the jury finds that one of the defendants was 51 percent responsible, that defendant still might have to pay all of the plaintiff's damages if the other defendant is unable to pay anything.

The basic premises of joint and several liability are that a plaintiff should recover all of his damages and they should be recovered from the wrongdoers in proportion to their percentage of fault. In actual practice, joint and several liability usually forces many defendants to pay for the wrongdoing of other defendants, and still does not assure a plaintiff will recover all his damages.

These premises need to be reconsidered because joint and several liability is extremely wasteful as well as frequently unjust and ineffective.

Another legal doctrine called vicarious liability is even worse. It allows a plaintiff to collect from a defendant who was not responsible for any part of the plaintiff's injuries. Vicarious liability is based on a relationship under which one person is liable for the wrongdoing of another without regard to fault. For example, under this doctrine, employers are liable for the acts of employees even when the employer did nothing wrong.

Courts have over-extended the doctrine of vicarious liability. Automobile and truck rental companies are forced to charge greatly inflated prices because they might be liable for damages caused by operators of their vehicles even if the operators have their own insurance.

Strict products liability law generates a significant percentage of the tort liability tax described by Peter W. Huber above. Under this law one who sells or distributes a defective product is liable for injuries or damage to persons or property caused by a defect in the product.

In principle, this law seems impregnable to opposition. A person who negligently or otherwise causes injury or damage should be liable for the damages his fault causes. No reasonable person quarrels with that. What many critics condemn is the use (or abuse) of strict product liability law to find fault where none exists. It is the egregious application of strict product liability law that creates massive injustice and excessive expense.

Making a product "defective" is a challenge to the imagination and ingenuity of lawyers who want to cash in on a products liability lawsuit against a manufacturer or distributor. Often the alleged defect is contrived and it later is discovered there was no negligence or defect.

Many times the fault or carelessness was that of the user. Examples that prove this are reflected in startling warnings that accompany a product such as the following:

> On a Swedish chainsaw: "Do not attempt to stop chain with your hands or genitals."

On a child's superman costume: "Warning: This garment does not enable you to fly."

On Sunsbury's peanuts: "Warning: contains nuts."

On most brands of Christmas tree lights: "For indoor or outdoor use only."

On Nytol sleep aid: "Warning: May cause drowsiness."

On Boot's Children cough medicine: "Do not drive or operate machinery after taking this medication."

On packaging for a Rowenta iron: "Do not iron clothes on body."

On Marks & Spencer bread pudding: "Product will be hot after heating."

On some Swanson frozen dinners: "Serving suggestion: defrost."

On a Sears hair dryer: "Do not use while sleeping."

Family court cases such as dissolution (divorce) and child support proceedings are another example of lawsuit waste. Only in America, literally, do couples, married or not, spend such vast amounts of time fighting over children and property – through their lawyers to whom they pay fortunes in legal fees. Other societies say it proves Americans are crazy.

For example, in China, the most populous nation in the world, couples do not go to court for a divorce. The family council of elders decides all family matters and files notice of the divorce. Which of these processes is the more sensible and civilized?

Of course, these are different cultures with different traditions. In China, family elders are held in far greater esteem than in our country. In fact, elders in American families often are considered old-fashioned or antiquated rather than reservoirs of wisdom.

Still, the mad-hatter squabbling that occurs thousands of times daily in our nation's divorce courts can be reduced enormously in magnitude by using neutral professionals and experts to make recommendations or even decisions on child custody, visitation and support, and property division issues.

Instead of artificial and rigid rules on child support and maintenance (formerly alimony), neutral, level-headed experts can recommend or decide what is reasonable in each situation. Using unbiased experts in family court cases is described in Chapter 16 of Part III. Maybe the proposed reforms will restore a semblance of sanity in resolving family controversies.

Courts in Minnesota, as in most of the United States, often are very inefficient. Many times a large group of cases is scheduled for the same time, such as 9:00 a.m. or 1:00 p.m. to be heard by one judge. This is common for criminal, juvenile, unlawful detainer and conciliation court cases. Rarely does the judge start on time. People and lawyers mill around for hours waiting to have their case heard.

Chapter 16 in Part III includes reforms to streamline our grossly inefficient and excessively expensive legal system to make it far more cost and service effective.

Cases That Concern Minor Matters

Tort liability and family court cases are not the only major villains in lawsuit wasteland. Public officials spend an inordinate amount of time and resources on relatively trivial matters while far more significant conditions persist or worsen because of a shortage of personnel to address them. For example, parking and minor traffic cases combined comprise more than 70 percent of the total cases filed in Minnesota in 2003.

The total number of court cases opened in Minnesota state courts in 2003 was 2,106,117. Two of the categories and the number of cases in each category were:

Traffic (excluding DWI)	778,993
Parking	701,805
Total	1,480,798

Issuing citations, processing tickets, maintaining records, and collecting fines for 1,480,798 cases requires the time and services of unknown numbers of Minnesota police officers and administrative personnel. In the meantime, drug use and distribution offenses are exploding. So is gang crime and warfare.

No one we know of denies that traffic and parking control are important. Rather, making these matters official court cases and treating them the same way as we treat matters that are far more serious is not only farcical but grossly inefficient. These matters should not be classified as court cases or even be in the court system. An administrative system will more than suffice.

Diverting minor parking and traffic matters to automated systems operated by an administrative agency will free up many police officer positions that can be focused on major social ills. Chapter 16 in Part III describes potential automated systems that could accomplish this.

Three percent of the cases filed in 2003, 63,293 in number, were conciliation court cases. Since each case involved at least two parties, over 100,000 people were involved in these cases. That is a significant number of people and they are very poorly served. Under the current system, each must prepare his or her claim or defense and present it effectively to a judge or referee in a few minutes. The average person is not trained to do this. Attempts are made in many instances to force the parties to mediate their dispute, but this takes place at the last minute and is virtually unorganized.

Other categories of cases such as unlawful detainer (late rent payment cases, 23,755), and minor DWI (26,866) cases take a significant amount of time — court time. Reforms that will simplify the processing and resolution of these and other categories of cases, and save significant amounts of public and private money, will be proposed in our next book.

Case Reduction Will Save Money and Increase Justice

A very important reason for eliminating case overload in our courts is that this will avoid expense to society that is both wasteful and unnecessary. Our booming prison population and recurring need for new prisons are due in part to a system that sends people to jail because the judge does not have time to decide each case carefully. Weeding out the masses of cases that can be processed administratively, or that never should have been brought in the first place, will give judges the time they need to be deliberative in every case.

In Chapter 16 – Make Justice Efficient, Affordable and Reasonable – of Part III, we propose a public low-cost claim preparation and file organization service. Such a service could be used in conciliation court cases to better achieve real justice in these cases. In Chapter 16, we propose quicker and more effective use of arbitration and mediation to resolve disputes. These alternative dispute resolution methods can be used in conciliation court cases in a much more organized way than at present. That could make conciliation courts much more satisfactory in fairly and efficiently resolving disputes.

Chapter 8
Contingent Fee Lawsuits

Contingent fee lawsuits fall into two general categories. One is class action lawsuits. This category is discussed in Chapter 9. The other category typically has a single plaintiff, although there can be more as in an automobile accident case where more than one person is hurt.

In a contingent fee case, the lawyer is paid only if he or she wins the case. If the client – usually the plaintiff – loses, both the lawyer and the client get nothing. In other words, pay for the lawyer is contingent on winning the case.

When the plaintiff wins, the money is split between the lawyer and the plaintiff. Lawyers often get one-third of the net amount won. Net amount means what is left after expenses such as court fees, pay for expert witnesses, copies, and other out-of-pocket costs have been reimbursed. After these expenses have been subtracted, and the lawyer is paid his contingent fees, the plaintiff often receives less than half the money that was won. On the other hand, if the lawyer settles the case before going to trial, he may get only 25 percent of the net amount.

Lawyers argue that the high percentages they get are justified since they actually take all the risk and get nothing if they lose the case. But lawyers rarely take a contingent fee case unless they are confident they will win. And since court rules and general practice require the client to pay court fees and many out-of-pocket costs, the actual risk to the lawyer primarily is only loss of his or her time.

Trial lawyers also argue that allowing contingent fee cases benefits society because the process screens out meritless cases. If being paid depends on winning, they reason, lawyers will reject cases that appear to be losers. However, these lawyers also know that lawsuits are intimidating and it is usually possible to get a defendant to pay something even if the claims are meritless. And even an outrageous case can still be a winner because many defendants will pay a settlement to avoid the risks of a jury trial.

Contingent fee lawsuits are big business – really big. Legions of contingent fee lawyers are listed in the yellow pages of telephone directories often in very expensive full-page advertisements. Every business day hundreds of them sally forth to depose witnesses, haggle with insurance company lawyers, and perform before juries.

Back at their offices, they interview potential clients. They choose those who offer good opportunities to make money and leave the others to their own devices.

Contingent fee cases often are very profitable as shown by the $2.7 and $4.4 million dollar victories in the McDonalds and BMW cases discussed in Chapter 7. Recent suits by overweight plaintiffs against McDonalds and other fast food restaurants are based on the failure of the restaurant to tell patrons that a double cheeseburger, supersized fries, and a large drink are fattening.

The average person sees these suits as frivolous, but McDonalds takes them seriously, and it costs them plenty. The costs of litigation, no matter how absurd the claims may be, must be paid and are passed on to their customers in the form of higher prices.

Contingent fee suits against the tobacco industry became the Mother of contingent fee litigation. Contingent fee lawyers in private practice teamed with state government through their attorneys general to wrest $245 billion from tobacco manufacturers, tens of billions of which went to private practice lawyers. For centuries people knew that tobacco was addictive and unhealthy. No matter, these suits asserted, tobacco manufacturers should pay for sums spent by states caring for sick smokers. Better yet for the lawyers, they forced tobacco companies to pay hundreds of millions to law firms, most of it paid long before the states collected their share.

But it was not the tobacco companies that paid; it was tobacco consumers. Shortly after the tobacco industry settled the cases, cigarette prices jumped by 45¢ per pack. The effect was identical to a new tax – on smokers – not passed by any legislature, but by state attorneys general and contingent fee lawyers.

Catherine Crier, a former judge and host of *Catherine Crier*

Live on Court TV, said this about the corrupting effects of the tobacco contingent fee litigation cases in her book *The Case Against Lawyers* (Broadway Books, New York, 2002, page 11):

> "This type of litigation has also put dreams of riches into the minds of governors and attorneys general around the country. An incestuous relationship between these officials and private attorneys is growing. Here's how it works. The government decides to attack some 'dangerous' industry to protect its citizens. Instead of calling on lawyers already on the state payroll, the officials hire big outside firms—often the same firms that are major contributors to the political campaigns that put and keep the officials in office. These state executives get bragging rights with the voters for lawsuit awards that pump up the general revenue fund, the private attorneys get huge contingency fees, and often some of those fees recycle right back into the campaign coffers for the next election."

The United States is one of the very few countries in the world that permit contingent fee suits. Most nations think that tying lawyer fees to courtroom success creates a bad incentive. Most bar contingent fee suits. They do not want plaintiffs who have nothing at risk if they pursue a weak case.

In her book cited above, Judge Crier censured contingent fee lawsuits as follows (page 188):

> "England has another policy that should be adopted in this country. It does not permit contingency fee contracts. Here in the United States, this practice began as a means of obtaining payment from poor clients in worthwhile cases. Now almost every form of litigation uses this fee structure. This arrangement has become a form of high stakes gambling for the legal community. While the cost of challenging a major industry can be astronomical, so are the

rewards. In a speech last summer, Justice Sandra Day O'Connor noted that lawyers become 'business partners of plaintiffs in seeking large dollar recoveries rather than act as objective servants of the law.' She continued: 'Such arrangements have made more overnight millionaires than almost any other businesses and the perverse incentives and the untoward consequences they are creating within our profession are many.'

"Trial work has become a major stand-alone business within the legal community. What was once the place for good advice about the worthiness of a claim has become a gristmill for expanding rights and remedies. To enterprising attorneys, there are few unmerited lawsuits. Traditionally, lawyers were officers of the court who zealously represented clients within legal and ethical boundaries. The interests of justice were paramount, such that intentionally misleading a jury or using discovery simply to wear down an opponent or drain his pocketbook was degrading to the practitioner and unethical as well. Using court pleadings or the media as a litigation tactic to destroy an opponent was unacceptable. Attorneys now regularly solicit clients, conjure up creative and nuisance filings, and delay the trial process, all to line their own pockets."

The underlying premise of contingent fee litigation is that injured persons can only be compensated by the wrongdoers who caused their injuries, and that a lawsuit is the most cost-effective method of proving the wrongdoing and determining a fair dollar amount for damages. This premise is invalid.

Minnesotans, as well as other Americans, miss the fact that paying many tens of millions of dollars each year to contingent fee lawyers and defense lawyers in those cases is a huge waste. These sums can be paid directly to the people who were injured or damaged. They will be compensated in full and the leftover money can be used to reduce insurance premiums. Chapter 16, Part III explains how to achieve this.

Contingent fee lawsuits are bad for society in other ways. They corrupt it. It is routine for lawyers, expert witnesses, and the parties themselves to posture, distort, exaggerate, and even lie. Winning, not fairness, is the principal objective. Dishonesty is acceptable. Somehow, the participants do not connect this with the morals and mores of our culture.

Greed dominates contingent fee litigation. Such litigation encourages immoral behavior. If it is all right to lie and cheat in court, is this not also all right in other settings? Where should a person draw the line that separates the permissibility of such conduct?

Of course, contingent fee litigation is far from the only cause of social degeneration. Nonetheless, in litigious America, it is a prominent display of malignant conduct.

Still, it cannot be denied that contingent fee lawsuits give many plaintiffs the means they would not otherwise have to assert valid claims. The benefits of contingent fee lawsuits can be preserved and its abuses controlled. Chapter 16 in Part III proposes reforms to accomplish this.

Chapter 9
Class Actions

A class action is a lawsuit where a small number of people sue to recover damages for a large number of people. The people who start the lawsuit are called class action plaintiffs. They are the representatives of others, often thousands of people who are not named as plaintiffs but who are paid damages if the class action plaintiffs win the lawsuit.

Typically, a class action is brought against a large business. The class action brought against the manufacturers of breast implants is an example. In that suit, a few plaintiffs represented hundreds of thousands of women who claimed injuries from breast implants. Another example is the class action against manufacturers of asbestos on behalf of people who claimed injuries from inhaling asbestos dust.

Class actions generally are the idea of and are started by lawyers, not by the people who claim injury. There are law firms that specialize in class actions. The primary reason lawyers start class action lawsuits is to make money. And they do – millions and millions of dollars every year. On the other hand, class action plaintiffs and beneficiaries, the individuals who supposedly suffered the injuries, frequently recover less than 25 percent of the amount said to be their damages.

Class action lawyers and others contend that class actions benefit society. They argue that class actions give ordinary people the means of challenging big businesses and recovering for injuries or wrongs inflicted on people by their wrongdoing. They also argue that class actions stop corporate and big business fraud, deception, cheating and scams and deter such illegal behavior.

But the current cost to society is very high. Manufacturers have paid millions of dollars to settle class actions that alleged highly questionable defects. They passed these costs to consumers in the prices of their products. Products have been pulled from the market to avoid class action lawsuits. Hundreds of thousands of jobs have been lost because of class actions that bankrupted large employers.

Beginning of Class Actions

The development and emergence of class actions began in the twentieth century. Walter K. Olson describes the evolution of the class action industry as follows in his book *The Rule of Lawyers: How the New Litigation Elite Threatens America's Rule of Law* (Truman Tally Books, New York, 2003, page 84):

> "A typical example was the early 1990s flap over the briefly popular singing duo Milli Vanilli who, after fading in popularity with their teenage fans, were revealed not actually to have been singing at all; they had been lip-synching to tracks prerecorded by others. Most young fans appeared willing to shrug off the affair, but not so many of the nation's most prominent class action firms. They rushed to file more than two dozen suits against Arista Records charging fraud, deception, and all manner of other illegalities, demanding disgorgement by the company of every penny taken in from the sale of the group's albums, et cetera. The lawsuits invariably sought class action status. When the cases eventually settled, the record company offered a $3 rebate to any customer who could offer proof of having bought one of the band's albums, while the lawyers requested court-ordered fees approaching $2 million. How spontaneous were the litigants' grievances? 'Of the 49 plaintiffs in the Milli Vanilli cases, at least 41 appear to have had pre-existing relationships to lawyers, most of whom worked at firms specializing in class action cases. And many of the plaintiffs say they agreed to file suit at the suggestion of a lawyer,' reported *The Wall Street Journal's* Amy Stevens.

Attorneys 'found clients in their own law offices and contacted their friends with teenage children'; one 'didn't know she was a plaintiff until she read it in the newspaper.' As a matter of fact, the lawyers were doing very much the same thing that the record promoters had done: line up appealing if vacuous faces to lip-synch their own compositions. [footnote omitted]

"Multiply by hundreds if not thousands of actions, and you get the year-in, year-out business of the class action industry, which today files a more or less continual stream of shareholder and investor actions against big companies, consumer suits over credit card grace periods and bank check bouncing fees, airline frequent flier programs, magazine sweepstakes and premium promotions that arguably fall short of promises, and so forth. To find likely cases, some lawyers comb through mass market commercial agreements in search of slipups in the fine print, often highly technical. Others piggyback on government enforcement actions. Few class members opt out; and when the case settles, the accepted logic behind the lawyers' payday is that the suit has created a benefit for the class members, which entitles the lawyers to deduct a reasonable fee before the class is paid."

Class Action Abuse

The excesses of class action lawyers in pursuit of big fees have caused their damage to society to far exceed their benefits. Drug firms have been sued by plaintiffs who took an overdose, or because of an unknown reaction. Automobile manufacturers have paid millions to lawyers and plaintiffs to settle cases because of allegations that an accident was caused by a defective design. These costs, of course, are passed on to buyers.

For decades builders used asbestos in construction because of its insulation properties and perceived safety. In the 1960s and 1970s, asbestos manufacturers learned with the rest of society of the dangers of asbestos – respiratory illness, cancer, and other illnesses. Class action suits targeted the manufacturers as solely responsible for society's ignorance. The resulting litigation redistributed tens of billions of dollars, bankrupted scores of large companies, and resulted in hundreds of thousands of job losses, even though there is substantial evidence that the type of asbestos used in insulation never caused cancer, although other forms do.

Breast implant class action litigation drove Dow Corning, a very large company, into bankruptcy even after the scientific basis of the claims was refuted. The final settlement package was $7 billion, including approximately $2 billion for the plaintiffs' class action lawyers.

A recent class action was based on the Super Bowl half-time show this past February 1, 2004 during which a male performer tore off a part of a female performer's clothes exposing her right breast.[38] Legal experts immediately pointed out that differences in the kinds of injuries people suffered as a result of this incident might prevent a class action.

Some experts said there would have to be a class action for women and another for men because of differences in injuries. For example, one prospective male plaintiff claimed that he choked on his beer and almost drowned. In contrast, the mother of a six-year-old boy said he demanded to know what the ruckus was all about and she was unable to explain it to him.

Resolution of these weighty legal issues might have been extremely difficult. We will never know what was decided. Fortunately, or unfortunately, the original plaintiff dismissed the suit.

Tort litigation based on alleged defects in products, or incidents like what occurred during the 2004 Super Bowl Halftime Show are not the only targets of class actions. Alleged fraud, money mismanagement, and deceptive practices are among the many other targets. Some of the class actions currently pending in Minnesota courts or that involve Minnesotans are:

> Lutheran Brotherhood Variable Insurance Products Co. Sales Practices Litigation, USDC Minnesota,

No. 99-MD-1309, in which the defendant is charged with conducting a campaign to sell life insurance in a deceptive manner.

In Re Xcel Energy, Inc. Securities Litigation, USDC Minnesota, No. 02-2677 (DSD/FLN), in which the defendant is alleged to have violated securities laws by issuing a series of material misrepresentations that artificially inflated the price of Xcel Energy securities.

Arent v. State Farm Mutual Automobile Insurance Co., Hennepin County District Court, No. MC 00-016521, in which the defendant is charged with illegally selling worthless life insurance to people over 65 years old.

Olson v. American Family Mutual Insurance Co., Hennepin County District Court, No. MC 00-01651, in which the defendant is charged with selling worthless insurance to people over 65 years old.

Tow Distributing v. Blue Cross Blue Shield of Minnesota, Dakota County District Court, No. 19-C4-02-009317, in which the plaintiff seeks distribution to policy holders of tobacco litigation proceeds.

In Re AOL Time Warner Inc. Securities and ERISA Litigation, New York, S.D.N.Y. M.D.L. No. 1500, in which the defendant is charged with breach of contract with subscribers, engaging in deceptive marketing practices, unjust enrichment, and false advertising.

In Re Monosodium Glutamate Antitrust Litigation, USDC Minnesota, No. MD-1328, in which the defendant is charged with illegally fixing the price for monosodium glutamate.

Alternatives to Class Actions

Class actions have their place and can serve society well. Overuse and abuse of this procedure are two of the problems, as are lawyers, who seek to enrich themselves above all else. The biggest problem, however, is the use of a class action to address a legal or social wrong when there is a far more effective and cheaper remedy.

For example, fraud and deception practiced by big business corporation executives are the basis for thousands of class actions. Why is this? Are there not laws that make such conduct unlawful? Enforcement of the law by government officials who already have that duty will do the trick in many cases – at no additional cost to the public. Eliot Spitzer, the Attorney General of the State of New York, exposed many scams and cleaned up whole industries by effectively performing his job. Class actions were not needed.

Corporate executives sometimes intentionally hide product defects, dangerous or unhealthy working conditions, environmental infractions and other corporate wrongdoing because they are confident these conditions will go undiscovered or, if discovered, that they will escape any penalty. This behavior can be thwarted without resort to class actions.

Corporate employees who know about such wrongdoing, but are afraid to speak up, can be protected and given strong incentive to disclose what they hear and see such as job protection and special compensation – paid for by the culprit. Corporations can be required to thoroughly educate employees on their legal duty to blow the whistle on corporate misbehavior.

Top corporate executives should be punished whenever there is corporate crime even if they supposedly knew nothing about it. If they face significant consequence, you can bet their efforts to find and eradicate such practices will more than double.

There is an example of this. Under the Foreign Corrupt Practices Act,[39] which concerns bribing foreign governments or companies to win a contract or for other gain, top executives of the bribing company are punished if they knew or should have known of illegal bribes even if they claim they had no knowledge. This works. You occasionally hear of such bribes but not nearly to the same extent as corporate fraud in America.

The excesses of class action lawyers in pursuit of lawsuits and the lawyers who start them can be controlled. Establishing a rule that 85 percent of the proceeds of a class action must be paid to class action beneficiaries, imposing sanctions on class action lawyers who pursue meritless cases, and implementing the so-called English Rule that requires the losing party and their attorneys to pay some or all the legal fees and litigation costs of the winning party will sharply reduce class action abuse. These and other reforms will reduce the number of class actions and correspondingly reduce the class action tax that goes with excessive use. These reforms are proposed and discussed in Chapter 16, Part III, Making Justice Efficient, Affordable and Reasonable.

Chapter 10
Public Pretenders

A public defender is a lawyer who is appointed by a judge to represent a poor person who cannot pay for the services of a lawyer. Only indigent people – those who meet the official standard of living in poverty – can get a public defender. A public defender is assigned only for certain kinds of cases such as a case where a person is charged with a crime or is involved in a juvenile court case.

Most Minnesota public defenders are full-time employees of the Minnesota Office of the State Public Defender. They are very dedicated to their work. They also are experienced, very capable, and very hard workers who often work up to 60 hours or more per week.

Part-time public defenders, almost all of whom are lawyers in the private practice of law, also are assigned to represent indigent clients. Most are conscientious and capable. However, the legal fees they receive for this work is very little per case compared to their regular clients. Perhaps because of that, they usually spend very little time working on the cases of their public defendant clients.

Sadly, there are part-time public defenders who seem to be more interested in the money they are paid and care little about what happens to their indigent clients. The work of many of these lawyers is very poor in quality. An illustration of this is what happened to Mother's 11-year-old son in the case of "The Young Sex Perverts."

Despite their good intentions, hard work and capabilities, public defenders have a bad reputation. They frequently are referred to as "public pretenders." This is because their service on each case generally is very inadequate.

Lack of Time and Resources

The biggest problems of public defenders are lack of time and resources. Currently, there are about 350 equivalent full-time public defenders in the whole State of Minnesota. During 2003, they opened 166,807 cases as follows: felony – 24,277; CHIPS (Children in Need of Protection) – 8,518; gross misdemeanor/other – 43,267; misdemeanor – 61,557; and juvenile – 29,238.[40] In 2003, each equivalent full-time public defender had an average of 915 cases. Public defenders often work on more than 20 cases per day. They spend an average of less than 30 minutes with their client in most of their cases. That is far less than what is needed to properly represent a defendant charged with a crime. It is barely enough time to work out a plea bargain.

A plea bargain is a deal made between the prosecutor and the defendant. If the defendant agrees to plead guilty to some crime and accepts the penalty, the prosecutor agrees to drop other generally more serious charges and recommend a lighter sentence than the defendant might get after a trial. Many defendants agree to a plea bargain even though they did nothing wrong and did not commit any crime. They feel they have no choice.

There is virtually no money available to public defenders for expert witnesses, investigators, and depositions (getting information from people to prepare for trial). The result is that in all but a very few cases a public defender cannot provide a fair defense in a criminal case or keep a parent from losing her children in juvenile proceedings.

Lack of Justice

The inability of public defenders to provide adequate services for their clients is described in an October 13, 2003 newspaper story (Brainerd Dispatch):

> "The 27-year-old man's legs jittered up and down beneath the small table in the stark jail interview room, although he appeared more resigned than nervous.
>
> "Nearby, names of others who had sat in the same chair were etched into the paint on the window frame

separating the interview room from the rest of the jail.

> "Across the table the man's public defender leaned forward and went over the options again–continue the case in court or accept an offer from the prosecution, which amounted to five years in prison with the possibility to get out in four.
>
> "It was one of about 100 cases facing the Crow Wing County Public Defender's Office Oct. 13. In a court day that ran from 9 a.m. until nearly 6:30 p.m., the court system churned through case after case.
>
> "'When you have a calendar of 105 (cases), you can't humanly do justice,' said David Hermerding, managing attorney for the Crow Wing County Public Defender's office. 'That's not justice. It's not. We are reaching a true crisis here. If we as a society really want a true justice system we need to adjust to some of the problems that are coming up here and coming up quickly.'"

U. S. Supreme Court Justice Hugo Black said the following in Gideon v. Wainwright:[41]

> "From the very beginning, our state and national constitutions and laws have laid great emphasis on procedural and substantive safeguards designed to assure fair trials before impartial tribunals in which every defendant stands equal before the law. This noble ideal cannot be realized if the poor man charged with a crime has to face his accusers without a lawyer to assist him." (372 U.S. at 344)

OVERWHELMED

The problem is getting worse. As a result of budget cuts, loss of lawyer positions, and an additional responsibility (child protection cases) annual caseloads of individual public defenders have increased as follows:

2000	757
2001	795
2002	864
2003	over 900

A recommendation contained in a National Advisory Commission is that lawyers take no more than 400 case units a year, which equals 400 misdemeanors, 275 gross misdemeanors, or 150 felonies. Minnesota's public defenders have nearly twice that load.

Value of Public Defenders

Many people believe that if a person is charged with a crime, he most likely is guilty of some wrongdoing. Police officers, they reason, do not arrest someone without good cause. Nor do prosecutors and grand juries indict a person unless they believe there is significant evidence of guilt.

But even people who believe most charged defendants are guilty of something believe all defendants should have access to a lawyer to assure procedural fairness. Many, however, draw the line at giving every defendant the full array of legal weapons needed for a vigorous defense. Why, they ask, should we provide guilty defendants with the chance to escape paying for their crimes? Why waste public funds on guilty people?

This argument, although based on logic, is wrong-headed. If people charged with committing a crime cannot get a fair defense, we have changed America's longstanding legal standard. Instead of innocent until proven guilty, it is guilty if charged.

No doubt many defendants are guilty – but certainly not all. There are instances of mistaken identity, confusion, false charges, poor investigation, overzealous and sometimes wrongful prosecution, and even falsified evidence. As illustrated by the cases of "The Cops From Hell" and "The Godzilla Conspiracy," there are instances of unjustified conviction. News stories have reported instances of people spending years in prison for a crime they did not commit. In some cases, a person was sentenced to die for committing a murder that later investigation proved was committed by someone else.

With respect to juvenile court proceedings, there is a comparable dialogue. Child protection workers, guardians ad litem and family court officers are thought of by most as very good-hearted people who are simply recommending what is in the best interests of the children who are the subjects of juvenile court proceedings. And if one of these public officers recommends terminating a person's parental rights to his or her child, or transferring custody to a third person, it is assumed that it probably is for compelling reasons. Therefore, the argument goes, it not only is a waste of public money, but also bad public policy to provide these parents with the means to keep custody of their children.

The above arguments also are logical, but they are based on false premises – that the public officers named are always right in their judgments and always well-intentioned. Public officers like those named can be and have been badly mistaken, negligent, and even intentionally unprofessional as shown by the cases of "The Young Sex Perverts," "Insanity in Wonderland," and "The Infant Trade."

Yet another argument against providing public defenders with the time and resources needed to adequately represent defendants in criminal cases and respondents in juvenile court proceedings is that there simply is not enough public money to do so. Minnesota's budget problems are well known. Because of budget deficits and a faltering economy, government already has cut many vital services that need to be restored before providing more than the about $50 million per year the state currently pays for public defender services.

The above arguments for limiting public defender services to the current level are short-sighted. Far more than lawyers in private practice, public defenders do not help people get away with crimes or help bad parents keep custody of their children. They have neither the time nor incentive for this. If a defendant admits guilt, the public defender almost always urges him or her to plead guilty, accept a reasonable penalty, and change his or her ways. No humane public defender would ever knowingly hurt a child by fighting to keep the child in a damaging environment. Public defenders have no obligation or reason to do that.

Effective Public Defenders Are Worth the Cost

Are public defender services a waste of money or are they cost-effective? We don't know. That is because we don't know how many people have been wrongfully or unjustly convicted of crimes. Nor do we know how many times children have unnecessarily or unjustifiably been placed in foster care or severely damaged emotionally by being separated from a parent.

From statistics published by the Supreme Court of Minnesota, we know that in 2003 there were 57,041 major criminal cases, 26,866 DWI cases, 15,049 5th degree assault cases, and 63,002 major juvenile cases. The total of these categories is 161,958, of which 98,956 were major criminal cases. We know that only a tiny percentage of this group had the many thousands of dollars it takes to pay for lawyer services through trial.

Data on the number or percentage of the 161,958 cases handled by a public defender are not available. An unknown number of the defendants in criminal cases represented themselves. In some cases, it was because it was their only option. In others, it was because they had no confidence in public defenders.

Although actual data on representation in criminal cases is unavailable, it is safe to assume that in over 90 percent of these cases either a public defender represented the defendant or the defendant represented himself or herself.

Determining how much public money was wasted because of wrongful convictions, or because defendants agreed to plead to a crime they did not commit as part of a plea agreement, is not possible without knowing the number of such convictions. What is known is that providing for the needs and supervision of a state prisoner costs Minnesota taxpayers about $80 per day, or $30,000 per year.[42]

This means that close to $30 million of public money was wasted if just 1 percent of the defendants in the 98,956 criminal cases were wrongfully convicted of a crime and imprisoned for a year. (989.5 x $30,000 = $29,685,000). This does not include the money spent to service prisoners before and after imprisonment or costs incurred by law enforcement officers, prosecutors, and the courts.

We believe the cost to society of grossly inadequate public defender services is staggering – many times more than the cost it would take to provide the legal services poor people should have. Significant sums of money are wasted when spent on prisoners who go to jail for a crime they did not commit. The damage to each person wrongfully sent to jail, and to that person's family, is enormous. More money is wasted on foster care, counseling and related services when a child is unjustifiably removed from the home of his or her parent. In many cases, a wrongful criminal conviction is followed by a family dissolution or families that resort to welfare programs which adds yet more to taxpayer cost.

The waste from wrongful termination of parental rights, unjustified placement of children in foster care, and other mishandled juvenile court proceedings is impossible to determine. Millions are spent for foster care, more millions for psychological counseling of children and parents, and an unascertainable amount for the services of child protection officers, other bureaucrats, and prosecutors. There is no way to measure the agony, grief and emotional damage caused by the destruction of a family.

Tens of thousands of Minnesotans are hurt by inadequate public defender services. Chapter 16 of Part III proposes reforms to remedy the huge amount of injustice and waste of taxpayer money experienced in Minnesota each year because indigent people cannot get effective legal representation.

Part III
Reforms

What reforms do you think will improve Minnesota's court and legal system? We would like to know your recommendations and, with your permission, may include them in our next book.

Send your recommendations:

By e-mail: dalenathan@usfamily.net

By mail:

Dale Nathan
PO Box 211284
Eagan, MN 55121

Judge's Court

Chapter 11
Make Judges, Public Officials and Lawyers Accountable

Common Sense Commission

Judges do not like seeing their name in print in connection with decisions that are obviously unjust. It embarrasses them. This fact can be used to give judges a powerful incentive to act responsibly. We propose a commission of ordinary citizens – the "Common Sense Commission." Its mission would be to review decisions referred to them by a party to a lawsuit, a lawyer, or anyone else.

Decisions like those in the horror cases summarized in Part I of this book that are outrageous or lacking in justice or common sense should be widely publicized in the media and the judges who made them exposed to the glare of public scrutiny. The commission also should have the authority to refer the judge and the case to a judicial discipline agency that is described later in this chapter.

Neither the Common Sense Commission nor the judicial discipline agency will be able to reverse or change any decision made by a judge. That would continue to be reserved exclusively to the appeals process.

The law that establishes the commission will require judges to give written notice to parties in each lawsuit of the Common Sense Commission and how to contact it. It also will provide for fines and possibly other sanctions if a judge fails to provide such a notice in a case.

Make Judges Pay Damages in Egregious Cases

Judges will act much more responsibly if they may be liable for damages when they injure a person intentionally or as a result of gross negligence. We recommend the creation of a new court, the "Minnesota Judges and Public Officials Court." Its exclusive jurisdiction will be limited to judges, prosecutors, government child protection and social workers, and law enforcement officers. This would be a special court independent of the state judicial branch of government. Judges of this court will be selected in the same manner as judges of the Minnesota Court of Appeals.

The only cases that would go before the Judges and Public Officials Court would be those that make a claim against a judge or public official for damages. Defendants will be liable for damages that result from gross negligence in performing his or her duties or from actions intended to wrongfully hurt a person.

To protect judges and public officials from harassment and frivolous or baseless claims or suits, each claim filed with the new court would be evaluated by a panel of three judges of the court. Following a process somewhat like a summary judgment proceeding[43] the panel would decide if there was enough substance to the claim to go to the next step. The person asserting the claim would have the burden of proving the case should go forward.

Similarly, claims against prosecutors and other public officials would first be evaluated by a panel of judges to determine if the case should be continued or be dismissed for lack of a sufficient basis.

A judge would be liable to pay damages if the Judges and Public Officials Court decides that the judge: (1) misinterpreted or misapplied the law either intentionally or as a result of gross negligence; (2) was clearly and unfairly biased against the person who makes the claim; (3) clearly was dishonest or untruthful; or (4) made a ruling so lacking in merit or grounds as to be clearly unjust. All judges, including judges of the Minnesota Court of Appeals and the Minnesota Supreme Court, and others who perform judge-like duties such as court referees, would be subject to the jurisdiction of the Judges and Public Officials Court.

Is establishing such a court controversial? Of course it is. Do judges and public officials want such a court? Of course not. It can be expected that they will find a thousand reasons why such a court is unneeded. They undoubtedly will argue that potential liability for damages will greatly impede their work. After all, judges and public officials will say, they all are good and well-meaning people who simply are doing their duty. And, they never make a mistake or, perish the thought, abuse their power.

But the reality is that judges and public officials need not worry if, in fact, they are as just described. Moreover, protections can be built in to shield them from vindictive and baseless claims. People who assert such claims frivolously would be subject to heavy fines and possibly other measures to discourage them from abusing judges and public officials. And, there would no litigation or other court cost to judges and public officials unless the evaluation panel finds sufficient cause to proceed against the defendant.

If voters believe that power corrupts, and that some judges and public officials abuse their powers and unjustifiably cause great damage and needless suffering, and if voters want an end to that, a Judges and Public Officials Court makes great sense.

Certification of Court Decisions

A person who starts a lawsuit and his attorney are required to certify that there is a reasonable basis for the lawsuit. A person who brings a lawsuit in bad faith, or with no reasonable basis and thereby violates the certification can be fined (called "sanctions"). The lawyer also can be sanctioned. Because of this possibility, lawyers normally will refuse to sue out a case that is not supportable.

Based on this precedent, we believe judges should include a certification in each decision that the decision is based on the facts in the case, the law, and is just. A judge could be sanctioned and assessed damages payable to an injured party if the Judges and Public Officials Court finds that his or her decision was, intentionally or through gross negligence, dishonest, biased, contrary to law, or so lacking in merit as to be unjust.

Lawyer Reference Service

We suggest the creation of a reference service similar to the

Better Business Bureau to help people determine if a lawyer they want to hire has a reputation for honesty and reasonableness. Every lawyer would be required to inform potential clients of the Lawyer Reference Service and provide information on how to contact it.

The Lawyer Reference Service would list a lawyer if ten of his clients provide a signed written statement to the Lawyer Reference Service that the lawyer is honest and ethical. Nothing would be said by the Lawyer Reference Service about any lawyer who is not listed on its roster.

The Lawyer Reference Service could receive complaints about a lawyer and, if it determined they are justified, remove a lawyer from its roster. The Lawyer Reference Service would not be allowed to give a negative reference about any lawyer – merely whether or not a particular lawyer is listed on its roster. This reform would provide incentive for lawyers to develop and maintain a reputation of being ethical.

Judge Oversight

Oversight of judges, including effective discipline, currently is nonexistent. The agency now charged with that responsibility is the feckless Board on Judicial Standards. Lawyers know this board is a fraud and that referring judge misbehavior to it is folly.

What the current Board on Judicial Standards does most aggressively is prosecute judges who dare to criticize other judges or the system. Hennepin County Judges LaJune Thomas Lange and Jack Nordby, both of whom sharply criticized judicial wrongdoing, were tried by the Board on Judicial Standards for criticizing judges. Each barely hung on to his or her job.

As noted by the League of Women Voters in their publication "Choosing Minnesota's Judges," 1998, League of Women Voters of Minnesota, 550 Rice Street, St. Paul, MN 55103 (page 5):

> "About 85 percent of the complaints filed against judges are dismissed by the Board on Judicial Standards, according to the Board's Executive Secretary, who explains that most complaints are filed by people who are disappointed after losing a

> case or who have no real basis for filing ethics charges.
>
> "When the Board does discipline a Judge, it does so with discretion-the degree to which has aroused controversy. Critics point out that citizens should have access to information about judges against whom complaints have been filed or disciplinary action taken. [footnote omitted] The issue of the public's role in judicial discipline continues to provoke discussion."

Although the Board on Judicial Standards supposedly is an independent state agency, it is dominated and controlled by judges. Four of its ten members are active judges, two are lawyers with at least ten years in the practice of law, and four are members of the public.

The current Board on Judicial Standards should be replaced by a board that does not include judges as members. That is who the board watches. If input from judges is needed, the new board can ask for it.

The proposed name of the new board is the Judge Discipline and Removal Board. In addition to the powers of the current board, the new board would have the power to suspend a judge and require him or her to run in the next election for the right to continue in office. This would give the Judge Discipline and Removal Board ample power to deal with miscreant judges and would leave it to the voters to decide the fate of judges whose competence and integrity are questioned.

The new Judge Discipline and Removal Board would receive and evaluate cases referred to it by the Common Sense Commission and take appropriate action. If there are three or more such referrals in a year's time, the Judge Discipline and Removal Board would automatically suspend the judge involved and refer the matter to the voters. This will give the Common Sense Commission real clout.

All proceedings and records of the new board would be open to the public. There is no justification for secrecy.

Lawyer Oversight

Lawyer oversight currently is performed by the Office of Lawyers Professional Responsibility (Lawyer's Board). This agency reports to and works for the Minnesota Supreme Court. For the reasons given below, the current agency should be disbanded and its personnel replaced.

Few occupations are held in lower repute in Minnesota than lawyer. There are grounds for this bad reputation. Lying, distortion, exaggeration and dishonesty are endemic among lawyers. It is no secret that lawyers cheat, chase ambulances, contrive, bribe, gouge, trick, cover up, and do whatever it takes to get business and make money. The current Lawyer's Board tolerates this as well as the racism and other injustices of our current legal system. It has failed in its purpose and failed to protect people from unscrupulous lawyers.

Lawyers and staff of the current Lawyer's Board are much too preoccupied with punishing lawyers who criticize their boss – the judges. Recently, the Lawyer's Board prosecuted and the Minnesota Supreme Court found that a lawyer's criticism of judges did not have a basis they thought was sufficient and they indefinitely suspended that lawyer's license to practice. That this is an egregious violation of our cherished right of free speech was no hindrance to the Lawyer's Board or the Minnesota Supreme Court.

The relationship between the current Lawyer's Board and judges is much too cozy. Clearly, the Lawyer's Board should be completely independent of the judicial branch of government. It should be completely separate from a related agency as is almost every other agency that monitors professions such as those who regulate doctors, accountants, pharmacists, dentists, barbers, nurses, psychologists, and many others.

We propose a reconstituted Lawyer's Board with new personnel who will focus on clearing up the lawyer profession even if some targets are rich lawyers with big law firms that contribute the most in gratuities and campaign contributions to judges who are seeking reelection to office. As proposed for prosecutors, lawyers and staff of the new board will be subject to liability for damages for wrongful prosecution of a lawyer.

New law: new judges will be appointed solely on merit.
All in favor?

And, judges face the voters every four years
to have their performance reviewed.
Now all in favor?

Chapter 12 Get Politics out of Judge Selection

At least 15 states and the District of Columbia use a merit selection plan to choose their judges.[44] The Minnesota League of Women Voters believes such a plan should be considered.[45] Replacing election of judges with a merit selection plan is recommended by the American Bar Association.[46]

Under such a plan, candidates for judge are selected by nonpolitical councils. Membership of these councils can vary. We recommend a mix of civic leaders and citizens as well as some lawyers, but no judges. Council members would not only evaluate candidates for judge, they also would actively seek out lawyers they believe would be good judges and urge them to apply.

Minnesota has ten judicial districts. We propose one Judge Recruitment and Nominating Council for each of these districts. Using such a council to select nominees for judge relieves citizens of having to make choices they are not qualified or sufficiently informed to make – determining who is most likely to be a high-quality judge.

If the district councils are nonpolitical as we propose, political considerations would be greatly reduced and maybe even be almost eliminated as a factor in selecting judges. At the same time, participation by all citizens in finding highly motivated and qualified candidates for judge would be enhanced. This will happen if the public is invited to attend council meetings and if council meetings are held in as many communities within a district as is practical.

At these meetings, citizens can recommend candidates they

believe should be encouraged to apply. Such meetings would offer excellent opportunities to inform and educate the public on Minnesota's judicial system. This is not to suggest that the public would participate in the evaluation or nomination process. Those tasks would be performed by council members only in private.

Combining the selection process described above with retention elections and performance appraisals provided to voters before judge elections would give voters a major role to play in determining whether or not incumbent judges stay in office. Retention elections would serve the purposes of making judges accountable directly to the people and subject to their oversight. As is the process in plans in effect in other states, a judge would stand for election within two years after his or her initial appointment. Voters would be provided with an appraisal of the judge's performance during his or her initial period of service and would determine whether or not the judge should continue in office. A sample appraisal report to voters is shown in Chapter 13, "Report Cards for Judges."

An incumbent judge does not face an opponent in a retention election. Voters are asked to decide only if the named judge should be retained. To stay in office, the judge must receive a certain percentage of the vote. In some states, it is a majority of votes – more yes than no votes. In one state, the judge needs 60 percent of the votes cast in the judge election to stay in office. Our proposal is that to stay in office, an incumbent judge must receive a majority of the votes cast in the district in an election. For example, if the number of people who voted in the judicial district was 100,000, an incumbent judge would need 50,001 yes votes to continue in office. Such a threshold would motivate incumbent judges to seek out voters and win their approval.

District councils would consist of people who do not hold elective office and have not held an elective office or a political job such as campaign manager, campaign treasurer, or similar position. The composition of district councils could be predetermined in part by designating members by category such as the Minnesota Bar Association chairperson of the judicial district; one or two clergy members selected by designated organizations; the chair of the major chamber of commerce in the judicial district; designated civic organizations in the judicial district, and other sources of citizen leaders.

There are a variety of methods that can be considered to make the selection of district council members as nonpolitical as possible.

The process to be followed by each district council is straightforward. For each judge vacancy in the district, the district council evaluates applicants and submits a list of three nominees to the governor who can select the new judge only from that list. The judge appointed would face the voters within two years of appointment to determine if he or she will continue in office. If continued in office, that judge would face a retention election every four years thereafter. Prior to each such election, a report on the performance of the judge would be provided to each registered voter as well as widely published in the judge's judicial district so each voter can make an informed decision.

Candidates for appellate court judges would be evaluated and nominated by a statewide council. This council could consist of civic leaders, educators including deans of Minnesota's law schools, business-persons, clergy, representative citizens and other members. Lawyers could be members, but their number would be limited.

Many Minnesotans, probably the vast majority, agree that our state's current methods of selecting and retaining judges are seriously deficient. The truth is that well over 90 percent of our judges become judge by appointment, not by election as contemplated in Minnesota's Constitution. We should conform the law to current practices.

Instead of delegating the selection of all nominees for district court judge to a small committee in the governor's office, this task should be shifted to district councils that are much closer to the people and who are much more familiar with local lawyers. Under the proposed merit selection process, governors will not be able to select judges for political reasons. Perhaps best of all for incumbent judges, they will not face opponents at re-election time, or have to worry about debate on political issues. They will run on their records. Campaign finance needs will be greatly reduced and maybe even eliminated.

Several states have reformed the procedure for selecting and retaining judges to get politics out of the process, find and nominate the individuals who most likely will be the best judges, and give voters an informed and effective way to review the performance of their judges. Minnesota can do that.

All judges will be appointed to office under the proposed new process. New judges no longer would be elected to office.

The proposed process is a version of the Missouri Plan, which was the first plan implemented to choose judges on merit as much as possible instead of political connections. Fifteen states have adopted similar plans.

Read all about Judge Casper!

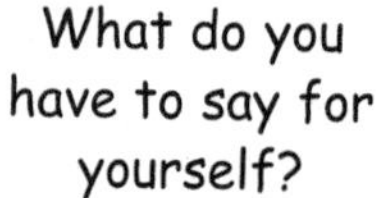

What do you have to say for yourself?

Chapter 13
Publish Report Cards on Judges at Re-Election Time

It is Tuesday, October 23. You have just returned home from work. As usual, work was hectic and demanding. The kids are not home yet. Only heaven knows what they are up to and it probably is not good. That worry can wait. Your spouse should be home soon and things will get better.

Inside the mailbox is a letter addressed to you. According to the return address, it is from the Minnesota Judicial Evaluation Commission. In the envelope is a report. It is about judges who are up for election in two weeks. The report tells how each of these judges has been performing his or her work. And it even has recommendations on which judges should be continued in office and which ones should be sent to pasture.

Unrealistic? Impossible? Not really. Since the 1980s, voters in Alaska have received such reports shortly before every judge election. An example of an actual report sent to Alaska voters by their judge evaluation commission is on the next page.[47] Now parts of Alaska may get colder than in Minnesota, but that does not mean Alaskans are smarter than Minnesotans. We can have reports on judges at election time just as they do.

Similar reports are sent to the voters in Colorado. They comment on the quality of the performance of each judge who is up for election or re-election. There is no reason Minnesota cannot follow the lead of these states and provide such a report to its voters.

Evaluate Every Judge's Work Annually

We propose a new state agency, not a part of the judicial branch of Minnesota government, that will review the work of each judge once a year and issue a report to the public on his or her performance. This agency, the "Minnesota Judicial Evaluation Commission," can be a small group of commissioners appointed by the district judge selection councils described in Chapter 12. In addition to evaluating the performance of each judge once a year, the proposed commission can publish a report at election time on each judge who seeks to be re-elected.

Reproduction of an Actual Report to Alaska Voters

THE ALASKA JUDICIAL COUNCIL
Finds THE FOLLOWING JUDGES
QUALIFIED
AND RECOMMENDS A "YES" VOTE ON THEIR RETENTION:

JUSTICE EDMOND W. BURKE, Supreme Court
JUSTICE JAY A. RABINOWITZ, Supreme Court

First Judicial District

JUDGE THOMAS M. JAHNKE, Superior Court
JUDGE GEORGE L. GUCKER, District Court

Third Judicial District

JUDGE JOHN BOSSARD, III, Superior Court
JUDGE RENE J. GONZALEZ, Superior Court
JUDGE KAREN L. HUNT, Superior Court
JUDGE JOAN M. KATZ, Superior Court
JUDGE PETER A. MICHALSKI, Superior Court
JUDGE MILTON SOUTER, Superior Court

JUDGE GLEN ANDERSON, District Court
JUDGE PETER G. ASHMAN, District Court
JUDGE NATALIE K. FINN, District Court
JUDGE WILLIAM H. FULD, District Court
JUDGE JOHN D. MASON, District Court

Fourth Judicial District

JUDGE MARY E. GREENE, Superior Court

THE ALASKA JUDICIAL COUNCIL FINDS
JUDGE KARL S. JOHNSTONE, SUPERIOR COURT,
THIRD JUDICIAL DISTRICT,
UNQUALIFIED
AND RECOMMENDS A "NO" VOTE ON HIS RETENTION

The Alaska Judicial Council has a statutory duty to conduct evaluations of each judge and justice standing for retention, and to provide information and recommendations to the public about these judges. The Council's evaluations were based on information from sources available to the Judicial Council at the time of its evaluation. These Sources included the Bar and Peace Officer mail surveys, a review of court and public records, professional and public testimony, investigation by Council staff and personal interviews.

The Judicial Council was established by the state's constitution as an agency of state government independent of the Court Systems and consists of seven members: three non-attorney members appointed by the Governor and confirmed by (the Legislature; three attorney members appointed by the Board of Governors of the Alaska Bar Association; and the Chief Justice, who serves as Chairman of the Council Exofficio).

Paid for by the Alaska Judicial Council, 1031 W. 4th Avenue, Suite 301, Anchorage 99501 – 279-2526

The proposed commission would be nonpartisan and independent. To assure independence, the commission would not be part of the judicial branch of state government. Its duties would be: (1) evaluate the performance of each state court judge once each year, and (2) publish a report on the performance of each judge who seeks re-election. The reports would be sent to each registered voter and would be widely published within the district of each judge who seeks re-election.

Evaluation of district court judges, court referees, and other judicial officials will be based on surveys of lawyers and people who were in lawsuits or court hearings, information on how many times the judge was reversed by a higher court, review of some of the judge's opinions, reports received by the Commission from people and lawyers, and other factors established by law or by the Commission.

Evaluation of appeals court judges could be based on surveys of lawyers, law school professors, house and senate committees on the judiciary, and the general public and reports received by the Commission from people and lawyers. A sample of opinions written by appeals court judges could be reviewed to gauge the clarity of his or her intellectual capacity.

The report issued on each judge who is seeking re-election will summarize the commission's information on and evaluation of that judge. It could recommend re-election or defeat. The report need not be long or overly-detailed. Contact information such as a website address, a telephone number, a mailing address can be included in the report. This will enable voters to get additional and even detailed information. To be fair, the reports should contain contact information provided by judges and candidates for judge so they can provide voters with the information they want voters to consider.

Annual performance evaluations will be an incentive, a very strong one, for judges to produce high-quality results. Despite occasional appearances to the contrary, judges want to be liked and respected. Few, if any, want to be regarded as incompetent or unqualified. And, most importantly, none wants to lose his or her job.

Which do you prefer: continuing the current system of voting for judges and judge candidates you know nothing about, or the proposed new system? Which system do you think will best promote justice in our courts?

"But Judge, This is for your re-election campaign," the lawyer said, begging the judge to take his money.

Chapter 14 Reform Campaign Finance for Judges

The need for incumbent judges to seek campaign contributions may disappear if Minnesota switches to retention elections instead of its current method of retaining incumbent judges. This switch is recommended in Chapter 12 – Get Politics Out of Judge Selection. In a retention election, only the incumbent judge is on the ballot. After reviewing information on the performance of an incumbent judge, voters determine whether or not the judge remains in office.

In contrast, Minnesota's current re-election process allows contested elections. If challenged, an incumbent judge needs to raise money to fight the challenger or challengers. There are many drawbacks to contested judge re-elections as described in Chapter 2 – Judge Election and Re-Election. But until the process is changed, incumbent judges and challengers need campaign funds.

Public Financing of Judge Elections

Public funding of judge elections is the interim solution we propose. Three states, North Carolina, Wisconsin and Montana, currently provide public funds to judge candidates,[48] and proposals have been made in four other states, Illinois, New Mexico, Pennsylvania and Texas to provide such funding.[49]

North Carolina's law that provides public funding to judges is the most recent and appears to be the best model. Key features of the North Carolina plan are:

- Full public funding is provided for qualified candidates who agree to fundraising and spending limits.

- Individual contributions to candidates are limited to specified amounts.

- Funds are available for both primary and general elections.

The North Carolina law applies only to candidates for Justice of the Supreme Court and Judge of the Court of Appeals. To qualify for public funds, a candidate must raise a "trigger" sum of money that comes only from "qualified" contributions. The trigger sum is the sum that opens the door to public funds. Qualified contributions are limited in amount and must be from a registered North Carolina voter.

A candidate for judge who wants to receive campaign funds from the state must file an application with the State Board of Elections. He must agree in his application to comply with contribution and expenditure limits and other terms. Then, he must within a specified period obtain contributions from 350 registered North Carolina voters that amount to not less than $10 nor more than $500.

Each candidate who satisfies the qualification criteria is certified as eligible to receive public funds. However, he actually receives public funds only if he is running against someone else for the same judge position, that is, in a contested election.

A certified candidate also is eligible to receive "rescue" funds. This additional amount is provided by the state if spending by a certified candidate's opponent will be higher than a second trigger amount. This means a certified candidate can get additional public funds if his opponent is set to spend an amount that is much higher than the limit agreed to by the certified candidate.

We propose a comparable plan for Minnesota. To run in the general election, a candidate for judge would have to receive a specified percentage of the total number of votes cast in the primary for the court seat being sought. A candidate could accept campaign contributions from anyone, including lawyers, for the primary race up to $50 per person. The balance remaining in the campaign account after the primary would be considered part of the public grant and the public grant would be reduced by that balance.

Each candidate who qualifies for the general election would receive a public grant if he or she agrees to certain terms. The candidate must agree to a spending limit and to not accept any contribution greater than a specified amount such as $300. If a candidate's opponent will be spending significantly more than the maximum agreed to by the candidate, additional state money will be provided to balance the election playing field.

Minnesota already has public funding of candidates for state executive and legislative offices. A candidate for one of these offices needs to raise a specific sum of money from contributions to his or her campaign in order to qualify for a public grant. This sum sometimes is referred to as the threshold sum. Each contribution received during the qualifying period counts as part of the threshold amount but only up to $50.

Threshold sums vary according to the office sought. In 2002, the threshold sum for a candidate for governor was $35,000. A candidate for governor who raised this amount within the qualifying period received a public grant of $216,463 after the primary elections. This grant came from an appropriation made by the Minnesota legislature for giving grants to candidates in 2002.

In addition to grants from this source, candidates who qualified for a public grant also received funds from tax check-off accounts. Tax check-off accounts come from tax check-offs made by taxpayers. Each taxpayer can check a box in his or her tax return to specify that he or she wants a portion of the taxes paid by him or her, up to a legal limit, to be given to the political party designated for distribution to that party's candidates.

Public grants can be made available to candidates for judge just as they are available to candidates for other elective state offices. It would take a somewhat different system particularly since candidates for judge do not run with a political party designation.

North Carolina has led the way in giving public grants to candidates for judge so they will not have to beg lawyers for big contributions. Minnesota should be quick to follow.

The law we propose would provide that members of law firms, lawyers and others who contribute to a judge's election or re-election campaign in the general election would not be allowed to appear before that judge in court for four years.

Judge elections would continue to be nonpartisan. All judge candidates who qualify to run in the general election and receive at least 5 percent of the vote in the primary would be eligible for a public grant.

The Cost of Publicly Funding Judge Elections

An important question is: how much will it cost to publicly fund judge elections? Only an estimate can be provided at this time, but available data makes such an estimate realistic.

In 2000, four Minnesota Supreme Court Justices ran for re-election. They spent a combined $505,121, or average of $126,280 each. In 2004, three Minnesota Supreme Court Justices are up for re-election. Using the 2000 average, we estimate they will spend a total of about $378,840 on their campaigns in 2004.

Of the sixteen judges on the Minnesota Court of Appeals, we believe eight will be running for re-election. In the past, there have been very few challenges to incumbent appeals court judges. We assume three will be challenged. Information obtained from the Minnesota Campaign Finance and Disclosure Board suggests that the average spent by each of these incumbent judges on their re-election campaign will be about $75,000. Based on this data, about $225,000 will be spent in appeals court judge elections.

About one-third of Minnesota's 271 district court judges will be on ballots in re-election campaigns. On the average, challenges to incumbent district court judges seeking re-election has been less than 10 percent. Data from the Campaign Finance and Disclosure Board show that in 2002 there were 15 contested district court judge elections and that individuals or incumbent judges who ran for election or re-election spent an average of about $25,000. If we assume there will be 25 contested district court judge elections in 2004 and that the average spent by each contestant will be $30,000, a total of $750,000 will be spent by candidates for the office of district court judge in 2004.

These estimates come to a total of $1,354,000. However, the plan proposed in this chapter still allows individual campaign contributions to incumbent judges and their challengers, although far less than the amounts now allowed. If we take these smaller contributions into account, the amount of public funds needed to finance these elections at the same level as in the past will be reduced. We estimate $54,000 in contributions will be made even if the new plan is implemented. This brings us to our estimate that $1,350,000 in pubic funds would be needed in 2004 if Minnesota had the proposed public funding plan in effect.

According to the Minnesota Population Center, University of Minnesota,[50] the estimated current population of Minnesota is just over 5 million and the projected population at the end of 2004 is close to 5.1 million. Since judge elections are held every other year, we have divided the computed estimate of $1,350,000 by two to get an estimated annual cost of $675,000. This leads to our belief that it would cost Minnesotans less than 14¢ ($675,000 divided by 5.1 million) per year per person to end judge bribery through campaign contributions.

Would public funding of judge elections result in offsetting savings? We think the answer is yes, and further that the savings would be much greater in amount than the funds expended to finance judge campaigns.

To begin with, lawyers and special interests do not really give campaign contributions to judges for civic reasons. Such contributions are considered by big law firms as a cost of doing business. Lawyers recover their contributions in some manner such as charging higher fees for their services. Most company moguls probably recover the contributions they make by including an amount in the prices they charge for their products and services for this expense. In the final analysis, this means that you, the consumer, actually pay the tab to re-elect judges. Eliminating the hundreds of thousands of dollars now donated by lawyers, law firms and corporate moguls to judges would be a huge savings.

If, as we and others think, re-elected judges return the favors accorded them by campaign contributions by slanting decisions in the direction of their contributors, we will save an incalculable sum by ending the corrupting effect of campaign contributions to judges.

If we could put a value on the peace of mind we would gain by eliminating the fear we experience when we go into court thinking the judge has been bought, the savings would be out of sight. Depending on your perspective, a person easily could conclude that the savings achieved by public financing of judge campaigns are many times more than the cost.

At its meeting in February 2004, the American Bar Association House of Delegates passed a resolution urging all states to consider public financing of judicial elections.[51] Consideration of this reform also is recommended by the Minnesota League of Women Voters.[52]

Public financing of judge elections gives incumbent judges the means to avoid selling justice for campaign contributions. It frees the public from the worry that judges have been bought. These benefits are well worth the surprisingly low cost. Serious consideration should be given to the reforms proposed in this chapter.

"I just want to give the judge his $150 gratuity,"
Lawyer Larson said.

Chapter 15
Abolish $150 Gratuities for Judges

> Judges are prohibited from accepting any gift that has more than a nominal value (almost no value) except that a judge can accept: (1) gifts from relatives, personal friends (if there is a history of such friendship and past exchanges of gifts), and members of the judiciary; (2) intra and inter-office gifts; (3) awards, an honorary degree, plaques; (4) food or refreshment of nominal value, meals or beverages consumed on the premises where purchased; and (5) things paid for by a unit of government. Judges who violate the gift ban law could be dismissed from office.[53] (emphasis added)

The prohibitions summarized above are in effect in the State of Illinois under its Gift Ban Law. Minnesota should have a similar law. The evils of lawyers giving gifts to judges and court personnel far outweigh any alleged benefit.

Unlike Illinois, in Minnesota lawyers and anyone else can give gifts to judges and court personnel – as much as a person wants. If the gift is $150 or less, it need not be reported. It can be kept anonymous. If it is over $150, it must be reported – to the Judicial Standards Board, where it is unlikely anyone will find out about it unless you visit this board and inquire.

The Minnesota Supreme Court, not the Minnesota legislature,

made the rule now in effect. It did so by order on November 1, 1995 that promulgated the rule in its current form. In pertinent part, Canon 4 of the Code of Judicial Conduct provides that a judge can accept:

> [A]ny other gift, bequest, favor or loan only if the donor is not a party or other person who has come or is likely to come or whose interests have come or are likely to come before the judge, and if its value exceeds $150, the judge reports it in the same manner as the judge reports compensation in Section 4H.

To get around the condition that the giver must not be a person who "has come or is likely to come before the judge," law firms who consider it smart to wine and dine judges and take good care of them designate a member of their firm as the firm's entertainer. That person does not appear before any judge and may not even perform legal duties.

The first reform proposed in this chapter is for the Minnesota legislature to pass a law that regulates gift giving to and gift accepting by judges, court personnel, and members of their families. Our proposed law would:

- Prohibit judges from accepting any gift from any lawyer just as current Minnesota law prohibits legislators and state executives from accepting gifts from lobbyists. The only exception would allow a judge or court employee to accept gifts from a lawyer who is a member of the judge's immediate family.

- Prohibit judges and court personnel from accepting any gift from any other person other than a member of his or her family.

- Prohibit lawyers and all others from giving any gift to any judge, member of a judge's immediate family, or any Minnesota court employee except for members of their immediate family.

- Require judges to file annual reports on the gifts they received from anyone and lawyers to file an annual report on the gifts they gave to judges and court personnel and their immediate families.

To establish uniformity in regulations that concern gift giving to public officials, the proposed law would be made a part of Minnesota Statutes 10A.071, the current law that prohibits gifts by lobbyists to public officials. (This law currently does not apply to judges or court personnel with one exception: it applies to judges of the Workers' Compensation Court of Appeals.) Definitions of the terms "gift" and "official" are contained in this law. These definitions have been interpreted and applied by the Minnesota Campaign Finance and Disclosure Board, which is responsible for administering Minnesota Statutes 10A.071.

Exceptions to the bans on gift giving and accepting for promotional items or items of nominal value are listed in Minnesota Statutes 10A.071 and can be made applicable to judges and court personnel. Interpretations of who are "givers" and "receivers" and classifications of the kinds of gifts that qualify as an item of nominal value have been promulgated by the Campaign Finance and Disclosure Board. These standards should be applied to judges and court personnel as well as all other government employees.

The intent of the proposed law is to abolish the current rule that allows a judge to accept an unlimited number of gratuities of up to $150 in amount. Such gifts may have the effect of influencing decisions. They create a perception of impropriety that degrades the public's perception of judge integrity.

Judges, lawyers and law firms would file a report each year with the Campaign Finance and Disclosure Board concerning gifts just as lobbyists now must do. In these reports, each judge would have to list each gift he or she received from a person who is not a member of the judge's immediate family, and the name and address of the donor.

Each lawyer and law firm would file a report with the Campaign Finance and Disclosure Board which lists any gift the lawyer or his firm, or any employee of his firm, gave directly or indirectly to a judge or court employee, the name of the judge to whom it was given, and the amount or value. In the case of a gift from an organization such as a bar association, corporation or other person, such as a fee for a speech or award, the donor will also be required to report the name and address of each source of the funds used to pay for the gift.

The second reform proposed in this chapter is to increase the salaries of judges enough to achieve two objectives: (1) cause the potential best judges to aspire to that office, and (2) eliminate the rationale for gratuities. To achieve these objectives, it is not necessary to pay judges the stratospheric amounts received by the highest-paid lawyers. It is sufficient if judge compensation leaves little need for a judge to forego his work as a judge for the financial benefit of his family.

A possible baseline for setting judge compensation is the median earnings of lawyers in the top 25 percent of lawyers in private practice. The agency that can make this determination and recommend the salary levels that are most likely to achieve our objectives is the Minnesota Compensation Council. This is a Minnesota executive commission authorized by Minnesota Statutes 15A.081 et seq. It is a balanced body that consists of members appointed by leaders of both the majority and minority political parties, the governor, and the Chief Justice of the Minnesota Supreme Court.

Once every two years, the commission submits a report to the legislature in which it recommends compensation amounts for the governor, constitutional officers, members of the Minnesota legislature, agency heads, judges, and other government officials. One of the factors the commission is required by law to consider is: "comparisons with other comparable positions in the public and private sectors."[54] With respect to judges, a legitimate comparison can be made between the position of judge and that of a senior partner in a successful law firm. The abilities and skills needed for each of these vocations are comparable. Their compensation also should be comparable.

The State of Illinois sanitized its legal system by barring gifts to judges by lawyers and others who have no legitimate reason to give them gifts. Minnesota's standard of morality in its legal system should be at least as high as the Illinois standard. As to judge compensation, we should not force our judges to sacrifice what they could earn in private practice for the privilege of serving us. There are two compelling reasons for this: the first is adherence to principle; the second is to attract the best possible judges.

Ridiculous! You lose - pay the winner's legal bills.

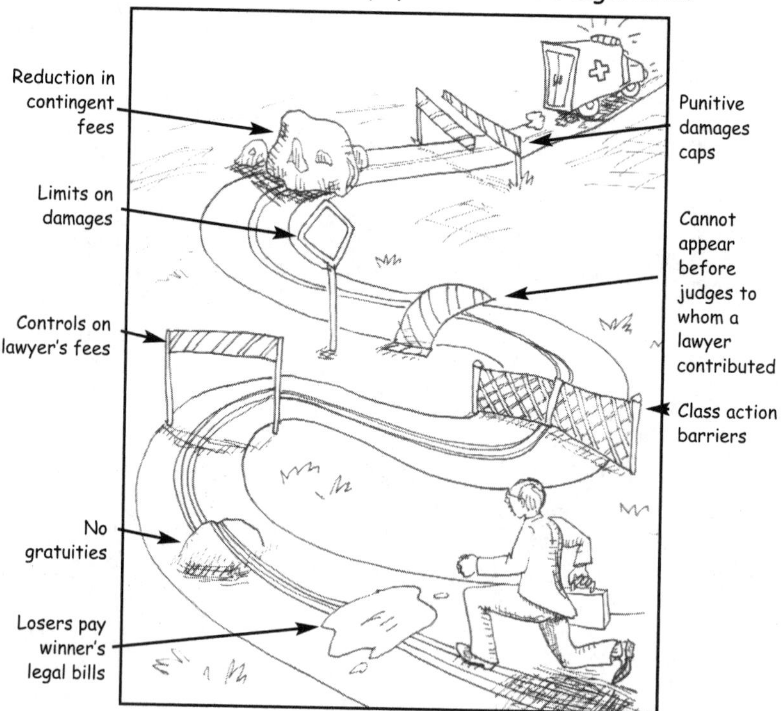

Chapter 16
Make Justice Efficient, Affordable and Reasonable

Justice is beyond the means of most people because of its cost. The average person does not have tens of thousands of dollars to spend to defend himself in a lawsuit or assert a just claim. The great poet Carl S. Sandberg said it this way:

When the lawyers are through
What is there left, Bob?
Can a mouse nibble at it
And find enough to fasten a tooth in?

The poet and writer Francóis Voltaire related, "I was never ruined but twice – once when I lost a lawsuit, and once when I gained one."

A pyrrhic win is not justice. To make justice available to everyone, we must reduce its cost.

Arbitration and Mediation

Early use of effective arbitration and mediation could resolve disputes with huge savings in time and expense. Waiting until shortly before trial to engage in arbitration or mediation is not necessary.

Arbitration and mediation are different, although the purpose of each is the same – to settle the dispute and end the lawsuit if there is one.

An arbitrator conducts an arbitration. Mediation is conducted by a mediator. Both are referred to as "neutrals."

Arbitration

Arbitration can be binding or non-binding. If it is binding, the arbitrator, after listening to the testimony and considering the evidence, makes a decision – very much like a judge. His or her decision settles the dispute. By law, the decision of the arbitrator is final and cannot be overturned on appeal unless the arbitrator exceeded his or her authority or did something illegal.

A non-binding arbitration does not result in a final settlement unless all parties to the dispute voluntarily accept the arbitrator's decision. In essence, the decision in a non-binding arbitration is advisory and reflects how the arbitrator thinks a judge would rule. Sometimes a non-binding arbitration helps the parties come to an agreement without proceeding further in the lawsuit.

As in court cases, there is a trial in an arbitration if the dispute is not resolved in advance of a trial. Prior to the trial, the parties typically submit summaries of the facts they expect to prove and their major arguments. The process at trial in an arbitration is about the same as in a court proceeding. Witnesses are sworn to tell the truth and give testimony. Parties submit documents and exhibits to back up their claims. However, the rules in arbitration are much more informal and far more flexible than in a court proceeding. Technical rules of evidence that bind a judge can be ignored in an arbitration.

After the arbitrator hears the testimony and considers the evidence (the exhibits) he or she issues a decision and informs the parties of it, generally sometime after the trial. Unlike judges, an arbitrator does not have to explain or back up his or her decision. Typically, the arbitrator announces the result only – that is, who wins and what relief or how much the winning party gets in money.

Mediation

The procedure in a mediation is very different from that in an arbitration. There is no trial in a mediation and the mediator usually meets with the parties separately until after there is a settlement if one is reached.

In a mediation, the parties typically sit in separate rooms during the mediation process. The mediator receives information in advance from each party telling the mediator that party's version of the facts and arguments, which the mediator reviews before the mediation. During the mediation, the mediator meets separately with each party to gain a better understanding of their positions and what is acceptable to each to settle the dispute.

After meeting with the parties one or more times, the mediator gives each party his or her analysis of that party's case. The mediator also makes a recommendation to each party on what would be a realistic and fair settlement.

The process of shuffling back and forth between the parties continues until there is agreement on a resolution of all issues – a settlement – or until everyone agrees a settlement cannot be reached.

Advantages of Arbitration and Mediation

Generally, arbitration and mediation are significantly cheaper than a court proceeding. Arbitrators and mediators usually are paid by the hour for their services, and there generally is a significant fee in an arbitration if it is conducted by an organization such as the American Arbitration Association. However, there are few other costs. Because both arbitration and mediation are far simpler and more flexible, they are many times faster than a court proceeding, which greatly reduces the cost.

It follows that there are many reasons for promoting arbitration and mediation as alternatives to a court proceeding. Courts are beginning to insist that parties to a lawsuit must attempt non-binding arbitration or mediation before the lawsuit will be allowed to proceed to trial. But currently, judges allow the court process to continue for an extended period before the parties must attempt arbitration or mediation. It may be that arbitration or mediation should be required early in a court proceeding. Combined with other proposed reforms – initial disclosures and a fact summary service, both described in this chapter – early arbitration or mediation could become much more feasible than they are currently.

To make arbitration and mediation affordable for parties in a lawsuit, partially funding them with public funds could be very cost effective in making justice far more available and in reducing the cost of maintaining our very expensive court system. One possibility is to pay retired judges an amount, say $35,000 per year, in addition to their retirement salary for services as part-time arbitrators and mediators. These services could be provided to parties in lawsuits at no charge if a settlement is reached and at moderate cost if there is no settlement. It is worth considering.

Lawsuit Costs Can Be Reduced

Actions that will reduce the cost of lawsuits include: (1) eliminate court fees of hundreds of dollars that must be paid to start or continue a lawsuit; (2) simplify the court process; (3) reduce the need for lawyer time, which is very expensive; (4) assess fines on lawyers and their clients who press meritless cases; and (5) provide independent, able and adequately funded public defenders to poor people who are charged with a crime or face losing custody of a child.

Court filing fees and other fees should be eliminated. Getting justice is a citizen's right and a government obligation. Deterring meritless lawsuits and actions can be accomplished by imposing fines and penalties as described below. This is far better than making justice unavailable because a person is too poor to pay court fees.

The court process can be simplified by requiring parties in a lawsuit to provide the other party with relevant information and documents up front as is the practice in federal courts. In those actions, this is called "initial disclosures," and it saves a lot of time and expense.

Court-provided independent experts to recommend damages awards to judges and juries will make the very expensive services of expert witnesses far less useful. The use of independent expert witnesses on property distribution issues and on child custody and visitation issues in dissolution cases also would make the services of party expert witnesses of doubtful value and thereby eliminate the expense of countering their testimony. Independent expert witnesses should have no connection with government agencies to assure they are not influenced by them.

Lawyer time, which often is $250 per hour or higher, can be reduced by providing case summary and file organization services to people. This public service would be at a reasonable cost, say $50 per hour. Legal advice would not be provided by this service. The service would gather information and documents, prepare a case summary that describes the situation, and assemble the documents into a file. The summary and file can be submitted to a lawyer. This would save the significant time it often takes for a lawyer to start providing legal advice and start legal actions.

Unjustified lawsuits by lawyers and their clients can be discouraged and greatly reduced by fines if the case is found to be meritless. Adoption of the English Rule that gives the winning party the right to recover their attorney's fees from the losing party also will deter meritless lawsuits.

Discouraging Wrongful Damage to Families

Public officials who abuse their power in actions that wrongly deprive a parent of custody of a child should be heavily penalized. So should judges who wrongfully permit a child to be taken away from his or her biological parents. The rule that children should not be separated from their biological parents except for grave and weighty reasons needs to be greatly strengthened.

Empowering the Poor

Providing able public defenders who have the resources they need to effectively represent poor defendants charged with a crime, or poor parents who face the loss of custody of a child, will substantially reduce the agony and huge expense of wrongful imprisonments, and the pitiful damage to parents and their children of separating them. It will save millions of tax dollars for foster care and related services. Keeping families together, like keeping innocent people out of jail, reduces overall government spending by significant amounts.

Authorizing defendants, if they choose, to submit the results of lie detector tests to the judge in non-jury cases can help dispose of hundreds, perhaps thousands, of cases where the entire evidence is the conflicting statements of the adversaries – "he said vs. she said."

The decision in these cases often is based on who is the better liar. Lie detector tests are routinely used by the Federal Bureau of Investigation (FBI) and even by police departments in internal investigations, and even by some commercial companies when the subject has consented. A judge may or may not be persuaded by the results of a lie detector test, but at least give the defendant (or party) the option of submitting such evidence to the judge.

The excessive use of contingent fee and class action lawsuits can be discouraged by rules applicable to these cases that: (1) require lawyers to keep track of the hours they spend on each contingent fee and class action case; (2) limit what a lawyer can charge in these cases to twice his regular hourly rate; (3) circumscribe a lawyer's compensation in class action and contingent fee cases to what is reasonable as determined by the judge; (4) make the English Rule that the loser pays the fees and costs of the prevailing party applicable to class action and contingent fee cases; (5) allow contingent fee cases only in a few categories such as personal injury and only when the charging party cannot afford to hire an attorney at an hourly rate; and (6) limit the fee collectable by lawyers in class action cases to a maximum of 15 percent of the net recovery.

Export Prisoners, Not Jobs

Many millions of dollars, maybe tens of millions of dollars, could be saved by reforming how we supervise, house and provide for prisoners. The corrections system is clearly associated with and some say is part of the legal system. Reducing the exploding cost of caring for prison inmates would be a boon to our economy.

A major topic of debate in today's highly charged political climate is outsourcing U.S. jobs. Advocates justify this on the basis that it reduces business costs even if it also deprives law-abiding workers of their likelihood.

If it is sensible to export citizens' jobs to save money, is it not just as sensible to export long-term prison residents for the same reason? Instead of paying $30,000 per year to care for a criminal, why not spend $5,000? The savings can be used to stimulate creation of replacement jobs and to reduce taxes the unemployed are less able to pay.

Opponents of exporting prisoners might argue that this would be a cruel and unusual punishment to separate prison inmates so far from their families. In earlier ages when a nation like Great Britain had prison colonies such as Australia, Louisiana or St. Helena, that argument had a firm foundation. Banishment to a foreign prison colony effectively cut off all contact between a prisoner and his family except perhaps for letters.

But conditions today are much different. Modern technology in the form of cell telephones enable people to talk regularly to each other and even to see the person to whom they are talking. Instead of pre-visit searches and a cramped jail cell, the conditions of visitation can be far more relaxed as well as more frequent.

In addition to dollar savings, a compelling reason for exporting prisoners is to provide an added incentive for avoiding crime. The threat of being outsourced could be the deciding factor in causing a person to not repeat crimes such as driving under the influence (DWI), assault, driving without a license or insurance, paying with a bad check, and other offenses that seem to be habitual to so many criminals. Conversely, the hope of returning to America could be the motivator in persuading a prisoner to earnestly educate, train and rehabilitate himself.

If selected with care, foreign custodians might surpass American prisons in rehabilitating criminals. Too many inmates in American jails and prisons spend their days in the exercise room and in watching American television programs such as the Jerry Springer Show, the content of which is questionable for character improvement. Contracts for the care of prisoners can specify that they should work at something to help pay for their keep, and should be trained in behaving lawfully as well as for a vocation.

Personnel now occupied with watching and caring for prisoners can be redirected to other tasks that need attention such as eradicating drug trading, curbing gang warfare, fighting terrorism and making our streets safe. Some of the savings realized by exporting prisoners can be used to construct affordable housing or reduce taxes instead of building more prisons.

Automate Enforcement of Parking and Traffic Rules

Tens of millions of dollars can be saved annually in Minnesota and law enforcement greatly expanded by automating parking and traffic management. License plate recognition (LPR) technology is the key. It is an image-processing technology used to identify vehicles by their license plate. It already is fully developed and is in extensive use.

This technology makes it possible to fully automate enforcement of parking rules. Parking meters become parking monitors as well. A scanner in the marking meter or meter stand reads the license plate. If payment is not made within some number of minutes after the vehicle is parked, or if the time paid for expires, an electronic record is created that results in a ticket. The ticket can be sent by a central administrative authority.

We propose a bold new system for parking meter administration. Our plan is to switch this task from municipalities to a state agency such as the Department of Transportation. This would greatly reduce the number of government employees in Minnesota who spend their work days processing parking tickets, accepting payment, and related activities. We further propose that all revenue from parking violations would go into the state's coffers. To offset this loss of local revenue, amounts provided by the state to local governments would be increased proportionately.

Payment for parking time no longer would be with coins. Parking cards, which already are in use, commercial credit cards, and even driver's license cards, would be used instead. People who use their driver's license cards would be invoiced for the parking fee plus a modest administrative charge, or would have to pay accumulated charges plus interest when they renew their license plate annually. There would be no need for police personnel to collect money from meters.

Hundreds of thousands of work hours now spent by police officers and personnel issuing and processing parking tickets would be saved. These employees could be assigned other tasks probably far more interesting and challenging.

Similarly, it is feasible to automate traffic control. Scanners already are in use that measure a vehicle's speed and flash a message showing what it is. Using LPR, an electronic device can catch speed violators and cause the issuance of a ticket. Similarly, such a device can catch traffic villains who make left turns at intersections when it is not authorized. Enforcement of traffic rules will be far more certain, which means our communities will be much safer.

Again, hundreds of thousands of work hours now spent by police officers lying in wait for traffic offenders can be diverted to work that protects citizens in other ways. Nor would it be necessary for officers to appear at court hearing for infractions that do not involve an accident.

That, some people argue, is exactly why automated traffic management never will work. Without a human involved, how could a person be prosecuted? How can people fight a machine that made a mistake?

As a practical matter, only a minuscule percent of people ticketed for a parking or traffic violation bother to contest it. How many times do you think it has been necessary for the officers who placed a parking ticket under a windshield wiper to appear in court to testify in support of his citation? With very rare exception, people do not contest parking or traffic citations. They do not have time for that. But, if necessary, we could add video scanners to the recording devices to get pictures of the offenders. Come to think of it, that is not a bad idea.

License plate recognition technology also offers another advantage. It enables the state to identify who has vehicle insurance and who does not by comparing scanned license plate numbers with information entered by insurance providers.

Prevent Driving Under the Influence with Vehicle Breathalyzers

Thirty-nine states, including Minnesota,[55] have laws that authorize the use of ignition interlocks. This is a device that prevents a person from starting a vehicle if he is intoxicated.

Before the vehicle will start, someone must breathe into a tube. If the alcohol concentration in the air blown into the device exceeds the legal limit, such as .08, the vehicle will not start.

Ignition interlock devices have proven to be very effective in sharply reducing repeat offenders of the crime of driving while intoxicated (DWI). A 1999 study entitled: *Effects of Ignition Interlock License Restrictions on Drivers*[56] of 1,387 multiple offenders who were randomly assigned to participate in an ignition interlock program found that: "Participation in the interlock program reduced offenders' risk of committing an alcohol traffic violation within the first year by about 65 percent." The study concluded: "Ignition interlock license restriction programs are effective at reducing recidivism among drivers with multiple alcohol offenses, at least while the restriction is in effect."

Ignition interlock systems, when used, prevent driving while drunk. If used extensively, they could dramatically reduce the thousands of cases annually in Minnesota of injuries and deaths because of intoxicated drivers, as well as the millions and millions of dollars spent for medical care and vehicle repair or replacement.

Doubting Thomases question the effectiveness of ignition interlocks with the argument that determined offenders can fool the device in several ways. One is to use a simple air pump to blow air into the device, or have a companion blow into it, or cover the tube with a filter before blowing into it.

Of course, few devices are entirely foolproof. But it is unrealistic to believe all individuals required to use an ignition interlock will circumvent it. If just a significant percentage use it properly, that most likely will result in a tremendous improvement in public safety.

Minnesota Statutes § 171.305 already provides a penalty for circumventing the use of an ignition interlock. The penalty can be made severe enough that few individuals will risk being apprehended driving while intoxicated in a vehicle that has an ignition interlock. In this connection, Minnesota Statutes § 171.305 requires that ignition interlocks: "be capable of recording information for later review that includes the date and time of any use of the vehicle or any attempt to use the vehicle, including all times that the vehicle engine was started or stopped and the alcohol concentration of each breath sample provided."

A person who intentionally circumvents use of an ignition interlock should be permanently deprived of a driver's license. That is incentive to faithfully use it.

As a further deterrent to drive a vehicle after a failed test, the following would happen if a second attempt to start the vehicle is made within one hour of the failed test:

1. An orange exterior light would start blinking and continue blinking for one hour; and

2. A message would go from the vehicle to 911 that contains the license number and the general location of the vehicle.

Our proposal is to give first time DWI offenders who were not involved in an accident and did not damage any property an alternative to the current procedure in such cases: agree to participate in an ignition interlock program. Under our proposal, the participant must:

1. Complete a substance-use evaluation and follow the recommendations of the evaluator.

2. Attend classes on avoiding substance abuse, listen intently, and seriously consider what is said.

3. Pay for the installation of an officially approved ignition interlock system.

4. Use an officially approved ignition system every time before driving any vehicle for a period of one year.

5. Agree that a conviction of driving while intoxicated within one year will result in permanent loss of his or her driving license.

6. Pay the fine assessed by the court.

7. Plead guilty to driving while intoxicated with the understanding that the sentence will be stayed for one year and dismissed if there are no violations during that period.

The driver's license of an offender who agrees to the above would be returned to him or her immediately. That by itself should sell the program. Few are likely to choose the current procedure: (1) pay from $3,000 to $8,000 for a lawyer; (2) complete a substance abuse evaluation; (3) complete classes on substance abuse; (4) lose the use of his or her driver's license for several months; (5) have a criminal record; and (6) pay sharply increased insurance premiums.

Former U.S. Supreme Court Chief Justice Warren E. Burger, a Minnesota native son, said:

> "Concepts of justice must have hands and feet to carry out justice in every case in the shortest possible time and at the lowest possible cost. This is the challenge to every lawyer and judge in America."

We are within sight of achieving the goal Chief Justice Burger set for us.

"He is such a nice judge!"
"He is sooo respectful to everyone."

Smile, Judge, you're on candid camera.

Chapter 17
Smile, Judge:
You're on Candid Camera

Systems that make video and sound records of court trials, hearings and sidebar discussions[57] will provide four worthwhile benefits:

1. Put a damper on judge abuse of parties, lawyers and witnesses;

2. Improve the accuracy of transcripts of proceedings;

3. Save some court reporter effort and expense; and

4. Preserve the visual and sound record of court trials and proceedings for historical and other purposes.

We propose to install a video camcorder in an inconspicuous location in every courtroom and a voice-activated sound recording system in every courtroom and judge's chambers. These systems would be under the control of court administrators.

Judges Should Be Respectful To People Who Appear Before Them

Most judges treat parties, lawyers, defendants in criminal cases, and witnesses courteously and respectfully. This is what they are supposed to do. Minnesota's Code of Judicial Conduct, Canon 3, rule A(4) states:

> "A judge shall be patient, dignified and courteous to litigants, jurors, witnesses and others dealt with in an official capacity."

Unfortunately, many judges ignore this rule and they make life in court miserable for those they abuse. These judges insult, belittle and castigate lawyers at will, except, perhaps, for those who gave them gratuities or campaign contributions. If so inclined, judges ridicule parties and witnesses and chastise those with whom they disagree unless it happens to be a case before a jury, and even then some judges send signals to the jury.

As a practical matter, there is little a lawyer, litigant or defendant can do. Lawyers know they may have to appear before the offending judge in other proceedings and cannot risk incurring his ill will. Litigants and defendants in criminal cases risk incurring the judge's wrath because he could retaliate by deciding the case against a protester or imposing a harsher sentence on a defendant who demurs.

Disrespectful treatment by judges of people and lawyers who appear before them will be greatly reduced if the judge knows he or she is being videotaped. Our proposal is to videotape the judge in every court hearing in a manner that will not disrupt or distract any hearing. To give these tapings real punch, we propose that evaluations of judges for the purpose of judge report cards at re-election time include random sampling of videotapes of trials and court hearings presided over by the judge being evaluated.

Videotaping a court hearing without disruption or distraction can be accomplished easily by installing video cameras in unobtrusive places accessible only to court personnel. Videotapes will be controlled by court administrators who will be authorized to release a videotape only as permitted by a law, rule or court order.

Everyone who appears before judges will have the right to get a videotape of a hearing involving him or her delivered by the court administrator's office directly to the state agency that has the power to discipline judges when they misbehave. They also will have the right to have the judge's conduct reviewed.

All testimony and discussions would be recorded including sidebar discussions and conversations in chambers. All persons who participate in the trial or proceeding would appear in the videotape except for jurors. The camcorder would be focused so as to never include any juror and there would be no sound record that would identify any juror.

Other Benefits of Videotaping and Recording

An accurate transcript of testimony at a trial can be essential in determining the outcome of an appeal. Such transcripts are produced by licensed court reporters. During a trial, the court reporter sits close to the witness and types what he or she hears on a machine called a stenotype. Modern stenotype machines store the typed characters on a disk. A transcript is produced from the disk.

Court reporters are very competent and rarely make a mistake. However, they are human and occasionally do not hear all that a witness says. Sometimes what they type in is incorrect. Such a mistake can be critical.

As a backup, most court reporters also tape record testimony on a sound recorder. If they need to check on portions of testimony, they can play the audio tape. These tapes are always in the court reporter's possession. They rarely are available to lawyers, parties or witnesses.

The change we propose is to install sound recording systems in all courthouses with microphones in every courtroom and in judge's chambers all connected to the central system. The system would record all testimony in court, all sidebar discussions, and all discussions in a judge's chambers. This will relieve court reporter's of the need to tape court testimony and save them time and effort.

Lawyers, parties and witnesses could purchase a copy of the audio record of part or all of a trial or court hearing. This would enable them to check the accuracy of a transcript produced by the court reporter. Some parties and witnesses might want such a recording simply for memory's sake.

Current rules prohibit audio and video coverage of trial court proceedings as well as broadcast and photographic equipment,[58] except as specifically permitted by a judge. These prohibitions seem to be aimed at the media. The objectives appear to be to prevent sensationalism of trials, disruption of proceedings, and embarrassment to parties and witnesses.

The system we propose can be installed and operated without creating any disruption or causing any embarrassment. Since the disks or other storage devices will be under the control of court administrators, sensationalism can be avoided.

At the same time, some trials of special significance can be preserved for future display after a sufficient lapse of time and for historical purposes. Trials already are open to the public except for special categories such as paternity cases. Recording public trials for the future is consistent with their public nature.

Videotaping and recording court proceedings have several advantages. We are not aware of any significant drawbacks. We think they are reforms whose times have arrived.

Judge Mouse

Chapter 18
Replace Incumbent Judges

There is one sure way to get judges to work for change: boot some of them out of office. That will not be easy. It will be hard to do.

Every two years, about one-third of Minnesota's incumbent judges run for re-election. We ask you to join us in voting against incumbent judges. They can be defeated. Most should be.

Defeating incumbent judges will send the remaining judges a message, a very, very important one: Minnesotans want changes in their legal system – very, very big changes. We want an end to thousands and thousands of gross injustices each year; we want affordable justice for all.

In the movie "Brewster's Millions," Richard Prior plays the part of a potential millionaire who conducts a political campaign in which he urges people to vote for "None of the Above." They did and None of the Above won. Voters can defeat incumbent judges and force them from office by voting for the same fictitious person. Voters can write in the name of a fictitious person in the space for a write-in vote just below the name of each incumbent judge who is running for re-election.

According to the Minnesota Secretary of State, each write-in vote must be counted even if it is for a fictitious person. If the majority of votes are for a fictitious person, that person is declared the winner. Because the fictitious person does not exist, the office becomes vacant. (Office of the Secretary of State, Elections, 651 215-1440; Minnesota Statutes, § 204C.22) In the case of a judgeship, that means the governor appoints a replacement.

We can defeat incumbent judges by casting our votes for the same fictitious person. Mickey Mouse is our candidate. He is an honest fellow who has a good sense of humor. You may wonder about his qualifications to be a judge. Actually, it does not make any difference. If you are like most voters, you don't know anything about the qualifications of the judge who is running for re-election. However, you may feel squeamish about voting for a cartoon character. An alternative is "New Judge." His qualifications are the same but his name is more dignified. This matter is open for debate.

An alternative to voting for a fictitious person is to vote for lawyers who challenge incumbent judges. The challenger to an incumbent judge is easy to identify because all incumbent judges running for re-election have the word "incumbent" just after their name on the ballot. However, there are downsides to this possibility. The first is that voters probably will know little about the challenger. He or she may be worse than the incumbent. The second is that highly qualified practicing attorneys, especially those who are successful, fear running against an incumbent judge because they know it generally is a lost cause and because judges retaliate against challengers.

Throwing out all judges running for re-election in the same year might seem excessive even if they are just one-third of the total number of judges. After all, the argument could be made, there are at least some good judges, maybe even many. Therefore, the argument continues, indiscriminately defeating all judges is equivalent to throwing out the baby with the bath water.

There are good judges, of course. Some are outstanding. By good, we mean a judge who is intelligent, compassionate, dedicated, honest and industrious. By outstanding, we do not mean an individual who has a great legal mind or is a genius, but rather an individual who uses common sense and basic values as well as the law in making judgments that are fair and sensible, that penalize people who commit crimes, fraud, and other illegal behavior, and who dispense justice to all who appear before him or her.

We agree that good judges should be retained – but only if they identify themselves to voters. As a practical matter, the average voter does not know who are good judges and who are not. Until there are legitimate reports on how judges are doing their jobs, good judges need to distinguish themselves from the others.

Good judges deserve our highest acclamation. Most could be earning several times what they earn as a judge merely by working as a lawyer in private practice. It is true as reported in Chapter 4 that Minnesota judges are paid annual salaries of between $116,300 and $147,000, which is high compared to the earnings of most Minnesotans. But these amounts are pale when compared to the hundreds of thousands of dollars typically earned by partners in law firms, especially big law firms. If a person is smart enough to be a judge, he or she probably could be a partner in a prosperous law firm.

Society owes sincere gratitude to good judges. They have put material gain second to public service. Their work in justly resolving disputes and applying the law properly contributes enormously to achieving one of the great goals of government: justice.

It would be a huge blessing if all judges were good judges. But that is not the case as shown by the horror cases in Part I of this book. There are other categories of judges. In *Anatomy of a Murder* (1958), Robert Traver divided judges into four classes. He wrote:

> Judges, like most people, may be divided roughly into four classes: Judges with neither head nor heart—they are to be avoided at all costs; judges with head but no heart—they are almost as bad; then judges with heart but no head—risky but better than the first two, and, finally, those rare judges who possess both head and a heart.[59]

We divided judges into three categories, the good judges mentioned above and two other categories of judges: incompetent and bad. Judges who fall into the latter two categories should be driven from office.

Little needs to be said on why our legal system should be cleansed of bad judges. Those who do not care whom they hurt or how badly, or who have intentionally wronged parents, children and others who were placed at their mercy, have betrayed justice and public service. Judges like those in the case of "The Godzilla Conspiracy," who knowingly let power barons enrich themselves by robbing innocent people, are monsters who have lost the right to public compensation and the honor and prestige that goes with the office of judge.

The second of our three categories consists of judges who are incompetent. It may be that these judges are honest, compassionate, well-meaning and dedicated. Unfortunately, they are lacking in intelligence, understanding, judgment or industriousness. Many of these judges do not have common sense.

An example is the judge in the case of "The Family Room Floor." She did not understand that it is extraordinarily abnormal to have a bare concrete floor in the ground level family room of a luxury home. She believed the tale of the homeowner that she wanted a bare concrete floor so her teenaged children would not dirty the carpet when they came in through the patio door. Based on that homeowner's testimony, the judge denied the concrete supplier any compensation for his materials and labor and socked him for thousands of dollars for a replacement floor supposedly to be installed in the future.

Another example is the judge in the case of "The Big Surprise." She did not know that a lawyer needs more time than one day to prepare for trial of a major issue. She understood that the defendant gave notice of a major new defense the day before trial. But because it was more important in her opinion to dispose of the case than to try it justly, she started the trial anyway, and completed it the same day. The plaintiff lost, of course. The Minnesota Court of Appeals reversed the obviously unfair ruling – at a cost of thousands of dollars to the plaintiff, and after months of delay.

Incompetent judges should be honorably excused from public service. No matter how pure their intent, they unwittingly cause great damage and suffering and give our legal system a very bad reputation. That unacceptably disrupts society.

This brings us back to the troublesome question: should we vote against all incumbent judges in the next election even if that costs us some good judges? Our answer, with one qualification, is yes, for three reasons: (1) this sends a much needed message; (2) it gets rid of incompetent and bad judges; and (3) it gives good judges strong incentive to take action to enable us to identify and keep them in office. The qualification is that we should vote for incumbent judges who convince us they are good judges.

Good judges have an obligation to speak up and inform us about their work. They should work to convince us to vote for them just as other elected officials need to do. They can attend meetings, give addresses, visit schools and publish articles telling us what they have done to alleviate the serious problems described in Part II of this book. Most importantly, they can listen – to the people – and respond.

We think good judges should work on the major headache of incompetent and bad judges – privately if not publicly. Good judges can approve and advocate for reforms such as: (1) a Common Sense Commission, (2) a Judges and Public Officials Court, (3) reports on judges' performance of their duties, (4) videotaping and recording events in court, and (5) others that put pressures on incompetent and bad judges to change their ways at the risk of being expelled from office if they do not.

Asking good judges to help Minnesotans get the justice they want and have been promised is not unreasonable. Nor is it asking too much. Good judges who refuse to make that effort do not deserve to be re-elected.

Among the bad judges who should be defeated in the next election are the Justices of the Minnesota Supreme Court and the judges of the Minnesota Court of Appeals who run for re-election. The courts they supervise do not reliably provide justice and often provide no justice at all. These leaders knowingly tolerate racism, racial profiling, and judge dishonesty, insensitivity, incompetence and abuse as illustrated by the horror cases in Part I of this book. With smiles, they happily accept gratuities of up to $150 in value that are hidden from the public and large campaign contributions from big law firms, rich lawyers, and corporate moguls with whom they are on cozy terms.

The Minnesota Supreme Court has done nothing effective to reduce lawsuit costs, lower the need for expensive lawyer time, shorten the court process, provide lawyers for destitute parents who face loss of a child in family court, give voters information on judges who run for re-election, outlaw bribes of judges through gratuities and campaign contributions, stop lawsuit abuse especially in contingent fee and class actions, and dam the avalanche of Minnesota's two million plus cases per year. They refuse to make any meaningful effort to banish these curses from our legal system. They are far more concerned with protecting their image.

The above are some of the reasons for rejecting incumbent Supreme Court Justices and judges of the Minnesota Court of Appeals in the next election. Another reason, even more important than any of those mentioned above, is to send a powerful message to Minnesota's political leadership, one they cannot fail to hear and heed.

Other Proposed Legal Reforms

If you believe there is a reform or are reforms that you think should be made, please tell us what they are and we will consider publishing them in our next book. Send them to us by e-mail at:

dalenathan@usfamily.net

Or by mail to:

Dale Nathan
P.O. Box 211284
Eagan, MN 55121

Here are some reforms we think should be considered:

Assure that medical, insurance, retirement and other benefits are paid to people, especially seniors, when due, and that the process for getting benefits is simple and pragmatic.

Require that a real human, not a mechanical voice, give you a responsible answer within one business day after you ask a question or make a claim by telephone about your benefits or rights.

Provide parents and children in juvenile court cases with a lawyer who has the time and resources needed to get a fair hearing and protect parents and their children.

Outlaw terms that make contracts one-sided and cost people their rights.

Bar Qwest and other companies from selling or releasing private data.

Stop unwanted telephone or e-mail solicitations and polling, and telemarketing and internet spam.

Give the Common Sense Commission the power and duty to widely publish decisions of judges that are lacking in fairness and common sense.

Give the Judge Discipline and Removal Board the power to suspend judges who are performing poorly and require that they stand for re-election at the next general election.

Take away the power of judges to put a person in jail, or fine a person more than $500, without first giving the person the right to a trial, by jury if demanded, before a different judge.

Protect home purchasers, homeowners and home-builders from irresponsible contractors by requiring them to use a trust fund for each project.

Assure that subcontractors are paid for materials and good workmanship by requiring contractors to use trust funds.

Make legal services more affordable for individuals and small businesses by allowing an individual or small business who win a lawsuit to recover attorney's fees from the other party.

Enact an equal access to justice law like the federal law that allows a person or small business to recover attorney's fees and litigation costs when he/it wins a lawsuit against a government agency.

Reduce the cost of appeals primarily by reducing the cost of transcripts so they are affordable by the person who wants to appeal, and by reducing fees and costs to be commensurate with the income of the person who wants to appeal.

Make expert witnesses liable for damages caused by testimony that is untruthful, grossly unsubstantiated, negligent or erroneous.

Create an independent, adequately funded organization to provide Guardians Ad Litem for children in juvenile cases.

Forbid judges from ordering a lawyer, clergyperson, or medical provider to disclose legally protected confidential information except that a judge may refer a matter to a state licensing board for investigation and discipline if it concerns a danger to society or a person.

Give all first time non-violent drug offenders alternative drug treatment sentencing instead of prison.

Use community service, home detention and current technology to ensure compliance with alternative sentences given first time nonviolent offenders.

Penalize municipalities, police departments, and police officers who engage in racial profiling.
Make it a crime for corporations and businesses to intentionally or through gross negligence fail to report a dangerous condition in their product such as

defective tires or tainted food, or to take prompt and effective corrective action.

Guarantee the civil and constitutional rights of and access to state and federal courts for all citizens living and/or doing business on Native American reservations.

Forbid criminals from collecting damages from citizens or businesses for injuries sustained during a criminal act, such as injuries resulting from attempts at self-defense for all.

Conclusion

Corruption

During a pilgrimage to North America in 1999, Pope John-Paul II gave a speech in Mexico in which he called for an end to "the corruption that permeates many institutions and many citizens." As Pope John-Paul observed then, and as is true now, corruption is rampant in America.

Massive accounting and investment fraud at Enron, WorldCom, Tyco, Adelphia, Qwest, Xcel, HealthSouth, Rite Aid, ImClone, and scores of other corporations cost investors and employees hundreds of billions of dollars. Hundreds of thousands of people lost their life savings and the comfortable retirement they worked so hard to get. Some participants in these schemes even laughed contemptuously at "little old ladies" in California who were the victims of artificially high utility prices.

Defrauding companies, employees, investors and the public was sport for these corporate executives and their associates who knew what they were doing was illegal and immoral. A few of them amassed huge fortunes through their fraud that they now are using to defend their ill-gotten gains and pay lawyers to spare them any consequence.

New federal laws recently were enacted to regulate wayward accounting firms that not only had allowed, but *helped* big corporations commit their frauds. And still, we read of new scams and scandals.

Millions of mutual fund investors learned recently that they too had been scammed. After-hours sales, tips, and other illegal behavior by brokers robbed millions of ordinary investors of as yet uncalculated billions of dollars - funds that had been reserved for college educations, retirement, legacy.

Even teachers got into the act, helping students cheat on tests so they could achieve mandated educational results. According to David Cay Johnson, author of the recent best seller *Perfectly Legal* (Portfolio, Published by Penguin Press, 2003) members of congress are contributing their fair share of shady dealing by passing law after law that enables large corporations and special interests to avoid paying their fair share of taxes.

Courts, lawyers and our legal system make corruption possible. Lawyers far and away are the principal enablers, architects or defenders of many fraudulent schemes. They are, after all, trained to obfuscate, distort, misrepresent, persuade, and convince. They, together with our judges and courts, are the protectors of far too many perpetrators of corruption.

Our society is sick with corruption. It is very sick.

Are you disturbed by the corruption you see all about you that has savaged so many people and so degraded our society? If so, what can and should we do about it?

Injustice

Injustice is part of the corruption that afflicts us. The horror cases in Part I of this book illustrate the bitter injustice meted out by Minnesota judges. Although no one can say for sure, it is safe to say that tens of thousands of Minnesotans are badly damaged or wronged each year as a result of bad judges and a dysfunctional justice system. It is likely that thousands of defendants plead guilty to an offense they did not commit because public defender services were unavailable. Hundreds and perhaps thousands of children are separated from their families each year for the same reason.

Small businesses and individuals suffer losses, or lose benefits they should have received because justice is so expensive it is not affordable. This is not how our society should operate.

Road to Change

A freshly minted priest was assigned to a rural parish as the first post in his pastoral career. For the first time, he was scheduled to preside at a burial service. An elderly member of a prominent family had passed away. Burial would be in the family burial grounds near the family home.

Not wanting to be late, the young priest set out in plenty of time and tried to follow the directions he had been given. But he was still unfamiliar with the area and became lost. The fine mist that was falling made the dirt roads muddy and slippery. This slowed him down. The scheduled time for the burial passed and he was still trying to find the burial site.

Now more than 50 minutes late, he was frantic. As he came around a bend, he saw two workers under a tent shoveling dirt into a good-sized hole. An elegant farmhouse stood in the background. To himself the priest thought, the family must have left already. It is only right, he concluded in his mind, that I perform the service even if the burial has already taken place.

The priest walked from his vehicle to the burial area. Approaching the two workers, he gave the peace sign and they returned it. Without further communication, the priest pulled his prayer book from his shirt pocket and performed the burial service. After the priest had made the final blessing and left, the older worker turned to the other and said, "I've been burying septic tanks for 20 years and I ain't never seen nothing like that."

We all know that reform of our court and legal system is urgently needed. Even so, we must not unthinkingly rush to make changes that prove to be ineffective or make the system even worse.

Comprehensive reform will not happen overnight. It must be developed over a period of time accompanied by much patience. The proposals in this book are not submitted as the only or the final answers. They are offered as starters of deliberation and debate. Their purpose is to generate thoughtful analysis, evaluation and creative thinking. This is what we believe is the realistic path to a vastly more efficient and less expensive court and legal system that makes true justice available and affordable for everyone.

Mission

We believe the key to getting the justice system we want, and that is attainable, is mission. By this, we mean first determining as a society what we want our justice system to be, and then following through aggressively until we achieve our objective.

History is replete with failed missions. Countless millions have died in crusades and rebellions, most of which accomplished nothing. Life's experiences have taught most of us that the probability of one person reforming the world is very small indeed. We should be mindful that irrational sacrifice is both foolish and valueless.

Having noted the possibility of failure, and recognizing the likelihood of fierce opposition by very powerful forces, there still remains a realistic possibility of success. Just as history is replete with failed missions, it also contains instances of great successes in the face of seemingly impossible odds. The successes of three such individuals, George Washington, William Wilberforce, and Aleksandr Solzhenitsyn, are described in the book *Character Counts* by Oz Guinness.

In the 1770s, after a small group of American colonists boldly declared their independence from England, a group asked George Washington to assume command of the nonexistent colonial army and battle the colossus of the day - The British Empire. Who would have given Washington any chance? No one would have blamed him if he had turned down a seemingly hopeless task in favor of his comfortable plantation life.

For more than four years Washington fought a hopeless battle - actually running all that time - and then, miracle of miracles, beat the British. Mission accomplished.

Few people have heard of William Wilberforce. Born in 1759 in England, he was a member of the British Parliament at age 28, destined, many said, to be the English Prime Minister. A mission intervened. He was asked to take on the British slave trade industry - the biggest industry of its day. A small group of people said it was wrong for British mariners to seize Africans, take them from their homes, and sell them into slavery in foreign lands.

It took more than 30 years, cost him his career in Parliament, resulted in beatings and bankruptcy, but Wilberforce prevailed. In 1833, shortly before his death at age 74, the English Parliament outlawed slave trading. He accomplished his mission even though few thought he could defeat an entire industry.

Aleksandr Solzhenitsyn is a modern example of the will to succeed despite the odds. In the 1940s and 1950s, he lived in the Union of Soviet Socialists Republics under the harsh rule of Russian dictator Joseph Stalin. Solzhenitsyn could have lived a luxurious life if only he had accommodated his country's iron dictatorship. He refused to do that. He insisted on writing about the plight of the Russian people and their suffering.

Stalin exiled Solzhenitsyn to Siberia. Still untamed, he wrote on scraps of paper if nothing else was available. He survived what was thought to be terminal cancer. Once freed from Siberia and exiled to the United States, Solzhenitsyn wrote *The Gulag Archipelago,* one of literature's greatest works. He is still recognized as one of the world's greatest fighters for morality.

In our time, a mere 40 years ago, there was a person who should inspire us. Dr. Martin Luther King, Jr. could have lived a comfortable life as an Atlanta, Georgia minister. He choose a different path. Instead of being at his Atlanta home with a loving family, he often was in jail for contempt of court - daring to march peacefully for the rights of his people. During these tumultuous times, the threat of violent death was King's constant companion.

King's mission certainly seemed hopeless and extremely foolish - get the white establishment to accept black Americans as equals. Most African-Americans opposed his efforts because they resulted in trouble for them, destruction of their property, injury and even death. Undaunted, and despite the refusal of three U.S. presidents to intervene and the opposition of an entire region of the United States, King pressed on until his life was taken from him. His mission was partially accomplished. His example as a fighter for justice still is a shining beacon.

For the author of this book, the greatest example of mission is Jesus of Nazareth. No one undertook a greater mission or sacrificed more for humanity. With His example before me, how could I not fight for justice for all my brethren? If Jesus was God Incarnate and made His sacrifices for me, surely I should continue the battle. If, like me, Jesus was a human, how can I not be moved by His sacrifice to continue His mission?

When all is said, we realize that we can change society as others have done before us. Our willingness to join together in a mission for justice is the key.

What You Can Do

Here is how you can help get reform of our court and legal system:

1. Vote
2. Write letters to your state legislators
3. Write letters to the governor and executive branch officials
4. Ask judges for information about their work and positions (see below)
5. Send emails to legislative and executive officials
6. Participate in discussion groups
7. Discuss the need for reform in conversations with your family and friends

We urge you to contact your government representatives at all levels - state, county and city - and let them know what you think about the content of this book. If you think change in our court and legal system is needed, please tell them. If you think some of the ideas in this book are worth pursuing, please tell let them that, too.

Do not let judges take your vote, or failure to vote, for granted in the coming election. In my website, mncourtreform.org, is a list of Minnesota judges who are running for re-election, and each candidate who wants to become a judge. The list includes (if available) email addresses, mail addresses, fax numbers and telephone numbers.

We urge you to contact each judge who is seeking to continue in office, and each candidate for judge, and ask for his or her schedule of public appearances where he or she will meet the people and answer questions about his or her work as a judge and what he or she will do to improve our court and legal system. Tell each judge and candidate for judge that you want to know their positions on issues such as:

Judge gratuities
Financing judge elections
Selecting judges on merit
Report cards on judges
Judge re-election

Lawsuit expense
Contingent fee cases
Class actions
Prison sentences
Judge accountability

Repeat DWI offenders
Abortion
Gay marriage
Prisoner rehabilitation
People's rights

Also included in my website are lists of candidates for state legislative and executive offices with contact information for each state legislator and state office holder and candidates for these offices. We urge you to contact your representatives and state executive officers and tell them your opinion on Minnesota's court and legal system and what changes you think are needed.

VOTE IN JUDGE ELECTIONS

Of course, your vote is by far the most powerful tool you have. We urge you to exercise it and to do so in each judge election. We urge you to vote in all judge elections.

We think judges who run for re-election, including justices of the Minnesota Supreme Court, and judges of the Minnesota Court of Appeals, should make their performance record known to you so you can make an informed decision on whether or not each should be re-elected to office. If they fail to do so, and you again are in the quandary of having to vote for only one person you know nothing about except for some newspaper advertisements, we urge you to cast a write-in vote for our candidate, Mickey Mouse.

Reform rarely initiates itself. It must be ignited. It generally starts with a message consisting of demands and actions. To get judicial reform, the message needs to be loud in the form of many votes. It needs to be a compelling message striking fear in the hearts of the judges who survive re-election.

You can and should help if you care about justice. Former U.S. Attorney General Robert F. Kennedy, speaking in South Africa during the apartheid era in that country, told them:

> Each time a man stands up for an ideal, or acts to improve the lot of others, or strikes out against injustice, he sends a tiny ripple of hope, and crossing each other from a million different centers of energy and daring, these ripples will build a current which can sweep down the mightiest walls of oppression and resistance.[60]

In *Beyond Power: On Women, Men and Morals* (1986), Marilyn French wrote: "We all have power—the capacity to influence, alter, affect the lives of those among us."[61]

Reform is rarely easy. Change will be fiercely opposed by those who will lose advantages they now enjoy. Powerful lawyers who control judges do not want change. Special interests, big business, and other power barons do not want to lose control over the people they now can exploit. Judges do not want to be without their gratuities. A free ride back into office is much more to their liking than a system that forces them to prove they deserve to be re-elected. As it has always been, greed dominates the actions of those who control society.

Massive opposition to legal system reform is likely. Corporate executives who defraud the public for their personal gain, stockholders like Martha Stewart who profit from insider tips, company officers who knowingly sell consumers defective products, all want a system that lets them get away with their wrongdoing. But however massive the opposition, it can be overcome. The glory of our country is that ultimate power resides with the people. If enough people will it, we can prevail through our votes in the privacy of the voting booth.

Echoing what we said in the prologue to this book, we do not lack the means of getting true justice. If we fail to get the justice we yearn for, it is because we lack the determination.

End Notes

1. C. M. Clark Ins. Agency, Inc. v. Reed, 390 F.Supp. 1056 (1975).

2. http://www.fa-ir.org/ai/nowrong.htm.

3. 48A C.J.S., Judges, §87.

4. Cameron v. Seitz, 38 F.3rd 264 (6th Cir. 1994).

5. 793 F.2d 1072 (9th Cir. 1986).

6. 435 U.S. 349 (1978).

7. Minn. Constit. Art. 6, §5.

8. In Re Scarrella, 221 N.W. 2d 562 (1974).

9. To run for district court judge, 1,000 names or 5 percent of the total votes in the district in the last election, whichever is lower. To run for a higher court, 2,000 names or 1 percent of the statewide vote.

10. Minn. Stat, Chapter 480B.

11. 122 S.Ct. 2528 (2002).

12. The Nation Magazine, 1/26/98, page 998.

13. 1999 WL3983729.

14. http://www.pbs.org/wgbh/pages/frontline/shows/justice.

15. 50 Catholic University Law Review 361.

16. USA Today, September 1, 2000, page 16A.

17. 122 S.Ct. 2525 (2002).

18. http://followthemoney.org/database/StateGlance/state_judicial_elections.phtlm?si=200.

19. ABA Report and Recommendations of the Task Force on Lawyers' Political Contributions, Part Two 6 (1998), http://www.abanet.org/media/jul98/play798.html, chair: John W. Martin, Jr., available from the American Bar Association, Chicago, IL, 1 800 285-2221.

20. http://www.pbs.org/wgbh/pages/frontline/shows/justice.

21. Frontline: Justice for Sale? *supra*, footnote 14.

22. 72 Southern California Law Review 505 (1999), at page 523.

23. The Wooing of Our Judges, http://www.mediatransparency.org/stories/wooing judges.htm, 4/1/04.

24. 198 N.W. 2d 152 (Minn 1972).

25. *Legislative Manuel,* (Blue Book), 2003-2004, published by the Minnesota Secretary of State, pages 36-46, Minnesota Compensation Council, 651-296-2963.

26. http://www.mnwfc.org/imi/salary.

27. From *The Quotable Lawyer* by Tony Lyons, The Lyons Press (2002) pages 317, 318, 322, 327, 331 and 332.

28. 536 US 765 (2002).

29. *The Quotable Lawyer* by Tony Lyons, pages 19 and 112.

30. *Id*, page 108.

31. *The Devil's Dictionary*, (1908).

32. *The Quotable Lawyer* by Tony Lyons (2002), page 173.

33. *Id*, page 120

34. http://criminal.justice.state/mn.us/courts_statistics.htm.

35. Minnesota Rules of Professional Conduct.

36. Liebeck v. McDonalds Corporation, CV-93-02479, N.M. District, 8-18-94.

37. BMW v. Gore, 1996 U.S. Lexis 3390, 646 So. 2d 619, 517 U.S. 559 (1996).

38. Mealet's Litigation Report Class Actions, 4/3/04, http://www.mealeys.com.

39. 15 U.S.C. § 78dd-1 et seq.

40. State of Minnesota Board of Public Defense, 331 Second Avenue South, Suite 900, Minneapolis, MN 55401, 612 349-2568.

41. 372 U.S. 335 (1963).

42. Minnesota Department of Corrections, 1450 Energy Park Drive, Suite 200, St. Paul, MN 55108, 651 642-0200.

43. In a summary judgment proceeding, the judge reviews undisputed facts, which are facts all parties agree on, and decides if there is enough merit to the claim to proceed further.

44. Alaska, Colorado, Connecticut, Delaware, District of Columbia, Hawaii, Iowa, Maryland, Massachusetts, Nebraska, New Mexico, Rhode Island, South Carolina, Utah, Vermont and Wyoming.

45. *Choosing Minnesota's Judges,* page 20, League of Women Voters, 550 Rice Street, St. Paul, MN 55103.

46. Patricia A. Garcia, *Judicial Selection: The Process of Choosing Judges*, American Bar Association Roadmaps Series, page 12.

47. *Electing Justice: A Handbook of Judicial Election Reforms*, Sara Mathias, American Judicature Society (1990), page 115.

48. North Carolina Statutes 163-278.61 et seq.; Mont. Code Ann §13-37-304 (1989); Wisc.Stat. §11.05 et seq.

49. *Electing Justice: A Handbook of Judicial Election Reforms*, Sara Mathias, American Judicature Society (1990), footnote 183; ComCauseNM@aol.com; http://www.ilcampaign.org/ issues/judicial/.

50. http://www.pop.umn.edu.

51. http://ncjudges.nevotered.com/media/release_10102002.html.

52. *Choosing Minnesota's Judges*, *id* note 45, page 20.

53. Illinois Statutes, 5 ILCS 425/1 et seq.

54. Minnesota Statutes § 15A.083, subd. 4.

55. Minnesota Statutes § 171.305.

56. American Public Health Association, 800 I Street N.W., Washington, DC 20001-3710, Phone: (202) 777-APHA, Fax: (202) 777-2534, Email: comments@apha.org.

57. A side bar discussion is a discussion at the judge's desk usually out of the hearing range of everyone else in the court.

58. Code of Judicial Conduct, Canon 3.

59. *The Quotable Lawyer*, (2002) by Tony Lyons, page 60.

60. *Id.*, page 200.

61. *Id.*, page 37.

Federal Statutes

Federal Cases

Minnesota Statutes

§ 204C.22 (write-in votes), 294
§ 480B (Judicial Merit Selection law), 172
§ 513.05 (statute of frauds), 149
§ 513.075 (property division), 120, 121, 123
§ 513.076 (property division), 122, 123
§ 514.74 (errors in mechanic's liens), 94
§ 517.01 (property division), 123
§ 517.08 (property division), 122
§ 518.166 (private interviews in custody cases), 70
§ 549.211 (sanctions), 193

Minnesota Cases

Carlson v. Olson, 122
256 N.W.2d 249 (Minn. 1977)

City of St. Paul v. Vaunhn, 143
237 N.W.2d 365 (Minn. 1975)

Custody of N.A.K., 127
649 N.W.2d 166 (Minn. 2002)

In Re Bartholet, 186
198 N.W.2d 152 (Minn. 1972)

In Re Scarrella, 171
221 N.W. 2d 562 (Minn. 1974)

State v. Barber, 143
241 N.W.2d 476 (Minn. 1976)

State v. Britton, 144, 145, 146
604 N.W. 2d 84 (Minn.2000)

State v. Curtis, 143
190 N.W.2d 631 (Minn. 1971)

State v. Encholm, 143
290 N.W.2d 780 (Minn. 1980)

State v. Hodgman, 143
257 N.W.2d 313 (Minn.1980)

State v. Victorsen, 146
2001 WL 410380 (Minn.App. 2001)

State v. Wicklund, 143
205 N.W.2d 509 (Minn.1973)

Cases – Other States

Candee v. Egan, 164
267 N.W. 2d 890 (Wis. 1978)

People v. Ingle, 144
36 N.Y.2d 413, 420, 369 N.Y.S.2d 67, 74, 330 N.E.2d 39, 44 (1975)

Selected Bibliography

Books

American Bar Association. *Report and Recommendations of the Task Force on Lawyers' Political Contributions*. Chicago, Illinois, 1998.

Bartlett, David L., and James B. Steele. *The Great American Tax Dodge*. New York: Little, Brown, 2000.

Berger, Raoul. *Government by Judiciary*. London: Howard University Press, 1977.

Boot, Max. *Out of Order*. New York: Basic Books, Inc., 1998.

Bork, Robert H. *The Tempting of America*. New York: MacMillan, Inc., 1990.

Corine, Jon. *Fathers' Rights*. New York: Walker and Company, 1989.

Crier, Catherine. *The Case Against Lawyers*. New York: Broadway Books, 2002.

Farrell, Warren. *The Father and Child Reunion*. New York: Jeremy P. Tarcher/Putnam, 2001.

Goulden, Joseph C. *The Benchwarmers*. New York: Ballantine Books, 1974.

Greider, William. *Who Will Tell the People*. New York: Simon & Shuster, 1992.

Gunnes, Oz. *Character Counts*. Grand Rapids, Michigan: Baker Books, 2001.

Howard, Philip K. *The Death of Common Sense*. New York: Random House, 1994.

Howard, Philip K. *The Collapse of the Common Good.* New York: Ballantine Books, 2001.

Huber, Peter W. *Liability*. New York: Basic Books, Inc., 1988.

Hubner, John and Jill Wolfson. *Somebody Else's Children.* New York: Crown Publishers, 1996.

Johnston, David Cay. *Perfectly Legal.* New York: Penguin Group, Inc., 2003.

League of Women Voters of Minnesota. *Choosing Minnesota's Judges.* 550 Rice Street, St. Paul, Minnesota 55103, 1998.

Leving, Jeffrey. *Father's Rights*. www.amazon.com; Harpercollins, Chicago, 1998.

Lyons, Tony. *The Quotable Lawyer.* Guilford, Connecticut: The Lyons Press, 2002.

Mathias, Sara. *Electing Justice: A Handbook of Judicial Election Reform.* Chicago, American Judicature Society, 1990.

National Center for State Courts. *Call To Reform*. Williamsburg, Virginia, 2002.

Olson, Walter K. *The Litigation Explosion*. New York: Penguin Books, Inc., 1991.

Olson, Walter K. *The Rule of Lawyers*. New York: St. Martin's Press, 2003.

Rothwax, Harold J. *The Collapse of Criminal Justice*. New York: Random House, 1996

Spannaus, Roy T. *A Trust Misplaced.* St. Paul, Minnesota: Ballista Books, 1990.

Spence, Gerry. *From Freedom to Slavery*. New York: Martin's Press, 1993.

Articles

Abrams, Kathryn. Some Realism About Electoralism in Rethinking Judicial Campaign Finance. 72 Southern California Law Review 505, 1999.

Anderson, Seth H. Judicial Retention Evaluation Programs. 34 Loyola of Los Angeles Law Review 1375, 2001.

Barnhizer, David. "On The Make": Campaign Funding and the The Corruption of the American Judiciary. 50 Catholic University Law Review 361, 2001.

Champagne, Anthony. Interest Groups and Judicial Elections. 34 Loyola of Los Angeles Law Review 1391, 2001.

Champagne, Anthony. Political Parties and Judicial Elections. 34 Loyola of Los Angeles Law Review 1411, 2001.

Croley, Steven P. The Majoritarian Difficulty: Elective Judiciaries and the Rule of Law. 62 The University of Chicago law Review 690, 1995.

Dann, Hon. B. Michael and Randall M. Hansen. Judicial Retention Elections. 34 Loyola of Los Angeles Law Review 1429, 2001.

Dove, Richard A. Judicial Campaign Conduct: Rules, Education, and Enforcement, 34 Loyola of Los Angeles Law Review 1361, 2001.

Engle v. R. J. Reynolds Tobacco Co.- No More Butts - Punitive Damages Have Gone Too Far, 34 Loyola of Los Angeles Law Review 1513, 2001.

Epstein, Richard A. and Alan O. Sykes. The Assault on Managed Care: Vicarious Liability, Class Actions and the Patient's Bill of Rights. John M. Olin Law & Economics Working Paper No. 112 (2d Series), http://papers.ssrn.com/paper.taf?abstract_id=253328,2000.

Geyh, Charles Gardner. Publicly Financed Judicial Elections: An Overview. 34 Loyola of Los Angeles Law Review 1467, 2001.

Kaplan, Sheila and Zoe Davidson. The Buying of the Bench. The Nation Magazine, January 26, 1998, page 10.

Mikva, Abner. The Wooing of Our Judges. http://www.mediatransparency.org/stories/wooing_judges.htm, Chicago, 2003

Schotland, Roy A. Campaign Finance in Judicial Elections. 34 Loyola of Los Angeles Law Review 1489, 2001.

Schotland, Roy A. Financing Judicial Elections, 2000: Change and Challenge. 2001 Law Review Michigan State University D.C.L. 849.

Schotland, Roy A. Summit on Improving Judicial Selection. 34 Loyola of Los Angeles Law Review 1361, 2001.

Schotland, Roy A. and David B. Rottman. What Makes Judicial Elections Unique. 34 Loyola of Los Angeles Law Review 1369, 2001.

Webster, Peter D. Selection and Retention of Judges: Is There One "Best" Method? 23 Florida State University Law Review 1, 1995.

Index

Meet Dale Nathan

Dale Nathan was born on July 4, 1934 in Louisville, Kentucky. He graduated from the University of Kentucky earning a B.A. in political science and psychology, LL.B., both in 1957. He financed his college education by working and earning scholarships. Dale served in the U. S. Army Medical Reserve during the Korean War. Dale's post-college employment included working as an administrative assistant for the City of Louisville, Kentucky; working as a contracts administrator for the U.S. Air Force (civilian); working as a contracts manager for government contractors; and working as a law editor.

Dale came to Minnesota in 1965 and was general counsel for the Sperry Univac Division of the Sperry Rand Corporation in St. Paul/Eagan, Minnesota, for 13 years. Dale also served as an adjunct professor and co-director of the Government Contracts Program, College (now University) of St. Thomas Graduate School of Business teaching contract management, government contract law, and negotiations. He also taught Religions of the World in two religious schools for over 10 years at Temple Israel in Minneapolis and Temple of Aaron in St. Paul.

He was admitted to the practice of law in Minnesota in its state and federal courts, before the United States Supreme Court and several federal courts of appeals, and the United States Court of Federal Claims. A past president of the National Contract Management Association, Dale was part of a historic cultural exchange mission in China in May-June, 1989 when the famous Tiananmen Square Massacre happened. For more than 30 years, Dale was a volunteer attorney with a legal aid organization, Southern Minnesota Regional Legal Services. He was Chair of the Independence Party Platform Committee and a member of his party's Executive Council. One of Dale's lawsuits was chosen by Law & Politics Magazine as one of the eleven lawsuits of the year for 2000. Dale is not currently practicing law. He is devoting all of his time to writing.

Dale is single and has never been married. He has no children, however, he served as a Dakota County foster parent for several years and had several foster children, both boys and girls.